T0311562

Franco Modigliani and Keynesian Economics

This book follows the intellectual path of Franco Modigliani, Nobel Prize winner and one of the most influential Keynesian economists of the twentieth century, tracing his development and examining the impact of his research.

The book begins with Modigliani's early work as a young law student in 1930s Italy and traces his development through his emigration to the U.S., his introduction to Keynes' *General Theory* at the New School for Social Research and his seminal 1944 article on Keynesian and classical economics. The book also discusses Modigliani's pioneering theory of savings: the life-cycle hypothesis with Richard Brumberg, further developed with Albert Ando, his contributions to decision-making under uncertainty and, finally, Modigliani's collaboration with the Federal Reserve Board for the building of its first macroeconometric model for the U.S. economy. The book argues that although Modigliani is placed amongst the most prominent Keynesian economists, if we look to his published works only, and with the exception of the 1944 article, his connections with Keynesian theory appears of secondary importance until the beginning of the 1960s when he joined MIT. Moreover, since then his contributions are much more on policy issues rather than theoretical ones.

This is the first book to place Modigliani's thought in its proper historical and intellectual context, showing how it related to wider economic concerns and possible policy solutions. It will be of interest to scholars in the history of economic thought, and especially post-war American Keynesian economics.

Antonella Rancan is Associate Professor of Economics at the University of Molise, Italy.

Perspectives in Economic and Social History
Series Editors: Andrew August and Jari Eloranta

For more information about this series, please visit: www.routledge.com/
series/PESHSeries\Perspectives in Economic and Social History.doc

Franco Modigliani and Keynesian Economics

Antonella Rancan

Routledge
Taylor & Francis Group

LONDON AND NEW YORK

First published 2020
by Routledge
2 Park Square, Milton Park, Abingdon, Oxon OX14 4RN

and by Routledge
52 Vanderbilt Avenue, New York, NY 10017

Routledge is an imprint of the Taylor & Francis Group, an informa business

British Library Cataloguing-in-Publication Data
A catalogue record for this book is available from the British Library

Library of Congress Cataloging-in-Publication Data
Names: Rancan, Antonella, author.
Title: Franco Modigliani and Keynesian economics : theory, facts and policy /
    Antonella Rancan.
Description: Abingdon, Oxon ; New York, NY : Routledge, 2020. |
    Series: Perspectives in social and economic history | Includes
    bibliographical references and index.
Identifiers: LCCN 2020002095 (print) | LCCN 2020002096 (ebook) |
    ISBN 9781848935013 (hardback) | ISBN 9781003047032 (ebook)
Subjects: LCSH: Modigliani, Franco. | Economists—Italy. | Keynesian
    economics.
Classification: LCC HB109.M63 R36 2020 (print) | LCC HB109.M63
    (ebook) | DDC 330.15/6—dc23
LC record available at https://lccn.loc.gov/2020002095
LC ebook record available at https://lccn.loc.gov/2020002096

ISBN: 978-1-848-93501-3 (hbk)
ISBN: 978-0-367-49701-9 (pbk)
ISBN: 978-1-003-04703-2 (ebk)

Typeset in Bembo
by Apex CoVantage, LLC

Contents

Introduction

Modigliani's Keynesianism and beyond

This book is an attempt to broadly outline the intellectual path of Franco Modigliani (1918–2003), who emigrated to the United States in 1939 to escape Mussolini's racial laws and took American citizenship a few years later, deciding not to come back to Italy at the end of WWII. In 1985 Modigliani was awarded the Royal Bank of Sweden Prize in Economic Science in Memory of Alfred Nobel for his pioneering theory of savings, the life cycle hypothesis (with Richard Brumberg), and for the Modigliani–Miller theorem (with Merton H. Miller), a cornerstone of modern theory of finance.

Although both achievements are not strictly related to postwar Keynesian macroeconomics, Modigliani is especially known as a leading Keynesian, and his name is associated with that of other prominent American Keynesians and Nobel Laureates: Lawrence Klein, Paul Samuelson, Robert Solow and James Tobin, who marked the U.S. postwar macroeconomics and its policy agenda.

Modigliani's (1944) seminal article on Keynes's involuntary unemployment and wage rigidity is recalled among the ones that set the basis of the neoclassical synthesis, that is, an interpretation of Keynes's macroeconomics within the neoclassical framework.[1] "I consider myself a Keynesian", Modigliani said in his conversation with Barnett and Solow (2000, p. 230) as in several other interviews and in his autobiography (Modigliani 2001). He also explained what he meant for "being a Keynesian": to know that "the system does not automatically tend to full employment without appropriate policies. Prices flexibility will not produce full employment, and therefore unemployment is always due to an insufficiency of real money" (Barnett and Solow 2000, p. 230), thus emphasizing what he considered "fundamental" in the Keynesian system: to recognize the limits of the market self-adjusting mechanisms, of the crucial role of money to explain unemployment and to believe in the effectiveness of policy actions. Modigliani also placed the research program he pursued all over his academic career within the context of postwar American Keynesianism. In the "Introduction" to his *Collected Papers*, he outlined his scientific endeavor as "dominated" by "sorting out" the lasting contributions of the Keynesian revolution, that is, to integrate the main building blocks of the *General Theory* with the neoclassical postulate of rational maximizing behavior; to empirically estimate and test the resulting theories; and to apply these results to policy issues (see Modigliani 1980, vol. 1, p. xi). Such basic building blocks are the consumption function, the investment function, the demand for and supply of money and other deposits and the mechanism determining wages and prices – the "Achilles's heel of macroeconomic analysis" as Modigliani puts it (Modigliani 1980, vol. 1, pp. xi–xii).

By outlining Modigliani's intellectual path, the book suggests that Modigliani's connections with the Keynesian theory appears of secondary importance until the beginning of the 1960s, when he joined MIT. In the late 1940s and 1950s, the years Modigliani defined as his most productive ones, he was working on consumption and savings behavior within the neoclassical optimization framework, on firms' production planning under uncertainty, on oligopoly theory and the theory of corporate finance. Although it is true that Modigliani's work on macroeconomics moved in that direction, being especially devoted to enlarge the perspective of marginal analysis by applying its tools to Keynesian macroeconomics, it is also true that Modigliani's most important contributions originated from a multifaceted intellectual context in which Keynesian developments were not central, and partly different from that of prominent Keynesians to whom his name is associated.[2]

The 1944 *Econometrica* article of the twenty-six-year-old economist was not followed by further developments in the 1940s and 1950s. Only in 1963 did Modigliani return to publish on Keynesian and classical economics with a more elaborate analysis along the lines began almost twenty years before. While his unfinished and unpublished work over the 1950s showed a *fil rouge* between the two models, in his published studies Modigliani's main interests seem to move in different directions.

In other words, it is only with Modigliani's arrival at MIT in 1962, and the beginning of the collaboration with the most important public institutions such as the Federal Reserve Board that Modigliani's image as a Keynesian takes full shape, permeating his previous works. It was in connection with the peak of the Keynesian and monetarist academic, intellectual and political dispute. From then Modigliani became fully engaged with Keynesian macroeconomics, especially with its translation in a macroeconometric model, to be delivered to policy makers. In fact, Oliver Blanchard in the *New Palgrave* (2008, pp. 635–636) will define the Federal Reserve Board, MIT and University of Pennsylvania macroeconometric model the "apotheosis" of the neoclassical synthesis, and the model was one of the main targets of Lucas's new classical macroeconomics over the late 1970s and 1980s. Modigliani himself saw in that macroeconometric model an attempt to put together the most relevant contributions of postwar economics in a large-scale, consistent model. The importance Modigliani ascribed to the Federal Reserve Board, MIT and University of Pennsylvania model is evident by the fact that with the exception of the 1944 and the 1963 articles, volume 1 of his *Collected Papers* devoted to his essays in (Keynesian) macroeconomics gathers papers Modigliani wrote in connection with its building.

Before his arrival at MIT, Modigliani went around different universities becoming part of different communities of academic economists from the

European émigrés of the New School for Social Research to Chicago University and the Cowles Commission, then he moved to the University of Illinois and in 1952 he joined the new Graduate School of Industrial Administration of the Carnegie Institute of Technology (now Carnegie Mellon University). Finally, ten years later he joined MIT, Samuelson and Solow, spending most of his time building the macroeconometric model for the Federal Reserve Board and intervening in policy issues. At MIT Modigliani accomplished his intellectual journey (and Keynesian adventure).

Modigliani's emphasis on market failures and his focus on wage and price behavior to distinguish between classical and Keynesian economics and on the active role of policy makers have a background that goes beyond American Keynesianism. Modigliani approached economics at the university during the fascist period in Italy when only corporative economics was taught. He recalled that he began to be interested in economic problems and to think about himself as an economist when translating German articles into Italian. He also began to write a few essays on price control and international trade whose *fil rouge* was a critique of classical economics with a highly rhetorical language (see Chapter 1). In other words, his reasoning on the relationships among public policies, market forces and individual choice began before his discovery of Keynes's *General Theory*, within the context of the corporative economics (he labeled "new economics").

He learned the tools of economic analysis at the New School as his Italian education was in humanities (classical studies and a degree in law), especially under Jacob Marschak who pursued an eclectic, anti-dogmatic and mathematical approach to economics and whose intellectual debt Modigliani has always accomplished and emphasized. Modigliani's 1944 Keynesian model originated from a quite unique intellectual context. He first encountered Keynes's *General Theory* through Marschak's classes, Oskar Lange's seminars and discussions with Abba Lerner and after having read Hicks's "Keynes and the Classics" (see Chapter 2). When he encountered Keynes's *General Theory*, he had already read the Keynes of the end of laissez-faire and national autarchy. Soon after his PhD dissertation, between 1944 and 1945, Modigliani returned to reasoning on the evolution of the capitalistic system and its failures, as he did in the 1930s, in an Italian article on the organization of a socialist economy (see Chapter 3).

At the New School he became associate professor and chief statistician of the Institute of World Affairs, founded and led by Hans Neisser, until 1948. With Neisser he was engaged with the building of a macroeconometric model for the world economy and came to work on long run and cyclical savings behavior, the starting point of the life cycle hypothesis (see Chapter 3). In 1948 he went to Chicago University with a six-month fellowship provided by Theodore Schultz, and soon after he joined the University of Illinois, whose Economics Department was at the center of a generational change being formed by a group of young mathematical and empirical economists. He was called to direct an interdisciplinary project, *Expectations and Business Fluctuation*, to which he was committed over the 1950s, when he moved to the new Graduate School of Industrial Administration of Carnegie Tech, whose research agenda set the basis for modern management science. There, Modigliani was part of an extraordinary research group formed by Lee Bach, Charles Holt, John Muth and Herbert Simon, working on firms' production planning behavior under uncertainty from which Muth's rational expectations, on the one side, and Simon's bounded rationality, on the other, emerged (see Chapters 4 and 5).

Over the 1950s Modigliani went on to work on consumption and savings behavior, a typically Keynesian topic that attracted the attention of most economists both because of the widespread concern about over savings, and "to solve" the intellectual puzzle of reconciling short- and long-run savings behavior (see Chapter 6). Modigliani and Richard Brumberg worked contemporarily on the microeconomic and macroeconomic aspects of their theory and established explicit connections with the Keynesian theory. However, these connections are only discussed in a section devoted to the Pigou effect of a paper longer than seventy pages that remained unpublished until Modigliani's *Collected Papers* (vol. 2, 1980). When Modigliani began to work on the savings function, he was much more interested in the possibility of its measuring, testing hypotheses and ability to forecast rather than in providing a theoretical framework for data. Later, when elaborating the life cycle theory with Brumberg, their main concern was not to have a theory consistent with the Keynesian one but with empirical evidence and the connections between micro and macroeconomic analysis. The macroeconomic implications of the life cycle theory were especially developed with Albert Ando in the 1960s as opposed to post-Keynesian theories of economic growth, whereas the life cycle implications for the Keynesian income multiplier were investigated through the Fed–MIT–Penn large-scale macroeconometric model of the late 1960s (see Chapter 7).

During the 1950s Modigliani was also working on a treatise on the theory of money and interest in a general equilibrium framework, and summarized these ideas in the 1963 article devoted to further develop the Keynesian framework he had set in 1944. However, these notes remained unpublished and were the result of different research lines emerging from an "eclectic" context, as was the Carnegie Institute of Technology of the 1950s (see Chapter 5).

The book provides a broad narrative of Modigliani's approach to economics from the 1940s to the 1970s. It is not comprehensive of all of Modigliani's most innovative and influential achievements, such as his work with Merton Miller on corporate finance, because I consider this as falling outside economics and particularly Keynesian economics. I also do not reconstruct the connections Modigliani established with Italian economists from the mid-1950s, and especially from the late 1960s, when he started to collaborate with the Bank of Italy to build its first macroeconometric model. From then he began to be increasingly involved in the Italian economic and policy situation as well (on this see Asso 2007; Camurri 2010, 2018).

Given Modigliani's versatility and prominence among Keynesian economists, Modigliani's achievements have been widely investigated. In 1980, Andrew Abel and Simon Johnson started to edit Modigliani's six volumes of *Collected Papers* (1980–1989), and in 2008 Michael Szenberg and Lall Ramrattan published "Franco Modigliani – Great Thinkers in Economics", a monograph devoted to

Modigliani's most relevant contributions, for the Macmillan Palgrave series. In 2005, the Italian Accademia Nazionale dei Lincei sponsored a conference, "Franco Modigliani between Economic Theory and Social Commitment", whose proceedings have been published by the *Banca Nazionale del Lavoro Quarterly Review*. Papers on specific topics of Modigliani's research have also been published.

With few exceptions, such as Harold Hagemann (2005) and, in Italian, Pier Francesco Asso (2007), Renato Camurri (2010, 2018), and Luca Michelini (2019), the abovementioned studies pursued a rational reconstruction of Modigliani's theories focusing on the internal logic of his achievements. Such literature, therefore, may be fruitfully integrated by looking at the historical and intellectual background in which Modigliani's theories originated. The contextualization of his most relevant achievements contributes to a better understanding of the meaning and evolution of his economic thought along with that of modern economics.

My reconstruction of some of Modigliani's main contributions to postwar economics is largely based on the Franco Modigliani Papers preserved at the David Rubinstein Rare Book and Manuscript Library of Duke University. Chapter 1, which deals with the articles Modigliani wrote between 1937 and 1938 and published in Italian fascist leading journals, largely benefits of the reading of Luca Michelini's manuscript on *Il nazional-fascismo del giovane Modigliani* (Michelini 2019), which made me aware of material I did not know about. I am grateful to Michelini for sharing with me his detailed and precious reconstruction of that period.

With the exception of Chapter 1, the rest of the book is based on results of research presented at conferences and seminars and Chapters 2, 5 and 7 are largely derived from articles already published, integrated with new material. I wish to thank all conference participants and anonymous referees for their helpful comments.

I am especially indebted and grateful to the historians of economics of Duke University whom I first met in 2007, when I began to work on Franco Modigliani papers, and then in 2008 and in 2018, for their continuous support and stimulating suggestions. Without the benefit of the Economists' Papers Project of Duke University (2007, 2008), a research grant from European Society for the History of Economic Thought (2007), the Center for the History of Political Economy fellowship from January to April 2018, and the Fulbright research grant for the 2018 semester, I could not have spent research periods at the Center for the History of Political Economy, which has been fundamental for my work. I also wish to thank the David M. Rubenstein Rare Book and Manuscript Library staff of Duke University for their precious and kind assistance.

Notes

1 Throughout the book I will use the term neoclassical synthesis and Keynesian economics as interchangeable, and I simply refer to attempts to integrate the neoclassical analysis (in the general equilibrium version) with Keynes's macroeconomics through the IS LM model and to demand policy management.
2 See for example Backhouse (2018) on Samuelson's intellectual biography and Dimand on Tobin (2014).

References

Asso, P. F., ed. 2007. *Franco Modigliani. L'impegno civile di un'economista*, Siena: Fondazione Monte dei Paschi.

Backhouse, R. 2018. *Founder of Modern Economics: Paul A. Samuelson: Volume 1: Becoming Samuelson, 1915–1948*. Oxford Studies in the History of Economics, Oxford: Oxford University Press.

Barnett, W. A., and R. Solow. 2000. "An Interview with Franco Modigliani November 5–6 1999", *Macroeconomic Dynamics*, 4: 222–256.

Blanchard, O. J. 2008. "Neoclassical Synthesis", in *The New Palgrave: Dictionary of Economics Second Edition*, ed. by S. N. Durlauf and L. E. Blume, vol. 5, London: Macmillan Press Ltd, 634–637.

Camurri, R., ed. 2010. *Franco Modigliani. L'Italia vista dall'America. Battaglie e riflessioni di un esule*, Turin: Bollati Boringhieri.

———. ed. 2018. *I modesti consigli di un premio Nobel. Franco Modigliani. Rischio Italia. L'Italia vista dall'America (1970–2003)*, Rome: Donzelli Editore.

Dimand, Robert, W. 2014. *James Tobin,* Basingstoke: Palgrave Macmillan.

Hagemann, H. 2005. "The influence of Jacob Marschak, Adolph Lowe, and Hans Neisser on the Formation of Franco Modigliani's work", in *Franco Modigliani and the Keynesian Legacy*, New York: Schwartz Center Conference at the New School University, April 14–15, 1–25.

Michelini, L. 2019. *Il nazionl-fascismo economico del giovane Franco Modigliani*, Firenze University. www.academia.edu/40986118/Il_nazional-fascismo_economico_del_giovane_Franco_ Modigliani.

Modigliani, F. 1944. "Liquidity Preference and the Theory of Interest and Money", *Econometrica*, 12 (January): 45–88.

———. 1980–1989. *The Collected Papers of Franco Modigliani* (5 voll.), ed. by A. Abel, Cambridge, MA: MIT Press.

———. 1987. "The 1985 Nobel Prize in Economics", in *Macroeconomics and Finance: Essays in Honors of Franco Modigliani*, ed. by R. Dornbusch, S. Fisher, and J. Bossons, Cambridge, MA: MIT Press, 29–35.

———. 2001. *Adventure of an Economist*, New York, London: Texere.

Szenberg, M., and L. Ramrattan. 2008. *Franco Modigliani a Mind That Never Rests*, Palgrave Macmillan.

1 Modigliani before Modigliani

Introduction

The *New York Times*, on September 23, 2003, published an open letter to protest the Distinguished Statesman Award the Anti-Defamation League offered to Silvio Berlusconi, at that time president of the Italian government. The letter is signed by three Nobel Laureates in Economics: Franco Modigliani and his MIT colleagues Paul Samuelson and Robert Solow. The news about the prize "is shocking", they wrote, because of Berlusconi's position towards fascism. He defined Benito Mussolini a "benevolent dictator" who "did not killed nobody . . . while he was responsible for the deportation of about 7000 Jews who death in the Nazi camps" (quoted from Repubblica.it, www.repubblica.it/2003/i/sezioni/politica/berlugiudici2/trenobel/trenobel.html; my translation).[1]

Modigliani's family was part of the Jewish community of Rome. He emigrated to Paris in September 1938 at the age of twenty and then to the United States because of the promulgation of the racial laws that excluded Jews from attending public school education or to hold public office.

His father, Enrico Modigliani, was a well-known social pediatrician, and his mother, Olga Flaschel, devoted herself to volunteering (Modigliani 2001, p. 1), both playing important roles in communicating the importance of civil and social commitment. Enrico Modigliani's contributions to pediatrics were both theoretical and applied. He was especially concerned with child nutrition disorders and infectious diseases, on which he published several studies in the beginning of the twentieth century. After WWI he was increasingly engaged in applied social pediatrics, assisting unmarried mothers and their children through the creation of institutions able to host them, providing psychological and practical assistance such as finding jobs. He also supported changing legislation to remove a child's status as illegitimate because a kind of discrimination.[2]

In his autobiography Franco Modigliani recalled that his stance towards the fascist regime was initially "neutral" because his family had no clear-cut position. Her mother "somewhat favored the regime" because of its laws regarding social assistance, whereas his father was "staunchly antifascist" (Modigliani 2001, p. 10). However, his premature death in 1931, when Modigliani was fourteen years old, left him without "firm guidance" (Modigliani 2001, p. 11).

Like most of his peers, his awareness of the regime seemed to mature gradually. According to the historian Renato Camurri (2010, 2018), Modigliani lacked strong reference points not only within his family but also outside it, within the social and policy context. He was among those young people Camurri labeled the "generation without myths" who, as in the case of Modigliani, had no organizational structure to refer to as it was the Communist Party for some of them (Camurri 2010, pp. xxiv–xxvi).

Modigliani enrolled at the Faculty of Law at the University of Rome in 1935, after having attended the Liceo classico Visconti, thus pursuing a humanist education with little mathematics in secondary school and not at all in the Faculty of Law. Here, there was some teaching of economics, at that time corporative economics. Modigliani recalled that his interest in economic problems was initially stimulated not by attending classes but from his translation of articles from German into Italian for the Traders' Federation. In 1937 he won the *Littorali della cultura*, a competition promoted by fascism, with a paper on price control, and since then, he began thinking of himself as an economist (Modigliani 2001, p. 9).

It is quite unknown that from 1937 to 1938 Modigliani wrote a few articles on economic issues that were published in leading fascist journals. The leitmotiv of his essays was a critique of classical economics, of its individualistic and hedonistic foundations, and of laissez-faire as opposed to the principles that inspired corporative economics. In other words, Modigliani first approach to economics was that of a young student influenced by the fascist propaganda of the 1930s.[3] With the exception of the 1937 paper by which he won the *Littorali* prize, Modigliani did not mention these essays in his autobiography or in his interviews, and they are not included in his 1986 bibliography. There are no references in his archive including his correspondence and other material. Although an English translation of some of Modigliani's articles was made available in 2007 by Daniela Parisi, subsequent biographies about Modigliani do not mention these essays, focusing on the American period. Gary Mongiovi (2015, p. 5) mentions them as politically naïve in a paper devoted to Modigliani's ideas on socialism (Modigliani 1947).[4]

In a recent book on *Il nazionl-fascismo economico del giovane Franco Modigliani* [*The Economic National-Fascism of the Young Franco Modigliani*], Luca Michelini calls attention to the four essays Parisi translated in English and two more articles Modigliani published between February and June 1938. Michelini investigates the cultural milieu in which he began to reason on economics through a detailed reconstruction of the intellectual and ideological profile of the journals that hosted Modigliani's writings, and their editors, along with the main topics that were discussed. Modigliani's articles cover a period from April 1937 to June 1938, just before the promulgation of the racial laws on September 1938, and his escape to Paris with his father-in-law's family before his graduation in July 1939.[5]

As Michelini remarks, the journals that hosted Modigliani's essays were among the leading fascist journals: *Lo Stato. Rivista di Scienze Politiche, Giuridiche ed Economiche*, founded by the jurist Carlo Costamagna, among the prominent intellectual of the fascism; *Il Ventuno. Rivista dei Littorali*, founded by Ettore Bernardo Rosboch, a scholar of Maffeo Panataleoni; and *La Dottrina Fascista,* directed by Nicolò Giani, who founded with Mussolini's brother *La scuola di mistica fascista*. All these journals were involved even before the promulgation of the racial laws in the anti–Semitic campaign.[6]

This chapter does not try to investigate the attitude the young Modigliani had towards the fascist regime in the 1930s; neither does it attempt to understand whether he sincerely believed in the principles of the corporative economics he supported in his articles or whether, on the contrary, his writing represented a way by which Modigliani protected himself from the regime, a sort of "cover" in case of necessity.[7] The chapter only testifies how, and in which context, Modigliani discovered the economic discipline.

Michelini's research, with his close attention to the economic issues Modigliani discussed and the intellectual context from which his writings originated, fills an important historiographical lacuna. Modigliani's early writings are important for a better understanding of the climate in which he first approached the study of economics, to investigate how much of this cultural experience he brought with him in the United States and whether there can be found any traces in his work during the 1940s and, eventually, later. Modigliani continued to reason about the relationships between state interventions and market system, ascribing to the institutional framework a crucial role in shaping economic phenomena; about self and collective interests and about the allocative and distributive functions of the price mechanism. The concrete working of a capitalistic economy, with its market imperfections and failures and the active role of government (Modigliani confidence on it), was the basis on which he built his economic theorizing. It is through his early readings and writings about corporative economics, and his critique of the classical theory, that Modigliani first met Keynes, not the Keynes of the *General Theory*, not yet available in Italy, but of the "End of Laissez Faire" and of "National Self-Sufficiency" published in the *Nuova Collana degli Economisti* by Giuseppe Bottai and Celestino Arena. It is in the context of the corporative economy that Modigliani embraced an idea of economics as a normative science committed with social and policy issues. Also later, despite postwar economics formalization, of which Modigliani became one of the main advocates, economics remained for him an applied science whose aim was to provide concrete answers to concrete problems.[8]

Discovering economics in Italy in the 1930s: price controls

Michelini explains that in the 1920s, there were two separate streams of thought supporting fascism: the liberal one, whose prominent figures were Enrico Barone, Maffeo Pantaleoni and Vilfredo Pareto and corporative-mercantilist thought led especially by jurists, political scientists, sociologists and historians.

They both shared an anti-socialism stance, defending private property. For both groups theory and policy were explicitly linked to each other. Whereas liberals like Pareto saw in fascism a way to restore the capitalistic system by developing an idea of state in terms of the élite, the "corporative" especially concentrated on a re-foundation of economic science by reversing the relationships among individuals, the market and the state with respect to the classical economy. It is to this current of thought that the young Modigliani referred to in his writings about the building of the "new (corporative) economics" (Michelini 2019, pp. 3–10).[9] Modigliani largely discussed the principles that should move the "new economics", whose foundations were to be found in the maximization of the social utility, in contrast with the classical hedonistic approach, and the subordination of individuals interests and the market mechanism to the state interests.

Modigliani's first published article is the one by which he won the *Littorali della cultura*. He decided to participate in the competition because he felt he was an expert on that year's (1936) subject – price control – about which he learned from his translation of German articles.[10] In his autobiography he recalled that the competition was particularly important to him for two reasons: because he began to think about himself as an economist and because, since then, he started to distance himself from fascism. Although the *Littorali* was a competition promoted by Mussolini, the cream of the antifascist youth also took part (Camurri 2010, p. 10). According to Italian historians, the *Littorali*, which comprised a variety of scientific, literary and artistic topics, was one of the most powerful instruments fascism used to reabsorb orthodoxy and dissent, playing a fundamental part in the pedagogical program of the regime (Camurri 2010, pp. xix–xx). Through his participation Modigliani entered in contact with a number of young antifascists who, Modigliani explained, helped him acquire an antifascist position (2001, pp. 9–11).[11] His recollection appears however in contrast with the publication in 1938 of further articles unless, as mentioned above, they were written to protect himself from a situation that was rapidly degenerating.

In any case, the thesis he wrote under Guglielmo Masci's supervision and defended in July 1939 to earn his doctoral degree in law had only minimal references to fascism and corporative economics, even if the issues Modigliani discussed were close to that of his previous articles, such as the overcoming of the capitalistic system based on market competition by industrial concentration.

The contents of Modigliani's articles are quite repetitive. Their starting point is a critique of the foundations of classical economics to which Modigliani opposed the preeminence of the principles of corporative economics. Despite the high standards of Italian economics in the beginning of the twentieth century, particularly regarding the development of marginal economics (see Schumpeter 1954 (1976), p. 855), and the debate about competitive and non-competitive market forms (Mosca 2018), Modigliani never refers to this literature. His approach is strongly rhetorical rather than analytical. There are no explicit and precise references to the classical or corporative economists and their theorizing. Only the two last articles, published in 1938, appear a little more elaborated.

The first three articles concern price control; two of them are summaries of the first one (the prize-winning article). This essay, titled *"Concetti generali sul controllo dei prezzi* [General Concepts on Price Control]" was published in *Lo Stato* in April 1937 under the feature of *"Problemi dell'economia nuova* [Problems of new economics]". The other appeared in the July–August issue of the same journal, and in *Il Ventuno. Rivista dei Littorali*, respectively. Two further essays (still in *Lo stato*) are devoted to the crisis of the capitalistic economy and the international division of labor (January 1938) and the principle of autarky (March 1938), both starting from a dismissal of Ricardo's theory of comparative advantages and Say's law. The last articles of February 1938 (in *Lo Stato*) and June 1938 (in *La Dottrina Fascista*) are still about national autarky, its important role and modernity.

At the center of Modigliani's discussions there are the foundations of the "new economics", which put the national and collective interest above individual selfishness. This is the departure point from which to criticize and reject the market system under theoretical and practical perspectives, thus dismissing the classical general equilibrium framework and its self-equilibrating mechanism, along with the "doctrine" of laissez-faire and free trade. Modigliani's radical position appears quite surprising because a few years later he embraced the marginal analysis and linked his image as an economist to his attempt to reconcile classical and Keynesian economics by reading the *General Theory* within a general equilibrium framework, thus reducing the revolutionary meaning of Keynes's theory (see Chapter 2).

In Modigliani's Italian articles the rejection of classical economics is desirable because of its individualistic approach to economic problems under the assumption of the coincidence of collective and individual interest'. This supposed consistency appears to Modigliani in contrast with the real working of the economy, where competitive markets have been replaced by monopolies whose profit maximization policies are against social utility.

In the first three articles, Modigliani discussed the principles and the effectiveness of the price control the fascist regime had imposed in 1935 to face the North Africa campaign, endorsed by a decree law in October 1936. As mentioned above, Modigliani's concern about the allocative and distributive functions of the price system, and about price formation, price flexibility and rigidity, will continue through the 1940s, although in a different context and with a much more rigorous language. Modigliani will apply the tools of marginal analysis and a quantitative approach in his empirical research with Hans Neisser on the relationships between production costs and the final prices of commodities. And in his influential 1944 Econometrica article he will distinguishes between classical and Keynesian economics on the basis of different price behaviors (see Chapters 2 and 3).

In "Concetti generali sul controllo dei prezzi" (April 1937) Modigliani distinguishes between price control conceived as a temporary policy imposed on a specific economic category (the retailers) and price controls as resulting from corporative economic principles. According to Modigliani, the former policy is both ineffective in the long run, because the "impossibility of compressing retail prices any further", and unfair, because it freezes only the prices of one kind of commodity, and therefore, it is "absolutely inadmissible within the ethical principles of Fascism" (1937 (2007), p. 18). On the other hand, the latter policy, based on sound economic principles, involves all kind of prices (of any goods and services), thus allowing for sharing of sacrifices among the entire collectivity.[12]

Modigliani emphasizes that price controls are necessary for better coordination of economic activity and to avoid the "exploitation of the consumer by a salesman", as in the case of monopolies:

> How could one possibly believe that Fascism, which aims to coordinate individual interests and subordinate them to the national interest in every field and most specifically in the economic field, would leave a function of such elevated importance as that of price setting completely at the mercy of individual interests? Can we imagine that the Fascist State would allow the exploitation of the consumer by a salesman, for example a monopolist salesman, letting the latter set the price in such a manner as to achieve the maximum benefit of the monopoly, or should we rather assume that it will intervene by setting the price at a level which, while ensuring that the monopolist obtains his just benefit, will guarantee the maximum gain for the collectivity?

(1937 (2007), p. 19)

As long as prices are set in a way to not ensure the maximization of social utility, "but only the advantage of the individual and the exploitation of the collectivity" the state, Modigliani argues, "has not only the right but also the duty to intervene" (1937 (2007), p. 20). However, he points out that differently from previous experience in Italy, Germany and France, price control must be *"complete, dynamic, continuous, and formative"* (1937 (2007), p. 22, italics in original). By *complete* Modigliani means that price controls must refer to the greatest possible number of commodities, from production to consumption and *dynamic, continuous*, and *formative* in the sense of not being an anchor to preserve the status quo. Prices, Modigliani remarks, should continuously adjust to the evolution of the national economy and to support the national interest. He insisted on the "dynamic nature" of controls that must follow the dynamics of business and must be able to "adapt continually and dynamically to even the slightest variations of the market" (1937 (2007), p. 22). In other words, price control must be capable of reproducing the market system behavior, avoiding, however, any form of market power. Modigliani's emphasis on price control in terms of a political instrument that must replicate market price behavior, acknowledged as a necessary device for an efficient allocation of resources, will be reaffirmed in the late 1940s in his essay on the organization of a socialist economy (Modigliani 1947) and in the so-called Meat Plan of 1947, in which however price control will be replaced by a system of fiscal incentives for only an indirect form of regulation.

Modigliani concluded the second article on the same topic, "*La funzione del partito nel controllo dei prezzi* [The Role of the Party in Controlling Prices]", arguing that the (fascist) party must conceive controls as "an elastic system ready to follow the alternating waves of the market, tamping them down only when it is right to do so" (1937 (2007), p. 33). In "*Prezzo politico e prezzo corporativo* [Political Price and Corporative Price]" (July–August 1937) Modigliani explains that price control, like the entire corporative system, acquires a precise significance in the context of a dismissal of the classical laws of economics. He rejects the idea of supply and demand as "a rigid and mathematical law", along with "equation individual = collectivity", and the existence of natural laws that "cannot be evaluated from the moral point of view" (1937 (2007), p. 41). According to Modigliani, the classical natural laws, he understood as mechanical, led to a "fatalistic conception of the economy". He wanted to replace the idea that market equilibrium "is restored spontaneously by virtue of the self-regulating forces" with a "strongly voluntaries conception" of equilibrium, which is at the basis of the corporative economics. Modigliani emphasized that the general equilibrium does not "take shape" but "is constructed and shaped" by state interventions and that the balance between supply and demand and the price level "*can* and *must* be created by the will of man" (1937 (2007), p. 41). In other words, Modigliani opposes the classical natural laws and a mechanical conception of the working of the economy with state interventions to reach the equilibrium. The idea of an equilibrium that is constructed through policy actions will remain in the background of Modigliani's economics although with reference to much more traditional Keynesians discretionary policies.

The faith Modigliani will demonstrate in identifying economic relationships and estimate economic variables appears closely related to his acceptance of a rational representation of the economy from which policy actions can be planned. Starting from a definition of the basic postulates of economic analysis as tools rather than an exact description of agents' behavior, Modigliani explained in his interview with Arjo Klamer (1984, p. 19) that the optimization assumption has the greater advantage of a unique answer. In other words, if you think of economics as a science to rationalize the decision process, you need such an assumption as a departure point. A rational organization is the required premise to plan state interventions.

Under this perspective, price control is not in Modigliani's view, a "ceiling price" or an isolated, exceptional intervention, but rather it is the "quintessentially internal action, eminently self-regulating, which aims – through direct cooperation with the categories involved" for a better coordination of economic activity. Public actions are needed because the economy is not self-adjusting: "once equilibrium has been shattered", it is no longer re-established spontaneously, and the door is open "to the worst forms of speculation, economic disruption and national ruin" (Modigliani 1937 (2007), pp. 41–43).

Discovering economics in Italy in the 1930s: national autarky

In the January 1938 essay in *Lo Stato*, Modigliani shifted attention to international trade. In *"La crisi dell'economia capitalistica. La divisione internazionale del lavoro"* ["The Crisis of the Capitalist Economy. The International Division of Labor]" (1938 (2007), pp. 9–30), the target is the policy of free trade and particularly Ricardo's theory of comparative advantages, Say's Law and the quantitative theory of money. To them Modigliani opposed Friedrich List's theory of infant industry, making for the first time explicit reference to the economic literature.

His departure point was the rejection of the classical definition of economics, which assumed as its model the "homo economicus", where the community has no meaning and adheres to an individual and utilitaristic conception of utility. For these reasons, Modigliani argued that "the judgement of 'pure economic theory' . . . is devoid of any significance: pure economic theory is not outside, but against reality. . . . The science of 'pure economics' either ignores the State or considers it an element of disturbance" (1938 (2007), p. 64). Once again Modigliani opposed the principles of the new economics based on social utility from which to evaluate the advantages of free trade. Modigliani followed an idea of economics as part of a unified science, quite common at that time, arguing that the question becomes whether protectionism is economically convenient for the collectivity as a whole, not only from an economic point of view but also from a political and a moral perspective, that is, from the perspective of a "Science of the State" whose meaning, however, Modigliani did not clarify.[13]

Modigliani read Ricardo's theory of free trade as originating from the economic and political supremacy of England over other countries in the beginning of the nineteenth century. In other words, classical faith in the laissez-faire is the result of a precise historical context, and therefore, its laws are not universally valid. It is from this perspective that Modigliani also rejected Say's law and the quantitative theory of money and ascribes to the classical theory no practical value.[14] To him, freedom and equality, that the classical theory would like to promote, remain "abstract and formal dogmas" until countries do not achieve similar development levels. Because of that, Modigliani remarked, List and American protectionists advocated customs barriers.

The historical contextualization from which Modigliani approached Ricardo's theory led him to criticize also its static and "fatalist" approach, in which specialization is the result of sorts of "natural gifts" (1938 (2007), p. 83), that implied a polarization of countries between industrialized on the one side and agricultural on the other.

According to Modigliani, once recognized that comparative costs had no role in controlling international trade, the "idyllic world of economic peace" disappears, leaving room for economic struggles such as the dumping system, state interventions to achieve the minimum price on the international market, wages reduction, manipulations of the exchange rate and devaluations. He concluded that in the light of the "gigantic progress made in the field of chemical . . . agricultural . . . etc. sciences are making it clear that man can, within constantly increasing limits, dominate the environment, reducing the extent of the divergence among costs and the importance of natural monopolies", thus reducing the premises of Ricardian laws to "useless" and "ridiculous" (1938 (2007), p. 84). What is required, he remarked once again, was to move closer to reality, to design a principle that is truly capable of eliminating the infinite, adverse effects of the current system of international trade. Such a principle is that embodied in autarky, a theoretical and practical principle of economic organization.[15]

In February 1938 Modigliani returned to support the principle of national autarky (*"L'Autarchia nazionale"*) in a paper partly devoted to the causes of the 1929 economic crisis. He identified a number of factors explaining it, such as the economic struggle prompted by free trade (as mentioned in his previous article); the disordered movements of capital and gold reserves among countries, which led to pathological phenomena such as inflation and speculation; the exploitation of the working class and of consumers from monopolies and the "excessive inequalities among populations" (1938, p. 80). Again, Modigliani argued that the world market cannot constitute an economic unit unless there is moral and political unity.

As Michelini (2019) shows, in this article Modigliani explicitly referred to the thesis of Enrico Corradini, a leading exponent of fascism, who denounced the international division among capitalistic and proletarian countries. Modigliani also discussed for the first time the problem of overproduction as due to an insufficient aggregate demand (without however explicit reference to Keynes),[16] concluding that economic crises are the result of classical liberalism and the inequalities it produces:

> One of the main reasons explaining overproduction crises . . . is the unequal international distribution of purchasing power. If it is true that these crises are characterized by a lack of demand, it is also true that this scarcity must be understood in a "relative sense". It does not mean that all consumption is already satisfied . . . but that it is satisfied that part of consumption whose purchasing power is high enough to demand goods at a remunerative price. The rest of consumption, instead of being satisfied, would still need those goods . . . but it is not able to contribute to the demand.

(1938, p. 81)

Finally, in his last article Modigliani published in *Dottrina fascista*, he explicit refers to the content of the journal and, especially, to Filippo Carli's ideas (a sociologist, economist and member of the fascist party). Carli believed in the possibility of establishing a national economic calculation and limiting free enterprise whenever in contrast with the superior national interest.[17] National economic equilibrium, Modigliani concluded, must be economic, political, spiritual, ethical and dynamic; in other words it must improve the situation of poorer classes. It must always be based on private property and individual initiative whenever exercised to promote the national interest (see Michelini 2019, p. 48).

Leaving Italy and the "new economics"

In September 1938 soon after the promulgation of the racial laws Modigliani left Italy with his father-in-law's family and moved to Paris. In 1938 Modigliani had not yet earnt his doctoral degree in law, and therefore, he came back secretly to Rome to defend the thesis in July 1939. Soon after they emigrated definitely to the United States.

In his dissertation, *La regolamentazione e la standardizzazione dei bilanci, della contabilità e del calcolo del prezzo di costo nei suoi aspetti teorici e nelle attuazioni all'estero* written while in Paris, Modigliani discussed many of the issues faced in his previous articles, focusing in particular on overcoming the capitalistic system. However, his attitude towards classical and neoclassical economics is less critical. In his autobiography Modigliani mentions Riccardo Bachi as his mentor in the study of economics (particularly of Marshall and the classics), while he never referred to his thesis supervisor Guglielmo Masci.[18] Federico Caffè describes Masci as an economist whose main contributions were on methodology and the classical and corporative economics (Caffè 1974). In *Saggi critici di metodologia* [*Critical Essays on Methodology*] (1934), Masci explains his preference for the hypothesis of causality rather than of interdependence in a general equilibrium framework as a proper representation of economic laws. To him, economic laws take place over time, in contrast with the atemporal conception of the mathematical economics.[19] Even if he was not against the general equilibrium theory, Masci was convinced that the discipline should also develop a partial equilibrium approach focusing on the study of the causes of economic phenomena for a more concrete approach to economic problems. Furthermore, the causality underlining economic laws also implied the possibility of their quantitative measurement.

As for his contribution to corporative economics, Masci published two monographs in 1935 and 1937 about industrial concentration and the creation of monopolies, the prevalence of fixed capital, the overcoming of perfect competition and the consequent need of state interventions to control market power, in which the influence of Marshall and Schumpeter is apparent, along with that of the Italian debate on such issues. As Mosca's (2018) historical reconstruction shows, the debate on monopoly, market power and competition were central especially within Italian marginalism already since the end of the nineteenth century and until the interwar period. Mosca remarks that this theorizing also originated from the evolution of the Italian economy towards modern forms of industrialization with a slow but progressive productive concentration, and it was devoted to provide policy answers.

All these issues are at the center of Modigliani's thesis as well. It is divided into four parts, the most interesting of which are part I and II, where he discussed the evolution of the capitalistic system, he justified state interventions for efficiency and not only equity reasons and elaborated in detail the appropriate method to measuring production costs.

Modigliani's starting point was the explanation of the origin of monopolies as the result of economies of scale and technological and financial reasons (easier access to credit). Modigliani's attitude did not appear hostile to industrial concentration, on the contrary, because of its economic advantages, such as a more efficient use of resources, a better coordination of the investment activity and a reduction of price fluctuations, the state should, in some cases, encourage mergers between firms. However, in doing so, it must also protect consumers from market power, understood as a monopolist's power to impose a selling price to maximize its own profit.

Although Modigliani's explicit reference to Marshall's *Industry and Trade* and the abovementioned widespread Italian literature on these issues, he did not apply the tools of marginal analysis, and with the exception of Masci, there is no reference to the contemporary literature.

Modigliani's starting point was a discussion of the evolution of market structures, from perfect competition to monopolies, through which he introduced the central theme of the dissertation concerning the advantages of applying standard rules in firms' accounting, particularly for a rational and standardize determination of production costs and prices. Differently from his earlier writings, here Modigliani acknowledged that the economic theory has demonstrated that under perfect competition, free market prices lead to the maximization of individual and social welfare. Therefore, state interventions are not justified. Nonetheless, because the capitalistic system has evolved towards the creation of monopolies characterized by an increasing specialization of machineries and production processes, the classical ideas of capital mobility and Say's law do not apply anymore. Firms encounter increasing difficulties to adjust their production to continuous changes of market conditions, with the costs of their adjustments that weigh on collectivity. The advantages, he acknowledged, and disadvantages of industrial concentration depend on the monopolies' use of their market power. Most important, according to Modigliani, the overcoming of perfect competition leads to the disappearance of the reasons preventing state interventions. Modigliani recalled that the need for state action was first recognized by fascism with the creation of the corporative system, defined as a "regime of organized and methodic state intervention in the economic field" (1939, p. 24, my translation).

Modigliani envisaged two kinds of public intervention: to control and to direct economic activities. The state has to exercise control over large companies' behavior to protect consumers (he mentioned the control of telephone and transportation rates), along with savers, who play a crucial role for the development of private enterprise, and over the banking system also by managing interest rates. State control is finally required for fiscal and statistical reasons. Statistical information is especially important to acquire precise knowledge of the economic phenomena the state needs to control (1939, p. 26).

Regarding state directive function, it must be devoted to encourage the merging of firms, to regulate the creation of new equipment, to promote the socialization in some cases of big companies, to coordinate economic activity through the elaboration of economic plans and finally to organize financial activity. This latter refers to changes of the discount rate and monetary management. In other words, through its directive function the state replaces competitive markets in coordinating individual activities.

With respect to his previous essays, Modigliani's discussion of the evolution of market structures and the consequent evolution of the relationships among state, market and individuals is now based not on an a priori (ideological) rejection of classical liberalism, and its abstract conceptions but on the awareness that perfect competition, which represents the necessary premise for the application of the classical economic principles, has been replaced by monopolies.

Once the need of state intervention to control and to organize the economic activities is recognized, Modigliani introduced and discussed in the second part of the thesis the advantages of applying standard budget rules. He remarked that the "unification of concepts, terminology and measurement" (p. 34) would lead to an exact calculation of costs by all firms, and an exact knowledge of their own business, which are necessary to plan their production activity. Standard rules also give the possibility of comparing firms' behavior.

To demonstrate the advantages of an objective and standard calculation of production costs, Modigliani introduced several numerical examples. On this ground, he finally returned to discuss price control, arguing that the precise knowledge of costs allows firms to protect themselves by asking policy makers to set prices not lower than their costs. A similar application refers to workers with the implementation of a common evaluation method of their contribution to production and, thus, for a standardization of their returns. More in general the application of standard rules helps the state to exercise effective control over economic activities, providing extensive economic documentation that is effective over the economic life.

Modigliani further developed all these aspects about competition, monopolies and state interventions soon after his PhD at the New School for Social Research in the context of the organization of a socialist economy (see Chapter 3), showing that Modigliani, also after his arrival in the United States and especially after his famous 1944 *Econometrica* article, was still reasoning on the topics he discussed in the 1930s.

Despite Modigliani definitely distancing himself from the fascism, and despite his disillusion with "new economics" (the principles of corporative economics), he did not lose his confidence in policy and government interventions, in the state and its democratic institutions and the roles they play for an equal and more efficient organization of economic activities.

Notes

1 Also see Camurri (2018) "Tre Nobel dicono no a Berlusconi. Con Paul Samuelson e Robert Solow" (pp. 239–240). The letter was signed also by Henry Rosovsky (emeritus professor at Harvard), Joshua Cohen, and Franklin M. Fisher (emeritus professors at MIT).
2 For a biography of Enrico Modigliani, see Italo Farnetani (2011). Among Enrico Modigliani's initiatives there were the founding in 1918 of the "*Opera di assistenza materna – Maternal care institution*" that assisted several unmarried mothers and the creation of children's kitchens for free food distribution. He strongly believed that among the main causes of child mortality, which was double for illegitimate children, there was malnutrition (www.treccani.it/enciclopedia/enrico-modigliani. Last access November 6, 2019).
3 Modigliani recalled that at the time (the year 1936) the course in economics he had at the Faculty of Law was about "the theory and institutions of the so-called 'Corporative State', which had nothing to do with modern economic theory" (2001, p. 10).
4 There are some references to Modigliani's writings in *Franco Modigliani (Ideological Profile of Economics Laureates)*: https://econjwatch.org ModiglianiIPEL.
5 With the promulgation of racial laws, many academic professors lost their positions, as in the case of the economist and statistician Riccardo Bachi, who Modigliani mentioned as his guide in his first readings of economics (see later).
6 For a detailed account of the journals and their editors see Michelini (2019), on which this chapter is largely based.
7 See, for example, Camurri (2018) who refers to Modigliani's attendance at the *Centro giovanile per il fascismo universale* (Youth Center for Universal Fascism) directed by Ruggero Zangrandi. According to Camurri the center was a sort of "covering structure" for young anti conformists who believed on a universal and anti-imperialist fascism founded on a program of radical economic and social reforms (pp. xxiii–xvi).
8 On the postwar problem-solving approach to economics, see Bernstein (2001), who ascribed it to the use of economics during the war period.
9 On corporative economics and economy in Italy and its lines of thought, see Bini (2017), Guidi (2018) and Barucci et al. ed. (2018).
10 Modigliani also recalled the important support he had from his older cousin Piero Modigliani and about his surprise about the prize. He was than enrolled in his second year at the Faculty of Law.
11 Modigliani also referred to the reading of Benedetto Croce, suggested by his cousin while assisting him in the writing of the piece for the competition, and to Mussolini's support of the Spanish civil war, which was strongly criticized at that time.
12 Part of Modigliani's discussion on price controls is closely related with the devaluation of lira and the risk of a price-wage spiral. Thus, the introduction of price controls was also justified by the need to protect the value of lira and to avoid a redistribution of wealth to the exclusive advantage of those with a variable income.
13 About replacing the concept of homo economicus with "homo corporativus", and the idea of economics as a political and moral science, see, for example, F. Carli (1938), and Gino Arias and Ugo Spirito, on this see Bini (2017). In the 1960s and 1970s Modigliani established close relationships with the son of Filippo Carli, Guido Carli, governor of the Bank of Italy from 1962 to 1972, with which Modigliani collaborated on the building of the bank's macroeconometric model.
14 Modigliani referred to Say's law as having the merit of "supporting the necessary economic solidarity among nations" by recognizing that exports are conditional on the country's imports; thus, economic development of poor countries were desirable (1938,

p. 72). He finally emphasized the contradiction of applying to the national and international market behavior a theory based on individual interest because the nation is not the sum of individuals, as social utility is not merely the sum of individual utility.

15 Modigliani returned to this subject in a short article in March 1938 and then in June. In *"Ancora intorno al principio di autarchia"* he clarified that autarky is economically advantageous only in the context of the "new economics", which shifts the attention from the individual to the national collectivity, organized in the form of the state, and therefore cannot be extended to the lesser units such as provinces or municipalities. Within a nation could not exist any particular interest, being subordinate to the national ends.

16 Keynes's reasoning was however quite known in Italy at that time and mentioned also within the literature about the corporative economy (see Michelini, 2019, pp. 47–48).

17 As noticed by Michelini (2019, p. 34) in his critique to the liberal egalitarianism, Modigliani appears also inspired by Pareto's and Spencer's Darwinism.

18 Riccardo Bachi was professor of economics at the University of Parma working on methodology and on economic cycles. Mussolini asked him to be involved in the organization of a statistical department for the Ministry of Finance. However, with the promulgation of racial laws, he lost his academic position and moved to Palestine. He came back to Italy in 1946, but he did not return to study economics.

19 See Caffè (1974).

References

Barucci, P., P. Bini, and L. Conigliello ed. 2018. *Il Corporativismo nell'Italia di Mussolini. Dal declino delle Istituzioni liberali alla Costituzione Repubblicana*, Firenze: Firenze University Press.

Bernstein, M. A. 2001. *A Perilous Progress*, Princeton, NJ: Economists and Public Purpose in Twenty–Century America, University Press.

Bini, P. 2017. "Corporative Economics and the Making of Economic Policy in Italy during the Interwar Years (1922–1940)", in *Business Cycles in Economic Though: A History*, ed. by A. Alcouffe, M. Poettinger, and B. Schefold, Abingdon, UK: Routledge.

Caffè, F. 1974. "Il tempo nel pensiero di Guglielmo Masci", *Il Giornale degli Economisti e Annali di Economia*, nuova serie, 33 (9/10), September–October: 679–683.

Camurri, R., ed. 2010. *Franco Modigliani. L'Italia vista dall'America. Battaglie e riflessioni di un esule*, Turin: Bollati Boringhieri.

———, ed. 2018. *I modesti consigli di un premio Nobel. Franco Modigliani. Rischio Italia. L'Italia vista dall'America (1970–2003)*, Rome: Donzelli Editore.

Carli, F. 1938. *Le basi storiche e dottrinario dell'economia coporativa*, Padova: Cedam.

Farnetani, I. 2011. "Enrico Modigliani", *Treccani, Dizionario Biografico degli Italiani*, 75. www.treccani.it/enciclopedia/enrico-modigliani_(Dizionario-Biografico). Last access November 6, 2019.

Franco Modigliani Papers, David M. Rubenstein Rare Book and Manuscript Library.

Guidi, M. E. L. 2018. *Corporate Economics and the Italian Tradition of Economic Thought: A Survey*. http://eprints.adm.unipi.it/1275/1/guidi.htm.

Klamer, A. 1984. *The New Classical Macroeconomics: Conversations with the New Classical Economists and Their Opponents*, Brighton: Harvester Press.

Klein, D. B., R. Daza, and V. D. Giovinazzo. 2013. "Franco Modigliani (Ideological Profile of Economics Laureates)", *Econ Journal Watch*, 10 (3), September. https://econjwatch.org›ModiglianiIPEL. Last access November 29, 2019.

Markowitz, H. 1952. "Portfolio selection". *Journal of Finance*, 7: 77–91.

Masci, G. 1934. *Saggi critici di metodologia*, Catania: Studio Editoriale Moderno.

Michelini, L. 2019. *Il nazionl-fascismo economico del giovane Franco Modigliani*, Firenze University Press. www.academia.edu/40986118/Il_nazional-fascismo_economico_del_giovane_Franco_Modigliani.

Modigliani, F. 1937 (2007). *Crisi del sistema economico, prezzi politici e autarchia. Cinque articoli giovanili: The Crisis of the Economic System, Political Prices and Autarky: Five Early Works (Roma 1937–1938)*, ed. by D. Parisi, Vita e Pensiero.

———. 1938. "L'autarchia nazionale", *Lo Stato. Rivista di Scienze Politiche, Giuridiche ed Economiche*, fascicolo 2: pp. 76–96.

———. 1939. "La regolamentazione e la standardizzazione dei bilanci, della contabilità e del calcolo del prezzo del costo nei suoi aspetti teorici e nelle sue attuazioni all'estero", Franco Modigliani Papers.

———. 1947. "L'Organizzazione e la Direzione della Produzione in un'Economia Socialista", *Giornali degli Economisti e Annali di Economia*, 6: 441–514.

———. 1985. Franco Modigliani. Biographical, The Sveriges Riksbank Prize in Economic Sciences in Memory of Alfred Nobel 1985 https://www.nobelprize.org/prizes/economic-sciences/1985/modigliani/biographical/

———. 2001. *Adventure of an Economist*, Texere.

———. Undated. "Plan to Meet the Problem of Rising Meat and Other Food Prices Without Bureaucratic Controls", Franco Modigliani Papers.

Mongiovi, G. 2015. "Franco Modigliani and the Socialist State", *Preliminary Draft*: 1–22. http://qcpages.qc.cuny.edu/~lussher/mongiovi05.pdfpp. Last access November 29, 2019.

Mosca, M. 2018. *Monopoly Power and Competition. The Italian Marginalist Perspective*, Cheltenham: Edward Elgar.

Schumpeter, J. A. 1954 (1976). *Storia dell'analisi economica*, Torino: Bollati Boringhieri.

2 Approaching Keynes and American Keynesianism

Introduction

Modigliani arrived in New York with his wife Serena Calabi and her family in August 1939 at the age of twenty-one. He enrolled soon after in the Graduate Faculty of Political and Social Sciences of the New School for Social Research, thanks to the Italian jurist Paolo Contini, who put Modigliani in contact with Max Ascoli, a political scientist among the founding members of the graduate school (see Camurri 2010, p. xxxvii; Mongiovi 2005, p. 429).[1] Modigliani spent almost ten years at the New School (until 1948) that were of fundamental importance for his education in economics, shaping his approach to the discipline. An intellectual debt, especially towards his mentor Jacob Marschak, Modigliani always mentioned, he "took me in his hands" he recalled, "he was very instrumental in giving me a style . . . a combination of theory, that is modelling, with testing empirical facts" (Klamer 1984, p. 115).[2] Modigliani joined the New School with an education in the humanities (Liceo Classico Visconti and a degree in law) with no training in mathematics and statistics, and from an intellectual context so much different from the New School:

> I worked hard but, nonetheless, remember that period as an exciting one, as I was discovering my passion for economics, thanks also to excellent teachers, including Adolph Lowe and above all Jacob Marschak to whom I owe a debt of gratitude beyond words. He helped me develop solid foundations in economics and econometrics, some mathematical foundations, introduced me to the great issues of the day and gave me, together with his unforgettable kindness, constant encouragement. In particular I owe to him that blend of theory and empirical analysis, theories that can be tested and empirical work guided by theory – that has characterized a good deal of my later work. Marschak also provided me with an experience that contributed to my development, by inviting me to participate in an informal seminar which met in New York around 1940–41, whose members included, among others, Abraham Wald, Tjalling Koopmans and Oscar Lange.

(Modigliani 1985, www.nobelprize.org/prizes/economic-sciences/1985/modigliani/biographical/;
see also Modigliani 2001, p. 19)

Since his arrival in the United States, Modigliani took part in a unique and stimulating intellectual milieu, which was placing the economic discipline on a new frontier, becoming the avant-garde of new mainstream economics that would be soon after pursued at the Cowles Commission under Marschak's directorship (see Düppe and Weintraub 2013).

As Modigliani acknowledged, he began his research when the profession was absorbing two important revolutions: the theory of choice under uncertainty (by Von Neumann and Morgenstern) and statistical inference from non-experimental observations, inspired by Haavelmo. The other revolution Modigliani confronted at the New School was the Keynesian one. He first approached Keynes's theory thanks to seminars organized by Oskar Lange, to long discussions with Abba Lerner and with Jacob Marschak. All of them were familiar with Keynes's theory and clearly shaped Modigliani's reading within a general equilibrium system of equations.

This chapter is devoted to Modigliani's 1944 *Econometrica* article on Keynesian and classical economics and to his PhD dissertation, which introduced him in the community of prominent economists when he was only twenty-six years old. I discuss the origin, the meaning and prevailing reading of his first article since his arrival in United States. I also investigate whether and under what respect there are any connections with his previous reasoning about economics or whether this article marked Modigliani's break with his past as a self-taught economist.

The economic science at the New School

The New School for Social Research was also known as the "University in Exile" for a number of European refugees, especially the German-speaking scholars it hosted, becoming at that time a "general center for modern continental European culture" (Hageman 2011, p. 653). Alvin Johnson established and directed in 1933 the University in Exile as part of the New School with the support of the Rockefeller Foundation and the Committee in Aid of German Scholars (Mongiovi 2005, pp. 427–428). As Mongiovi (2005) explains, to convince American institutions and foundations about his project, Johnson emphasized the benefits the United States could have by attracting European scholars.[3] Thus, in an undated memorandum Johnson described his plan as follows:

> The project is conceived, not as a charity but as a plan for enriching the American educational system the enlistment of first-class scholars displaced from their positions. It follow that in every case proposed to the New School for consideration a careful study must be made of the record and quality of the scholar in question. . . . Since our object is to bring over scholars who may be expected to strengthen the American educational system, we are interested only in scholars who have proved themselves and who still have many productive years ahead of them.

(quoted from Mongiovi 2005, p. 428)

The Graduate Faculty pursued an interdisciplinary approach to social sciences with its most influential professors who covered different fields: the sociologist Hans Speier, the psychologist Rudolf Arnheim, and the economists Fritz Lehmann and especially Adolph Lowe, Hans Neisser and Jacob Marschak. In his reconstruction of the economics that was practiced at the New School, Mongiovi (2005) also remarked they all shared an anti-dogmatic attitude to social sciences that was critical and methodologically eclectic. The group of German-speaking economists had a lot in common, sharing a Marxian mathematical education and having already occupied prominent academic and political positions in their countries (Mongiovi 2005, pp. 428–430; Hagemann 2011, 2005). They had been economic planners but were fascinated by the rigor and formalism of marginal analysis, thus attempting to overcome its limits, and not as sympathetic about Keynes's General Theory. According to Mongiovi, Lederer (1936) and Neisser's (1936) "lukewarm" reviews of Keynes are emblematic of the New School attitude towards the Keynesian revolution. Neisser, for example, was critical about Keynes's identification of full capacity utilization with full employment. To him, capital stock might be insufficient to provide employment for all the available labor. He was also critical of Keynes's neglecting the problem of technological unemployment and structural dynamics and was not convinced that a fall in wages would lead to an expected fall in profits and, therefore, of investment. Neisser also see Keynes's theory as not inconstent with the "orthodox doctrine" (Mongiovi 2005, p. 433, 2015, p. 4). An approach that would explain attempts such as that of Modigliani to apply the tools of marginal analysis to Keynes's macroeconomics.

The New School economists agreed, instead, that the effective demand was usually insufficient to guarantee full employment, and therefore, they believed in policy interventions.[4] Because of their small interest in Keynes's *General Theory*, the Graduate Faculty did not contribute so much to the widespread literature on money interest and effective demand (Mongiovi 2005, p. 433). Modigliani himself recalled his interest in classical and Keynesian economics had been especially due to the arrival at the New School of Abba Lerner in 1942. However, the PhD supervisor who followed Modigliani's research since the beginning was not Lerner but Marschak, as their correspondence clearly shows, who was very influential in stimulating Modigliani's research interests.

Marschak's ability to work with several paradigms is among the main features of his research activity, as Cherrier (2010) emphasizes, arguing that his multifaceted contributions to economics run across many fields: rational choice, economics as a social engineering, uncertainty and the stochastic approach to economics. This eclectic attitude was certainly appreciated by the young Modigliani, whose research, especially in the 1940s and still in the 1950s, revolved around a number of micro and macroeconomics issues. Marschak was particularly interested in monetary macroeconomics already since his dissertation on the quantity theory of money (see Dimand and Hagemann 2019, pp. 3–4), an interest that he probably transmitted to Modigliani, whose first readings of economics came through his translations to Italian of German books about price control. Marschak is considered a pioneer in the field of portfolio theory with his paper on "Money and the Theory of Assets" (1938), which he wrote while at Oxford. According to Mehrling (2010), and Dimand and Hagemann (2019), his attempts to have a Walrasian system with a money demand equation incorporated set the agenda for subsequent research in this direction contributing to the development of the postwar "monetary Walrasian economics", as Mehrling characterizes also Modigliani's macroeconomics, and especially Markowitz (1952), Patinkin (1956) and Tobin (1958), which became dominant in the postwar period.

At the New School, Marschak also worked on topics related to Keynesian macroeconomics: the effects of animal spirits on investment decisions, the role of government in stabilizing the economy, linking Keynesian macroeconomics to earlier Swedish monetary economics and Knut Wicksell's natural and market rates of interest. He also went on to study money illusion in demand analysis, which represents a continuation of the line of thought he pursued when at Oxford and preserved his interest on simultaneous equations macroeconomic models, which became entangled with his interest in econometrics (see Dimand and Hagemann 2019, p. 11; also see Hagemann 2005; Mehrling 2002).

Marschak was the founding director of the Oxford Institute of Statistics in 1935, while in New York he organized seminars on econometrics and mathematical economics "which proved to be the catalyst of the development of econometrics in the US" (Cherrier 2010, p. 3, quoted from Koopmans 1978, p. ix; also see Christ 1985).

Modigliani approaching Keynesian economics

In the beginning, the study of Keynesian economics was not at the center of Modigliani's interests as it was not at the New School. It appears from his handwritten notes that he was still fascinated by the study of market forms, particularly monopolies in relation to the achievement of social welfare, a topic on which he had written in the 1930s, discussing the evolution of the capitalistic system from competitive to monopolistic because of the process of industrial concentration, with firms that set prices to maximize their profits at the expenses of consumers and social utility. As reconstructed in the previous chapter, these topics were however faced from an ideological perspective, with few reference to the literature and the tools of economic analysis.

Marschak, in a letter from January 1942 suggested Modigliani read the *Economic Journal* 1941 December review of the E A. G. Robinson book on monopoly because it "seems to touch closely upon your same subject", also asking for a review or an article for the *Social Research* (Marschak to Modigliani: January 22, 1942, MP).[5] Again, a few months later, in June, he wrote

Modigliani whether he thought "feasible that we might (you and I) present a joint report on monopoly and welfare which would give an outline of all our 4 (or 8) sub-problems and may be . . . of general interest, both because of the practical and of the methodological aspect" (June 25, 1945, MP). Still, in July Modigliani sent him a paper "on a problem not strictly related to our problem but on which I have been interested in these last days" about firms' location "which was first dealt with by Hotelling". Modigliani also added that he "intend[s] to write soon another paper referring to the monopoly problem (possibly next week). . . . I am using your Gibson book extensively. . . . I have been at the New School and made my application for the Doctor degree as you told me" (July 17, 1942, MP).

Marschak was supportive, encouraging the young Modigliani to carry on his studies: "I should like to know whether you are making some progress with your thesis. Your future will very much depend on your ability to concentrate and publish something really new. I am sure you *can do it,* whatever the external circumstances" (Marschak to Modigliani: January 22, 1942, MP).

In his autobiography Modigliani (2001, p. 43) recalled that his attention towards Keynesian economics especially related with the arrival of Lerner. Indeed, Modigliani's lengthy discussions with Lerner represented the departure point for his "Liquidity Preference" article. The paper was intended as his answer to Lerner's "functional finance" that Modigliani described as follows in his autobiography:[6]

> The function of [public] expenditure must not be the traditional one of providing the necessarily public service, and that of taxes must not be to pay for the public services but, rather, to stabilize employment by increasing or diminishing disposable income and aggregate demand. I rejected this formulation because it presupposed that the so-called limit case of Keynes was the prevailing situation in the market economies.

(2001, pp. 43–44)[7]

Modigliani wanted to challenge the idea that only fiscal policy worked. By contrast, his 1944 article and his PhD dissertation focused on the role of expansionary monetary policy to achieve full employment. Nonetheless, in the dissertation and, later, in a long essay on the working of a socialist economy (apparently written between 1944 and 1945), Modigliani also stressed the role of public expenditures to be financed, however, by the creation of new money (see next chapter).

Thus, Modigliani and Lerner's discussions revolved around the interpretation of Keynesian and classical economics, particularly the so-called Keynesian case (Keynes's liquidity trap) as well as Lerner's monetary explanation of interest rates (as determined by the liquidity preference schedule rather that by the savings and investment schedules). Following Hicks's (1937) IS-LM model, Modigliani distinguished between classical and Keynesian economics on the basis of the interest rate elasticity of liquidity preference. According to him, high levels of interest are in line with the classical theory in which the demand for money is only function of income – the price of liquidity is too high – therefore, any small shift in the propensity to save will cause the interest rate to fall to induce borrowers to borrow more, leaving income and employment unchanged. Nonetheless, if in the relevant range the LM curve were moderately bent, then an increase in the propensity to save requires some adjustment to money wages to maintain full employment:

> Even though [the classical economists] did not foresee that a change in the propensity to consume might require a cut in money wage, they were perfectly right in maintaining that a cut in wage would lead to full employment. And this continues to hold true until the range of "low" interest rate is reached where the LL [LM] curve becomes perpendicular to the interest rate axis. It is at this point that Keynes's analysis becomes really relevant. . . . [Y]ou wanted to deny that any change in investment could occur unless people changed their desire to hold cash.

(Modigliani to Lerner: June 2nd 1943, MP)

In his reply Lerner pointed out that Modigliani was ascribing to classical Keynes reasoning based on the effect of a fall in income on the rate of interest through a reduction in the need for cash "so that the investors have a signal that they should increase investments" (June 2, 1943, MP). Lerner also specified that the classical conclusions did not hold "whenever the liquidity preference is less than infinite but only when this elasticity is zero" (June 2, 1943, MP). In this case, an infinitesimal decrease in employment is sufficient to bring about any necessary fall in the rate of interest. When the liquidity preference is not vertical,

> It is possible for investments to fill the gap made by the increased propensity to save only when wages and prices have fallen as much as is necessary to reduce the rate of interest. I deny that this is the classical argument, because it differs from it not only in the mechanism but also in the conclusion. . . . The similarity is only in that both arguments finally show full employment with less consumption and more investment. The differences are that the classical theory did not indicate any necessity for wages and prices to fall while it is essential (except for the limiting cases), and that the classical theory did say that the real wage must be less, which is not necessary at all. . . . Some minor points . . . when you say the classical economists are perfectly right in saying that a cut in money wages would lead to full employment, you are disregarding the reasons they gave for it but notice that the conclusions are right for reasons given by Keynes.

(Lerner to Modigliani, June 2, 1943, MP)

To explain the determinants of interest rates and their connection with employment levels was one of Modigliani's major aims of the *Econometrica* article, defending the indirect role savings and investment still play in Keynesian economics when nominal wages are rigid. Although Lerner and Modigliani had different theories of interest rate determination, they both believed in the theoretical equivalence of wage deflation and expansionary monetary policy, around which the first part of Modigliani's article was constructed. Both also denied any practical relevance to wage cuts once their effects on income distribution and expectations are taken into consideration, as discussed in Lerner (1939) and Modigliani's PhD dissertation.

That Modigliani's interest in Keynes's *General Theory* was about his monetary and interest theory is also apparent from his correspondence with Marschak and Lange. In a letter to Marschak dated July 1943, Modigliani wrote:

> *I have just finished to write an article on the theory of the rate of interest which, you may perhaps remember had been in my mind for a long time. I don't believe it is any great achievement but it may help to clarify a few points;* in any event it is very important for me because it is the first time since I am in this country that I manage to carry a research to the end. . . . I would like to mail you a copy of the manuscript and to ask you for your advice on one or two mathematical points which I would like to include in the paper but of which I am not sure.

(July 16, 1943, emphasis added, MP)

A few months later, Lange asked Modigliani – probably at Marschak's suggestion – to send "one or more articles for *Econometrica* . . . I know you have been working on several subjects like consumer surplus, the Hotelling theory, Says' law, interest, etc." (October 5, 1943, MP).[8]

Although the subsequent literature on Modigliani's 1944 article concentrated on the relation between wage rigidity and Keynesian unemployment, Modigliani considered the last section of his paper, devoted to the construction of a "general theory of the rate of interest and money", his original and most relevant contribution. In sending the manuscript to *Econometrica* he "recommend[ed] especially . . . attention [in the editing of the English parts] to the last chapter of the paper, *which I feel is the most important of all*" (Modigliani to Mr. Leavens: managing editor of *Econometrica*: December 14, 1943, emphasis added, MP).[9] He did not equally emphasize the wage rigidity assumption probably because he knew that the interpretation of Keynes's unemployment equilibrium in terms of a horizontal labor supply was not new in the literature. That a mere discussion on the relation between wage behavior and involuntary unemployment as such did not represent Modigliani's main object of investigation is also suggested by his decision to omit from the overly long draft of the article the section devoted to the analysis of wage cutting and unemployment policies because "the chapter is not necessary for the main argument. If Prof. Lange and the referee feel it is worthwhile, it could be published in some future issue of *Econometrica*" (Modigliani to Mr. Leavens: December 14, 1943, MP).

Modigliani's monetary theory of unemployment

Modigliani introduced the 1944 article stating that his aim was to elaborate a general theory of interest alternative to Lerner's and Hicks's monetary theory, Modigliani derived from his reading of classical and Keynesian economics.[10] Therefore, the first part of the paper was devoted to a "brief reexamination" of the Keynesian theory to determine the role in it of liquidity preference and nominal wage rigidity and to specify the properties of systems in which one or both Keynesian hypotheses are abandoned. The classical theory of money and the dichotomy of real and monetary variables were also analyzed for logical consistency.[11] Modigliani aimed at extending the validity of Keynesian theory behind the special case of the liquidity trap, shifting the attention on the role played by wage rigidity – a more general and realistic hypothesis – to obtain Keynesian outcomes, in particular with reference to the influence of money supply on employment levels.

With respect to Hicks (1937), who assumed exogenously fixed nominal wage in both classical and Keynesian systems, Modigliani explicitly introduced the labor market and confronted the real and monetary mechanisms underlying the two models as the result of different wage behavior. His emphasis on wage rigidity versus classical flexibility did not mean, however, an attempt to reconcile the two systems. On the contrary, Modigliani intended to make clear the working of a monetary economy in respect to the economy analyzed by classical theory: "Systems with rigid wages share the common property that the equilibrium value of 'real variables' is determined essentially by monetary conditions rather than by 'real' factors" (1944b, p. 65).[12]

From the mere counting of unknowns and equations, he demonstrated that under flexible wages, the classical dichotomy holds because the monetary and real parts of the model formed two determinate subsystems. The money equation, either quantity theory or liquidity preference, only determines the price level, whereas the rate of interest and the employment level do not depend on money.

In contrast, under wage rigidity, the classical dichotomy breaks down. The monetary side of the system, defined by the liquidity preference, the supply of and demand for saving and its equilibrium condition, determines the equilibrium level of money income and interest rates, from which all real variables now depend. Once the equilibrium in the money market is established, the equilibrium value of real variables is also determined. In particular, to each money income there corresponds (for given price and technical conditions) a definite equilibrium level of employment and output, which Modigliani pointed out, does not tend to correspond with full employment "except by mere chance" (1944b, p. 66).

The reading of Keynes's theory in terms of given nominal wage and quantity of money, with the employment level depending on money income was common in the early 1940s, but Modigliani also demonstrated that it was possible to derive from a general system of equations, either classical or Keynesian outcomes, depending only on wage behavior.[13] Most important, he was challenging the traditional Keynesian view of unemployment as explained by the lack of investment rather than the scarcity of money. To illustrate the monetary transmission mechanism, Modigliani started from the hypothesis of a fall in the marginal efficiency of investment and discussed its effects on employment levels through change in the demand for money. According to him, the resulting fall in interest rates leads to an excess demand for money as an asset. If the supply of money is not properly increased, money income has to fall to restore, by a fall in the transaction demand, the equilibrium in the money market. Under the condition of flexible wages, this means a fall in money wages and prices without affecting real variables. Under wage rigidity instead,

> The reduction in money income made necessary by the fall in the rate of interest becomes a reduction in real income and employment as well. The effect of a shift of the investment schedule is now to start a typical process of contraction so frequently described in Keynesian literature. As producers of investment goods make losses, they have no other choice than to dismiss workers, even though their physical productivity is unchanged. . . . The fall in money income increases the supply of money to hold; the fall in real income decreases savings and rises its marginal efficiency above the level r_1. . . . [T]his double set of reactions leads finally to a new equilibrium, with a smaller money and real income, less employment, higher real wages and a rate of interest somewhere below r_0 and above the new "full employment" interest r_1.

(1944b, p. 73)

Differently from Lange (1938) and Hicks (1937), who concentrated on the effects on investment of a fall in its marginal efficiency, Modigliani looked at the monetary side of the system.[14] His focal point was the disequilibrium in the money market that starts the Keynesian process of a reduction in real income and employment to clear the money market.[15] Modigliani pointed out that changes in the marginal efficiency of investment had no direct influence on employment, as shown by the classical case in which its variation affects only the rate of interest. To him the reduced level of employment and investment is "not the result of causal relationship" but "a symptom of monetary disturbances, investments are low because employment is low and not the other way around" (1944b, p. 77). Therefore, by an increase in the quantity of money, or "at worst" reducing wages, employment will rise in "every field of production including investment" (1944b, p. 77).

Modigliani deeply discussed the theoretical equivalence of monetary and wage policy in his PhD dissertation on *The General Theory of Employment, Interest and Money under the Assumption of Flexible Prices and Fixed Prices*, which he defended in May 1944 after the publication of the article.

Modigliani's PhD dissertation: unemployment and money supply

Modigliani's dissertation was an extended version of the "Liquidity Preference" article with additional sections on the functioning of the labor market and the effects of wage cuts and expansionary monetary policy on employment levels. The dissertation further testifies how Modigliani was especially interested in the analysis of the monetary aspects of Keynesian economics and their policy implications. First, he introduced a graphical representation of equilibrium under classical and Keynesian systems, somewhat different from the analysis carried out in the article. Following Lange (1938, p. 31), in the article Modigliani read the wage rigidity hypothesis as equivalent to a perfect elastic labor supply as long as the demand for labor is less than full employment. Therefore, he measured unemployment as the distance from their intersection – which denotes the equilibrium level of employment – and the kink of labor supply, to which corresponds full employment. In the PhD dissertation, instead, he introduced an increasing demand for and a decreasing supply of labor in a real wage-employment plan. Their intersection now determines what level of employment would be full employment, with no necessary connection with the equilibrium one. Any given price equal to the marginal labor cost corresponds, in fact, to the equilibrium level of output and hence of employment, which lies only on the labor demand. Its distance from the labor supply measures unemployment. In other words, differently from the horizontal labor supply – which implies an equilibrium in the labor market – unemployment is now associated with an excess supply in this market. Modigliani explained that under wager rigidity, the actual equilibrium level of employment (N) – that is for which prices (P) are equal to marginal cost – that tends to rule the system has no necessary connection with full employment because every point in the demand for labor curve, and not only the full employment one, gives a possible position of equilibrium. "What point on this curve will actually be established depends on the price level that is consistent with the quantity of active money in the system" (1944a, p. 42, MP). In other words, the price and the employment can only take such value as to satisfy the money equation $M = L\ [r(N), PX\ (N)]$.[16] There will be full employment only in such cases in which the money supply is so adjusted to be consistent with the full employment price level, and, Modigliani pointed out, "[T]here is of course no automatic mechanism ensuring this adjustment. Since the relevant quantity for the determination of the level of employment is the ratio W/P if an attempt is made at fixing wages in real terms under conditions of under employment, no amount of monetary management will be successful in bringing about full employment" (1944a, p. 43, MP).

With respect to the article, there is also a section on "Generalization of the Argument to Other Price Rigidities" and a section devoted to discuss the policy implications of his Keynesian economics. As for the former section, Modigliani enlarged the case of rigidity to other services or commodities "whose price is 'fixed' in money terms" (1944a, p. 44 MP). Here Modigliani ascribed a money illusion (with implicitly explained wage rigidity) also to entrepreneurs. He justified his focus on wage rather than price rigidity because of the institutional and quantitative importance of labor, arguing that however also the behavior of "the price charged by entrepreneurs for the use of their equipment" is equally important. According to him, if entrepreneurs are "money minded (as labor is)" they may compute the depreciation charge of their equipment not on the basis of the actual replacement cost of similar equipment but on the basis of the cost originally paid. This "money minded rationality" will refrain from using equipment unless this cost can be recovered (1944a, p. 46, MP). Then, as in the case of rigid wage, the level of employment and output depend on the quantity of active money. Indeed any fall in the quantity of money will decrease the price level and "entrepreneurs, finding that they cannot recover the money cost, will begin to reduce the amount of equipment used . . . as in the case of simple wage rigidity, there will be one quantity of active money and relative price level that will produce an optimum situation" (1944a, p. 47 MP). This equilibrium does not necessarily correspond to full employment, but it is "optimum" in the sense that "the depreciation charge will, once more, correspond to the true cost for the community of the marginal use of equipment, and the real wage rate will be equal to the marginal product of labor" (1944a, p. 47 MP).

Modigliani concluded that even if a money illusion is not justified from a rational point of view, it is widespread among workers as well as entrepreneurs.

Part II of the dissertation is partly devoted to the policy implications of his interpretation of the Keynesian theory (probably the sections omitted in the article), pointing out that "in stressing so much the monetary aspect of the unemployment problem we are not only interested in a more correct theoretical formulation, for this formulation has also important implications concerning the concrete forms of economic policies indicated to relieve unemployment" (1944a, p. 52, MP). Modigliani distinguished between "the normal case" and the "Keynesian case" re-affirming once again that in the normal situation unemployment "is merely due to the scarcity of money in relation to the schedule of liquidity preference and the money fixed prices"; therefore, the main tool of intervention should be an increase in the quantity of money. If properly carried out, "investment will take care for themselves, rising together with employment and income" (1944a, p. 52, MP). He also clarified that he did not refer only to open market policy, but interesting enough, a rise of money will be much more effective if injected directly through the income stream rather than through the money market. Modigliani remarked that "public investments would be undertaken for the purpose of increasing the quantity of money and not just for the purpose of increasing investment". For this reason public investment *"should be financed with newly created money and not with money borrowed from the public, or even worse, with the proceed of taxation"* (1944a, p. 52, MP, emphasis in the original). Otherwise, Modigliani concluded it relieves unemployment only temporarily but does nothing to attack the true causes of the problem, namely, the scarcity of cash. For the same reason, if government expenditures are financed by borrowing from the money market, the rate of interest will tend to rise, and public investment will be partly offset by a fall in private investment, with the former that merely substitutes the latter. Finally, newly created money avoids the rising of national debt. Modigliani also pointed out that in the Keynesian case even if monetary policy breaks down, the argument of financing public investment by money created ad hoc still holds.

In the concluding section, accompanied by a mathematical appendix, Modigliani discussed the effects of wage cuts, a problem that "has caused much confusion and some definite mistakes" (1944a, p. 70, MP), and expansionary monetary policy, on the employment level and income distribution among workers, entrepreneurs and fixed income receivers. A topic on which Modigliani devoted much attention over the 1930s with reference to price controls.

Modigliani's starting point was Tarshis's (1939) empirical demonstration of a direct correlation between money and real wage rates. Before Tarshis (1939), Dunlop (1938) and Kalecki (1938) had challenged empirically Keynes's conclusion on the inverse relation of nominal and real wages based on his acceptance of the law of decreasing returns and the assumption of a constant degree of competition during the cycle. They disputed the validity of the law of rising marginal (labor) costs (except at the peak of the boom) because in many industries there is excess capacity. According to them during the boom the employment expansion (due to a rise in the aggregate demand) was accompanied by a rise of nominal and real wage rate. A conclusion shared by Modigliani who stated that with low employment and much unused capacity of plants and organization, labor productivity will be high and not greatly affected by the expansion of employment.[17] Furthermore, if the elasticity of the demand for labor with respect to real wage is more than one, which is likely to occur as long as the employment level remains low, the employment expansion is accompanied by an increase rather than a fall of the real wage bill. Therefore, he concluded, wage cuts was not against the interest of the labor class (1944a, p. 72, MP).[18]

However, according to Modigliani, the most interesting result refers to the behavior of profits: if the fall in price level "is considerable, entrepreneurs may very well find that . . . their real net profits are actually reduced" (1944a, p. 73, MP).[19] Therefore, Modigliani emphasized that the class that asked for wage cuts as the "only sound way of reducing unemployment" would be the only one to lose out. These negative consequences are worsened by expectations: wage cuts may become a dangerous source of entrepreneurial loss and thus lead to further contractions: "Realized losses are sure to create a mood of pessimistic expectation and thus adversely affect the level of economic activity" (1944a, pp. 75–76, MP). Modigliani considered expectations as the most important argument against wage cuts: "a fall in the price level may lead to the expectation of a further fall and thus create a speculative demand for money. If this happens, a cut in money wage is likely to cause a fall rather than an increase in employment" (1944a, n. 1, p. 76, MP). However, he did not develop the argument further because, being dynamic, it was excluded by his simplifying assumption of unity elasticity of expectations.

The crucial role of expectations, not only to determine a full employment equilibrium but, first of all, for the existence of the system solution, was analyzed more in depth in the 1950s. In some lengthy notes he prepared for his classes and that also served as a basis for a book on the theory of money and interest Modigliani analyzed the conditions for the existence and stability of equilibrium in which expectations played a crucial role (see Chapter 6). Discussing the validity of the Pigou effect, Modigliani will emphasize the potential instability of a system with flexible prices.[20]

What Modigliani meant by a monetary explanation of unemployment and the significance he ascribed to wage rigidity also emerges from his correspondence with Don Patinkin.

From the monetary to wage rigidity interpretation of Keynes's unemployment (Modigliani and Patinkin correspondence)

Since its appearance, Modigliani's article has been read as a reassessment of the relevance of Keynes's revolution. His demonstration that Keynesian outcomes could be derived from a classical system by the wage rigidity hypothesis especially called the attention of neoclassical economists, who read it as an attempt to make Keynes's theory consistent with neoclassical economics. Leontief, in a letter to Modigliani, defined the article as "one of the best expositions of the Keynesian theory in its relation to a Classical theory. . . . You might be interested that in his answer to my discussion of the homogeneity assumption in 1936 *QJE* Mr. Keynes acknowledged the existence of his non-homogeneity assumption" (July 3, 1944, MP). Haberler referred to Modigliani's analysis as a "remarkable demonstration of the crucial role of wage rigidity" to deny the novelty of Keynes's theory (1946, p. 190, n. 11). Schumpeter even considered the article as one of the highest examples of anti-Keynesianism:

> It is really an injustice to Keynes's achievement to reduce it to the bare bones of its logical structure and then to reason on these bones as if they were all. Nevertheless, great interest attaches to the attempts that have been made to cast his system into exact form. I want in particular to mention: W. B. Reddaway's review . . . 1936; R. F. Harrod . . . 1937, J. E. Maeade . . . 1937, J.R. Hicks . . . 1937; O. Lange . . . 1938; P.A. Lerner 1938. . . . In the hand of economists less in sympathy with the spirit of Keynesian economics, some of the result presented in these papers might have been turned into serious criticisms. This is still more true of F. Modigliani "Liquidity Preference".

(1946, pp. 510–511, n. 26)

On the other hand, the main developments of Keynesian economics during the 1940s and 1950s were basically devoted to investigate the relations among effective demand, real output and the employment level.[21] Klein (1947), Hansen (1946, 1949) and Samuelson (1948) did not explicitly refer to Modigliani's monetary analysis and especially concentrated on the role of investment. Hansen (1946, p. 186, n. 10) rejected the possibility that an orderly reduction in wages, "which are relatively rigid", could promote an increase in employment via a fall in the interest rate. He criticized, in a short footnote, Modigliani's excessive emphasis on expansionary monetary policy, focusing instead on the limited investment opportunities. Samuelson's representation of Keynes's theory in his *Economics* textbook by the income-expenditure model neglected the monetary side and focused on the role of income multipliers. Klein's *The Keynesian Revolution* (1947), although suggesting an interpretation of Keynes's involuntary unemployment in terms of a perfectly elastic labor supply (1966 (1947), p. 74), denied that wage rigidity is a necessary condition to explain its emergence: "with the assumption of various frictions, imperfections, and rigidities of the real word, an explanation of unemployment is not difficult, either in the classical or the Keynesian system . . . the numerous remarks throughout the recent literature that Keynes relied upon wage inflexibilities to obtain his result are entirely unsubstantiated" (1966 (1947), pp. 87–90).[22] By focusing on the elasticity of the liquidity preference schedule with respect to interest rate, Klein also rejected wage cut as "an easy-money policy" (1966 (1947), p. 88). However, he maintained the necessity of wage rigidity to avoid a cumulative deflation process when the interest rate is negative.

Klein's approach was followed by Patinkin, who welcomed Klein's critique of the wage rigidity interpretation of Keynes's unemployment.[23] Patinkin became one of the most known critics of Modigliani's 1944 article.

In 1946 Patinkin began a correspondence with Modigliani while working on his PhD dissertation *On the Consistency of Economic Models: A Theory of Involuntary Unemployment* under Marschak's supervision. As reconstructed by Rubin (2002, 2012), after having searched for a compromise between Keynes's involuntary unemployment theory and the Walrasian framework, Patinkin abandoned the equilibrium approach in favor of a disequilibrium interpretation of Keynes's theory (see Rubin 2012, p. 6). His emphasis on the involuntary aspect of unemployment, defined in terms of workers being off their labor supply, is also evident in his critique of Modigliani's wage rigidity hypothesis and his reading of unemployment as an equilibrium phenomenon. Their correspondence helps clarify Modigliani's position on it because, in his reply to Patinkin, instead of defending the key role played by wage rigidity, as emphasized in the 1944 article, he concentrated on its instrumental role in making explicit the monetary aspects of unemployment.[24]

Under Marschak's suggestion, Patinkin embarked on a correspondence with Modigliani that begins with a critique to Modigliani's use of a perfectly elastic labor supply, asking for references in the *General Theory*. Whereas Modigliani focused on Keynes's Chapter 2, about workers' resistance to money wage cuts, Patinkin's reading concentrated on Chapter 19 about falling wage, shifting the attention from Modigliani's explanation of unemployment through wage rigidity to the inability of wage cuts to restore full employment, stressing that Keynes's unemployment was a disequilibrium rather than equilibrium phenomenon:[25]

> It is hard for me to believe that wage rigidity is the essence of the Keynesian system. . . . It seems to me obvious that we cannot have a situation of unemployment equilibrium unless there are rigid wages. Here I agree with your statement of section 12 ["Underemployment equilibrium and Liquidity Preference] of your paper. . . . However, I do not think it is necessary to prove this by an elaborate exposition. One need merely point out that if there is flexibility of wages then by definition the wage rate will change unless there is full employment. Hence, there cannot be equilibrium if there is unemployment. Now, if the whole purpose of Keynes is to say that with rigid wages we can have unemployment 'equilibrium', I really do not see his contribution. . . . The . . . major contribution of Keynesian economics is not in pointing out that there may be an unemployment equilibrium but in stressing the dangers of unemployment *dis*equilibrium. In other word, Keynes emphasized that the policies advocated by the Classical school (flexibility of all kinds of prices and wages) might work very slowly. . . . This seems to me essentially his argument in chapter 19. And this argument can be maintained without assuming any type of wage rigidity.

(Patinkin to Modigliani: April 7, 1948, MP)

In his reply, Modigliani insisted that his main point was about the monetary implications of wage rigidity. His focal point was the working of a monetary economy that emerges from a combination of liquidity preference and wage rigidity. In Modigliani's words,

> All I tried to do was to schematize what appeared to me the basic system underlying most of the reasoning of *The General Theory*. I do not maintain that my supply of labor equation, as such, is "the essence of the Keynesian system". Indeed, on the one hand, I have stated that this equation does over simplify the matter and on the other hand I have laid great stress on the liquidity preference. . . . *It was, by no means, my intention to show that the purpose of Keynes is to say that with rigid wages we can have unemployment equilibrium.* What I tried to show was that all the essential conclusions of the General Theory follow from a combination . . . about the nature of the wage bargain and about liquidity preference. It follows from this primarily that wage policy (under unity elasticity of expectations) is strictly equivalent to monetary policy.

(Modigliani to Patinkin: July 2, 1948, emphasis added, MP)[26]

Differently from Patinkin, Modigliani was not interested in discussing the involuntary aspect of unemployment. His major aim was to demonstrate the crucial role of money in determining the equilibrium level of output and employment and the consistency of unemployment with an equilibrium position, defined as a situation of rest. His analysis was essentially static, moving to dynamics only to discuss the policy implications of his model (in the PhD dissertation), rejecting the efficacy of wage deflation policy when expectations and changes in income distribution were taken into account.

Finally, to answer to Patinkin's critique of the possibility of reaching an unemployment equilibrium position even in Keynes's liquidity trap, Modigliani referred to wage rigidity as a stability condition to describe "a reality . . . which does not know a processes of infinite deflation. . . . As I would like to put it, this assumption must be introduced to explain the stability of the price level not under employment of factors" (Modigliani to Patinkin: July 2, 1948, MP).[27] A point further investigated in the 1950s when he analyzed the case of a negative equilibrium rate of interest or, if positive, below the interest floor, arguing that in this case, wage flexibility leads to a cumulative deflation process because it implies ineradicable excess supplies in some markets.

Modigliani concluded his correspondence with Patinkin arguing that he was not sure what Patinkin was driving at (Modigliani to Patinkin: July 2, 1948, MP). He did not understand the significance of Patinkin's critique because of their different perspectives. Modigliani aimed at extending the validity of the Keynesian theory, emphasizing its closeness to reality trough the wage rigidity hypothesis and the analysis of the working of a monetary economy. Patinkin looked for "a synthesis between the macroeconomics inspired by the *General Theory* and the Walrasian theory of price, with the emphasis put on the logical consistency of the general apparatus" (see Rubin 2004, p. 211).[28] Nonetheless, Modigliani's and Patinkin's different research programs emerged from a common intellectual background, and their contributions to subsequent developments of Keynesian economics have been often associated.

Keynesian unemployment in the 1940s

Both Modigliani and Patinkin had Marschak as a PhD supervisor; they attended Lange's seminars on Keynesian economics at New York and the Cowles Commission. Lange and Marschak clearly shaped their mathematical approach to Keynes's theory, particularly the reading within a general equilibrium framework.[29] However, Modigliani's and Patinkin's analyses show different insights of Lange's and Marschak's eclectic approach to Keynes's theory.[30] Lange, in *Price Flexibility and Employment* (1944), considered the reading of Keynes's unemployment in terms of a perfect elastic labor supply and of an excess in the labor market as equivalent, which choice was merely a matter of convenience (1944, p. 6, n. 4). Although to Patinkin the two notions were irreconcilable (see Boianovsky 2006, p. 204),[31] Modigliani referred alternatively to both representations in the *Econometrica* article and the dissertation, respectively. The market clearing definition of equilibrium, implied in the horizontal labor supply, coexists with a conception of unemployment in terms of an excess labor supply and a definition of equilibrium as a position of rest, in which there is no automatic tendency for economic variables to change. Unlike Patinkin, Modigliani did not see any inconsistency between the concept of involuntary unemployment defined as workers' inability to fulfill their desires, and the notion of equilibrium because "in a free capitalistic economy production is guided by prices and not by desires and since the money wage is rigid, this desire fails to be translated into an economic stimulus" (1944, p. 66).

Lange (1944) may also have influenced Modigliani's discussion in the dissertation about the instability of systems with flexible wages once the expectations elasticity is larger than unity, as mentioned before. Both Modigliani and Lange also focused on wage and price flexibility versus wage and price rigidity as the dividing line between classical and Keynesian economics (see Backhouse and Boianovsky 2013, Chapter 3).

As in Lange (1938), Modigliani's assumed wage rigidity as an institutional or historical fact. He discussed rational behavior in regard to the homogeneity assumption to defend the validity of the classical dichotomy, referring only tacitly to the non-rational behavior behind the horizontal labor supply. Modigliani explicitly associated wage rigidity to money illusion in his dissertation, enlarging this non-rational behavior also to entrepreneurs (see above), and in the correspondence with Patinkin argued that "[t]he hypothesis that workers bargain primarily for money and not for real wages, that they will resist money wage cut even if there is unemployment . . . all these seem to me an essential part of the reasoning of the General Theory" (Modigliani to Patinkin: July 2, 1948, MP).

The role of money illusion to distinguish between classical and Keynesian outcomes was at the center of Marschak's interpretation of Keynes, as appears from his 1948–1949 classes on macroeconomics (Marschak 1951). In Marschak's analysis under the hypothesis of money illusion prices must enter the system of behavioral equations (decisions run in monetary rather than real terms) but, differently from Modigliani, money illusion did not imply wage rigidity and, therefore, did not prevent equilibrium in the labor market. To have an excess labor supply, it was necessary to introduce the additional hypothesis of wage rigidity. However, like Modigliani, Marschak as well ascribed money illusion not only to workers but to any economic agent. To him, when there is money illusion only in the demand sub-set – formed by private and public expenditures and liquidity preference – we have the classical case in which employment is determined by shifts in the supply curve through changes in the production function or in the demand for and supply of labor. Therefore, if workers are willing to accept lower real wages, employment will certainly increase; unemployment is always voluntary, and monetary and fiscal policy only shifts the demand curve, changing the price rather than the employment level (1951, pp. 68–69).

If money illusion refers to the supply sub-set only – formed by the labor market functions and the production function – we have the "extreme Keynes" case in which the aggregate demand is independent from prices (being horizontal with respect to the real income–price axis). Then, he distinguished between "free" and "unionized labor market" and two related different concepts of involuntary unemployment discussed by Keynes in the *General Theory*. In the case of flexible wages, any "revisions of workers' supply schedule" only affect prices and not the employment level (1951, p. 69). Nonetheless, the labor market is in equilibrium because all people willing to work at the existing money wage get jobs. There is involuntary unemployment only in the sense of a wage cut's inability to raise employment, as discussed by Keynes in Chapter 19.[32] The additional assumption of an exogenously fixed wage ("unionized labor market") leads to an excess labor supply over demand and to involuntary unemployment also in the sense that not all people willing to work at the existing money wage and price get jobs, discussed by Keynes in Chapter 2 (1951, pp. 69–70).

Marschak's reading of Keynes's unemployment disclosed elements of both Modigliani's and Patinkin's interpretations. The "extreme Keynes case" with flexible wage reminds Patinkin's explanation based on demand constraint and to his focus on Keynes's Chapter 19, although in Patinkin it leads to a disequilibrium rather than equilibrium in the labor market (see Boianovsky 2002, pp. 232–235). On the other hand, wage rigidity is a necessary condition to have unemployment in terms of an excess labor supply, as in Modigliani's PhD dissertation, a notion Marschak found in Chapter 2 of the General Theory, to which Modigliani as well referred, and for both involuntary unemployment was due to institutional reasons.

Marschak's influence on Modigliani and Patinkin was especially about the reading of Keynesian and classical theory within a general equilibrium system of equations, and the role of money. However, Modigliani's attention to price and wage behavior as the dividing line between the two systems also recalls under some respect his previous writings, in which he looked at the price system (and market forms) as the borderline between state interventions and laissez faire.

Finally, Modigliani's focus on money supply both to explain and to solve the unemployment problem (under wage rigidity), that is, his challenge to the Keynesian's mainstream and the neglecting of money for the determination of real variables, explains why Milton Friedman, years later, referred to Modigliani as a monetarist ante-litteram:

> I may say that I've always thought that Franco, insofar as you use these terms, has always been a monetarist, in very important ways. His famous 1944 paper certainly qualifies as a major element in the so-called monetarist structure.

(1977, p. 12)[33]

Modigliani will further analyzed the effects of monetary variables on the real ones over the 1950s and especially with his work on building the Federal Reserve's Board first macroeconometric model for the U.S. economy since the late 1960s.

Although the central role Modigliani ascribed to the quantity of money to explain unemployment, subsequent readings of the 1944 article especially concentrated on the wage rigidity hypothesis and the working of the labor market. Indeed, for Samuelson, it set Keynesian economics on its modern evolutionary path and probed its microfoundations in rigid, nonmarket clearing prices (Samuelson 1987, p. 29).

After the "Liquidity Preference" article, Modigliani did not return for almost twenty years to publish anything more closely connected with the Keynesian theory. His most known works of the 1950s are on microeconomics within the framework of marginal analysis, such as the life cycle hypothesis and the Modigliani and Miller theorem on finance.

But, before entering the 1950s, it is worthwhile to mention another less known article he published in 1947 in an Italian journal. It is of particular interest because it happened just when Modigliani was earning, thanks to the 1944 article, a reputation among U.S. leading economists, and because the "Liquidity Preference" testified the long way Modigliani had traveled in a few years, from the highly rhetorical articles of the 1930s to the new rigorous language of mathematical economics and economic modeling.

However, in between 1944 and 1945 he returned to reasoning about the shortcomings of the capitalist economy and he analyzed the working of a socialist economy. Even if he made a major reference to marginal analysis, which serves as the perspective from which to look at a socialist economy, his attitude and his language appears much more radical than that of the 1944 *Econometrica* article.

Notes

1 The chapter is largely based on Rancan (2017).

> Both Ascoli and Contini, along with Bruno Foa, emigrated for racial reasons. Johnson called Ascoli in 1933; see R. J. Tosiello (2000, pp. 107–140); also see Camurri (2012, pp. 166–194).

2 Still, in his interview with Barnett and Solow Modigliani pointed out that "Jasha Marschak was my mentor, we studied Keynes and the *GT* in classes with Marschak. . . . In addition [I] received a lot of advice and support from him. He suggested me readings and persuaded me of the importance of mathematical tools" (2000, p. 225, see also Breit and Hirsch 2009, p. 118). In his autobiography Modigliani also recalled that "Marschak at once took a liking to me and, first, gave me to understand that if I wanted to get ahead as an economist I should study more mathematics. That was a field I had no grounding – indeed, ever since secondary school I had felt some aversion to it. . . . I mugged up books of math and statistics . . . [a]ll of which was tremendously useful to me when I tried to develop my articles" (Modigliani 2001, p. 19).

3 Also see Hagemann (2011, p. 659) on Schumpeter's "priority list" about the most prominent European economists.

4 However, according to Mongiovi (2005, p. 431) having experimented with the destructive potential of the state they matured into a less pessimistic view about market mechanisms and embraced more traditional policy interventions with respect to economic planning. Moreover, none of them were any more actively engaged in the policy agenda.

5 Marschak referred to P. Sargant Florence's review of Robinson's book, published in the December 1941 issue.

6 In a letter to Marschak, Modigliani wrote about his relationship with Lerner: "we have been talking much about you with all our common friends, Lange, Loewe and especially Lerner. There seems to be a good deal of understanding between me and Lerner and genuine friendship is gradually developing with him of which I am very happy. I think

more and more that Lerner is an exceptionally good economist and I am often amazed at what he manages to do without using calculus. I have the impression that he is very often too extreme in his theories or rather too 'logically extreme' but this very fact makes discussion with him very fruitful because one always knows what one is talking about" (July 16, 1943, MP). See also Barnett and Solow (2000) and Modigliani (2001).

7 See in particular Lerner (1944, Chapter 24), according to which the size of the national debt was relatively unimportant, that the interest on the debt was not a burden on the nation, and that the nation could not be made "bankrupt" by internally held debt. Every debt has a corresponding credit. Only external debt is like individual debt and impoverishes a nation. On Lerner see Colander (1980) and de Scitovsky (1984).

8 Modigliani's article was reviewed by Leonid Hurwicz, who at that time was Lange's research assistant at the University of Chicago. From 1942 he was at the Cowles Commission working with Marschak and Koopmans.

9 Solow recalled that "the 1944 article was . . . mostly about Keynes's theory of interest. . . . [I]t is interesting then, that the main influence of the paper lay elsewhere" (2005, p. 12).

10 Modigliani concluded the article arguing that under wage flexibility, the long-run equilibrium rate of interest rate is determined by real factors (the classical explanation was still true); under wage rigidity it is determined by the quantity of money and indirectly by savings and investment schedules (1944b, pp. 87–88).

11 Modigliani agreed with Lange's dismissal of Say's law, but he still defended the validity of classical dichotomy. According to him the homogeneity assumption of zero degree of demand and supply functions, which explained such dichotomy, depends on the hypothesis of rationality, that is, no money illusion and not from Say's law.

12 For monetary economy Modigliani meant an economy in which the classical dichotomy breaks down and money is not neutral. He deeply analyzed the validity of classical dichotomy and neutrality of money in the mid-1950s in his long typewritten notes on money (see Chapter 6).

13 However, as Modigliani pointed out in his latest article, "The Keynesian Gospel" (2003), in which he returned to his early Keynesian model: "the difference between rigidity and perfect flexibility turns out to make an enormous difference in the monetary mechanism – the mechanism that ensures the clearing of the money market – and the understanding of unemployment" (2003, p. 3).

14 Modigliani did not explain possible reasons of a fall in the marginal efficiency of investment – whose factors are technological and psychological, such as expectations (1944b, p. 59 fn17). In his handwritten notes on Keynes's *General Theory*, Chapter 21 ("Incentive to Liquidity"), Modigliani only commented that he agreed with Keynes that "the difficulty of full employment follows 'from the association of a conventional and fairly stable long-run rate of interest with a . . . highly unstable marginal efficiency of capital'" (in *Keynes – General Theory, Notes and Remarks*, MP).

15 In his interview with Barnett and Solow (2000), Modigliani explained that "Keynes' unique achievement consisted not only in showing that unemployment is the variable that clears the money market; he also elaborated the mechanism by which an excess demand for money causes a decline of output and thus in the demand for money, until the demand matches the given nominal money supply. . . . And this starts the chain leading to lower output through a fall in investment, a fall in savings, and thus in income and employment. It is this fall, together with the rise in interest rate, that reduces the demand for money till it matches the supply" (p. 228).

16 Where M is the money supply, L the demand for money, r interest rate and PX money income.

17 Keynes replied to these criticisms acknowledging that their study suggested that there was much to think about and that it had seriously shaken the fundamental assumptions of the short-period theory of distribution. Nonetheless, he pointed out that their conclusions confirmed his idea that the causes of short period fluctuations are to be found

in changes in the demand for labor, associated to change in the aggregate demand, rather than in the real wage rate (Keynes 1939, p. 50).

18 Regarding fixed income receivers, because the price level falls, their real income necessarily rises.

19 His analysis on the effects of wage cuts on income distribution was based on data from *Census of Manufacturers for the Years 1925–1939* (1944a, p. 77).

20 Modigliani further developed the theoretical equivalence (not practical, as he remarked) between wage deflation and expansionary monetary policy in the 1955 "Preliminary Notes on Monetary Economics". Subsequent literature on the wage–employment relationship often associates the introduction of the wage rigidity hypothesis as implying the efficacy of wage cuts in restoring full employment. Colander (1996) argued that Keynes's reference to the existence of two opposing schools is less in evidence in the modern literature where "the contrasts take the form – initially prompted by Hansen, Klein, Modigliani and others early proponents of the 'rigid wage version' of Keynesian economics, that the economic system would be self-adjusting if (contrary to experience) wages and prices would adjust rapidly" (Colander, p. 29). See also Leijonhufvud (1968).

21 Apparently Modigliani's (1944b) article initially received little attention from scholars; it was not among the most cited articles published between 1936 and 1948 (ten or more citations in Moggridge 2000, p. 232).

22 Klein's book was an outgrowth of his PhD dissertation he wrote at MIT under Samuelson's supervision.

23 Regarding Klein's influence on Patinkin, see Patinkin (1956 (1965), p. 234 fn.4), Rubin (2002) and Boianovsky (2006).

24 Because Patinkin's interpretation of Keynes's theory has been largely reconstructed as well as his position in regard to Modigliani's (1944) article, I mainly concentrated on Modigliani's reply to Patinkin's critique. (see De Vroey 2002; Rubin 2002, 2004, 2012; Boianovsky 2002, 2006, among others)

25 Patinkin returned on Lange's and Modigliani's wage rigidity hypothesis in his influential *Money Income and Price,* rejecting once again their horizontal labor supply on the basis of the inefficacy of wage cuts to restore full employment: "we have shown that reductions in this rate [wage] are neither necessary nor a sufficient condition for the rapid reestablishment of full employment equilibrium" (Patinkin 1956 (1965), pp. 237–238).

26 Luigi Pasinetti, a long-lasting friend of Modigliani and leading post-Keynesian economist, illustrated well this point arguing that in Modigliani, wage rigidity was "a kind of *deus ex-machina* that solves most of his key problems. . . . Modigliani's method was simplification, which implies concentration on one single point, without bothering about the rest" (2005, pp. 13–15).

27 According to Patinkin "What would be true . . . is that the unemployment disequilibrium would continue for an indefinitely long time. What I mean by unemployment disequilibrium is that the amount of unemployment, the wage rate, and other variables in the system would continuously be changing" (Patinkin to Modigliani: April 7, 1948). Modigliani also explained that in the Keynesian case, the wage rigidity hypothesis is necessary to avoid over-determinacy of the system, "to which you refer on p. 51 of your Cowles Commission manuscript and which you treat at great length in Ch. 6 and 7" (Modigliani to Patinkin: July 2, 1948, MP).

28 Modigliani's and Patinkin's different readings of the wage rigidity assumption also reflected their different approaches to economic analysis. Where there was a choice between rigor and convenience, Modigliani chose the latter, thus he introduced wage rigidity because it "oversimplified the matter" (see, e.g., 1944b, p. 46), whereas Patinkin chose analytical rigor. On different approaches to macroeconomics see Mankiw (2006).

29 In his unpublished reply to Hahn's (1955) critique, Modigliani explained that his model was not stated in general equilibrium language "as it become fashionable since the time

of its appearance" (undated, MP). He however admitted he went further in that direction. Modigliani restated explicitly the 1944 model in Walrasian form in 1963 to reply to the so-called Patinkin controversy.

30 In the preface to the Chicago classes (1948–1949), it was stated that Marschak had set himself with the task of synthesizing the old and the new, distilling the best in both, and showing how to each set of assumptions corresponds different models with different implications (1951, pp. 3–4). As Lange's and Marschak's influence on Patinkin has been already reconstructed (see Boianovsky 2002, 2006; Rubin 2002, 2012), I only referred to Modigliani. Unfortunately from Modigliani–Marschak correspondence no important elements of Marschak's influence on Modigliani's interpretation of the Keynesian theory emerges; it can be traced only indirectly from Marschak' published works

31 Patinkin introduced the case of absolute wage rigidity "which has special importance for monetary theory" (1956) only in regard to Keynes's interest theory (repeating Modigliani's conclusions), discussing Keynes's unemployment theory separately as a real phenomenon; in Modigliani the unemployment and interest theories are both the result of the monetary mechanism which followed from the wage rigidity hypothesis.

32 During the 1930s Marschak was involved in an active movement, the Kiel–Heidelberg group, against wage-cut policy, which had a leading role in the Weimar debate. According to Marschak a wage cut implied a reallocation of purchasing power from workers to entrepreneurs with negative effects on the demand side: "[s]uch a reallocation of purchasing power naturally is associated with a change in the structural composition of production . . . a reallocation of purchasing power in favor of workers, which is associated with higher wages, will stimulate production since the goods consumed by workers are subjected to the law of mass production at higher degree than those goods consumed by the capitalist" (quoted from Hagemann 2005, pp. 16–17).

33 M. Friedman, "The Monetarist Controversy: Discussion by Milton Friedman and Franco Modigliani", *Federal Reserve Bank of San Francisco Economic Review*, Supplement, Spring 1977: 5–27.

References

Backhouse, R. E., and M. Boianovsky. 2013. *Transforming Modern Macroeconomics: Exploring Disequilibrium Microfoundations, 1956–2003*, Cambridge, NY: Cambridge University Press.

Barnett, W. A., and R. Solow. 2000. "An Interview with Franco Modigliani November 5–6 1999", *Macroeconomic Dynamics*, 4: 222–256.

Bodkin, R. G., L. Klein, and K. Marwah. 1991. *A History of Macroeconometric model-building*, Aldershot: Edward Elgar.

Boianovsky, M. 2002. "Don Patinkin, the Cowles Commission, and the Theory of Unemployment and Aggregate Supply", *European Journal of the History of Economic Thought*, 9 (2): 226–259.

———. 2006. "The Making of Chapters 13 and 14 of Patinkin's Money, Interest and Prices", *History of Political Economy*, 38 (2): 193–249.

Breit, W., and B. T. Hirsch, eds. 2009. *Lives of the Laureates: Twenty-three Nobel Economists*, 5th ed., Cambridge, MA: MIT Press.

Camurri, R. 2010. *Franco Modigliani. L'Italia vista dall'America. Battaglie e riflessioni di un esule*, Turin: Bollati Boringhieri.

———. 2012. "Max Ascoli: un esule non esule", in *Max Ascoli. Max Ascoli. Antifascista, intellettuale, giornalista*, ed. by Camurri, Franco Angeli, 166–194.

———. ed. 2018. *I modesti consigli di un premio Nobel. Franco Modigliani. Rischio Italia. L'Italia vista dall'America (1970–2003)*, Rome: Donzelli Editore.

Cherrier, B. 2010. "Rationalizing Human Organization in an Uncertain World: Jacob Marschak, from Ukrainian Prisons to Behavioral Science Laboratories", *History of Political Economy*, 42 (3): 443–467.

Christ, C. 1985. "Early Progress in Estimating Quantitative Economic Relationships in America", *American Economic Review*, 75 (6), 39–52.

Colander, D. 1980. "Post-Keynesian Economics, Abba Lerner and His Critics", *Social Research*, 47 (2): 352–360. "Lerner's Contributions to Economics", *Journal of Economic Literature*, 22 (4).

———. ed. 1996. *Beyond Microfoundations: Post Walrasian Macroeconomics*, Cambridge, NY: Cambridge University Press.

de Scitovsky, T. 1984. "Lerner's Contributions to Economics", *Journal of Economic Literature*, 22 (4): 1547–1571.

De Vroey, M. 2000. "IS-LM à la Hicks versus IS-LM à la Modigliani", *History of Political Economy*, 32 (6): 293–316.

———. 2002. "Can Slowly Adjusting Wages Explain Involuntary Unemployment? A Critical Re-examination of Patinkin's Theory of Involuntary Unemployment", *European Journal of the History of Economic Thought*, 9 (2): 293–307.

Dimand, R., and H. Hagemann. 2019. "Jacob Marschak and the Cowles Approaches to the Theory of Money and Assets", Cowles Foundation Discussion Paper no 2196. www.researchgate.net/publication/335677051. Last access November 29, 2019.

Düppe, T., and E. R. Weintraub. 2013. "Siting the New Economic Science: The Cowles Commission's Activity Analysis Conference of June 1949", *Science in Context*, 27 (3): 453–483.

Friedman, M. 1977. "The Monetarist Controversy: Discussion by Milton Friedman and Franco Modigliani", *Federal Reserve Bank of San Francisco Economic Review*, Supplement, Spring: 5–27.

Haberler, G. 1946. "The Place of the General Theory of Employment, Interest, and Money in the History of Economic Thought", *The Review of Economics and Statistics*, 28 (4), November: 187–194.

———. 2005. *The Influence of Jacob Marschak, Adolph Lowe, and Hans Neisser on the Formation of Franco Modigliani's Work*, Franco Modigliani and the Keynesian Legacy, Schwartz Center Conference at the New School University, New York, April 14–15: 1–25.

———. 2011. "European émigrés and the 'Americanization' of Economics", *The European Journal of the History of Economic Thought*, 18 (5): 643–671.

Hansen, A. H. 1946. "Keynes and the General Theory", *The Review of Economics and Statistics*, 28 (4), 182–187.

———. 1949. *Monetary Theory and Fiscal Policy*, New York: McGraw-Hill Book Co.

Hicks, J. R. 1937. "Mr. Keynes and the 'Classics': A Suggested Interpretation", *Econometrica*, 5 (2): 147–159.

Klamer, A. 1984. *The New Classical Macroeconomics: Conversations with the New Classical Economists and Their Opponents*, Brighton: Harvester Press.

Klein, L. 1947 (1966). *The Keynesian Revolution*, 2nd ed., New York: McMillan.

Koopmans, T. 1978. "Jacob Marschak, 1898–1977", *American Economic Review*, 68 (2): ix–xi.

Lange, O. 1938. "The Rate of Interest and the Optimum Propensity to Consume, the Rate of Interest and the Optimum Propensity to Consume", *Economica*, New Series, 5 (17): 12–32.

———. 1944. *Price Flexibility and Employment*, Cowles Commission for Research in Economics, Monograph No 8.

Lederer, E. 1936. "Commentary on Keynes. II", *Social Research*, 3 (4): 478–487.

Leijonhufvud, A. 1968. *On Keynesian Economics and the Economics of Keynes: A Study in Monetary Theory*, New York: Oxford University Press.

Leontief, W. 1936. "The Fundamental Assumption of Mr. *Keynes's* Monetary Theory of *Unemployment*", *Quarterly Journal of Economics*, 51 (1), November: 192–197.

Lerner, A. 1939. "The Relation of Wage Policies and Prices Policies", *American Economic Review*, 29 (1), Supplement: 158–169.

———. 1944. "Interest Theory: Supply and Demand for Loans or Supply and Demand for Cash", *The Review of Economics and Statistics*, 26 (2): 88–91.

Mankiw, N. G. 2006. "The Macroeconomist as Scientist and Engineer", *The Journal of Economic Perspective*, 20 (4), Fall: 29–46.

Marschak, J. 1943. "Money Illusion and Demand Analysis", *Review of Economics and Statistics*, 25: 40–48.

———. 1951. *Income, Employment and the Price Level: Notes of Lectures Given at the University of Chicago in Autumn 1948 and 1949*, ed. by D. I. Fand and H. Markowitz, New York: Augustus M. Kelley, Kelley Reprints of Economic Classics, 1965; Cowles Commission Discussion Paper no. 250, 1949 (as 20 Lectures on *Income, Employment and the Price Level*).

Mehrling, P. 2002. "Don Patinkin and the Origin of Postwar Monetary Orthodoxy", *European Journal of Economic Thought*, 9: 161–185.

———. 2010. "A Tale of Two Cities", *History of Political Economy*, 42: 201–219.

Franco Modigliani Papers, David M. Rubenstein Rare Book and Manuscript Library, Duke University.

Modigliani, F. 1944a. *The General Theory of Employment, Interest and Money under the Assumptions of Flexible Prices and of Fixed Prices*, Thesis, Doctorate for Social Science.

———. 1944b. "Liquidity Preference and the Theory of Interest and Money", *Econometrica*, 12, January: 45–88.

———. 1955. "Theory of Money and Interest in the Framework of the General Equilibrium Analysis", Preliminary Notes, Modigliani Papers.

———. 1963. "The Monetary Mechanism and Its Interaction with Real Phenomena", *The Review of Economics and Statistics*, 45 (1), Part 2, Supplement, February: 79–107.

———. 2001. *Adventure of an Economist*, New York and London: Texere.

———. 2003. "The Keynesian Gospel According to Modigliani", *American Economist*, Spring: 3–47.

Moggridge, D. E. 2000. "The Diffusion of the Keynesian Revolution: The Young and the Graduate Schools", in *History of Political Economy, Supplement*, 223–241.

Mongiovi, G. 2005. "Emigré Economists and American Neoclassical Economics", *Journal of the History of Economic Thought*, 27 (4): 427–437.

Neisser, H. 1936. "Commentary on Keynes", *Social Research*, 3 (4): 459–478.

———. 2015. "Franco Modigliani and the Socialist State", *Preliminary Draft*: 1–22. http://qcpages.qc.cuny.edu/~lussher/mongiovi05.pdfpp. Last access November 2019.

Pasinetti, L. L. 2005. *How Much of J. M. Keynes Can We Find in Franco Modigliani, in Franco Modigliani between Economic Theory and Social Commitment*, Proceeding of the International Conference Organized by the Accademia Nazionale dei Lincei, Roma, February 17–18, Banca Nazionale del Lavoro, Quarterly Review, 58: 21–40.

Patinkin, D. 1948. "Correspondence with Franco Modigliani", Patinkin Papers, Box 29.

———. 1956 (1965). *Money Interests and Prices: An Integration of Monetary and Value Theory*, 2nd ed., New York: Harper & Row.

Rancan, A. 2017. "The Wage-Employment Relationship in Modigliani's 1944 article", *European Journal of the History of Economic Thought* 24 (1): 143–174.

Rubin, G. 2002. "From Equilibrium to Disequilibrium: The Genesis of Don Patinkin's Interpretation of the Keynesian Theory", *European Journal of the History of Economic Thought*, 9 (2): 205–225.

———. 2004. "Patinkin on IS-LM: An Alternative to Modigliani", in *The IS-LM Model: Its Rise, Fall, and Strange Persistence:* History of Political Economy, ed. by M. De Vroey and K. D. Hoover, 36 Supplement: 90–216.

———. 2012. "*Don Patinkin's,* PhD Dissertation as the Prehistory of Disequilibrium Theories", *History of Political Economy*, 44 (2): 235–276.

Samuelson, P. A. 1948. *Economics: An Introductory Analysis*, New York: McGraw-Hill Book Co.

———. 1987. "The 1985 Nobel Prize in Economics", in *Macroeconomics and Finance: Essays in Honors of Franco Modigliani*, ed. by R. Dornbusch, S. Fisher, and J. Bossons, Cambridge, MA: MIT Press, 29–35.

———. 2005. *Franco: A Mind Never at Rest, Franco Modigliani between Economic Theory and Social Commitment*, Proceeding of the International Conference Organized by the Accademia Nazionale dei Lincei, Roma, February 17–18, Banca Nazionale del Lavoro, Quarterly Review, 58: 5–10.

Schumpeter, A. J. 1946. "The General Theory of Employment, Interest and Money by John Maynard Keynes", *Journal of the American Statistical Association*, 31 (196): 791–795.

———. 1946. "John Maynard Keynes 1883–1946", *American Economic Review*, 36 (4): 495–518.

Solow, R. 2005. "Modigliani and Keynes", *Franco Modigliani between Economic Theory and Social Commitment*, Proceeding of the International Conference Organized by the Accademia Nazionale dei Lincei, Roma, February 17–18, Banca Nazionale del Lavoro, Quarterly Review, 58: 11–20.

Tarshis, L. 1939. "Changes in Real and Money Wages", *The Economic Journal*, 49 (193): 150–154.

Tobin, J. 1958. "Liquidity Preference as Behavior Towards Risk", *Review of Economic Studies*, 25: 65–86.

Tosiello, J. R. 2000. "Max Ascoli: A Lifetime of Rockfeller Connections", in *The "Unacceptables": American Foundations and Refugees Scholars between the Two Wars and after*, ed. by G. Gemelli, Bruxel: Lang, 107–140.

3 Keynesian economics in between corporative and socialist economics

Introduction

The 1944 *Econometrica* article on Keynesian and classical economics provided to the twenty-six-year-old Modigliani a reputation among prominent American economists as the correspondence with Leontief, Samuelson and Solow, among others, testify (see Chapter 2). Beyond the content, the article also shows the long way Modigliani has traveled in a few years, from a self-taught economist and from his rhetorical essays on corporative economics to one of the most appreciated mathematical economists familiar with the tools of marginal and Keynesian analysis and the language of economic modeling.

Modigliani had begun to teach mathematical economics and statistics already during the PhD at the New School for Social Research, at the College for Women (Douglas College) of Rutgers University in New Jersey and since 1942 at Bard College of Columbia University (Modigliani 2001, pp. 44–45). In 1944 he came back to the New School as a research associate and chief statistician of the newly created Institute of World Affairs, led by Neisser. In his classes of Mathematical Economics, Modigliani taught macro and micro, static and dynamic economics. The reading list he suggested for the 1944–1945 academic year included texts on planning economy such as *Basic Social Controls of the Economy* by Alexander H. Pekelis, *Government in Business and Planning* and *Political and Economic Problems* by Arnold Brecht, along with *Reading in Political Philosophy: The Social Philosophy of Early Capitalism*.[1] The same year Lerner was teaching Economics and Planning. At that time Modigliani was also writing on the organization of a socialist economy to which this chapter is especially devoted.

In 1947 Modigliani joined the Institute of Word Affairs where he worked with Neisser on building a macroeconometric model for the world economy (among the first models of this kind that anticipated in some way Lawrence Klein's *Project Link* of the 1970s), under the influence of Gottfried Haberler's *Prosperity and Depression* (1937) and stimulated by Jan Tinbergen's pioneering work on business cycles (Tinbergen 1939).

Modigliani and Neisser's model (only published in 1953) analyzed the flow of imports and exports through linear homogeneous specifications of a country's balance of payments between the United States and the United Kingdom and Germany and France. Their aim was to understand how a change of income of a certain industrial country, with no change in any other exogenous variables, affects the other country's income through international trade (see Neisser and Modigliani 1953, pp. 6, 75; also see Szenberg and Ramrattan 2008, pp. 133–134). In his autobiography Modigliani recalled that with their econometric model, the world economy was seen for the first time as the result of the interactions among individual economies, all sensible to the trends of the international economy. Even if they still lacked proper estimate methods (developed soon after at the Cowles Commission), "The overall philosophy of the model was that of a simultaneous system . . . in which the behavior functions of the individual variables and individual countries were formalized with econometric methods (2001, p. 50).

As appears from Modigliani's correspondence, while working on this model, he was particularly interested in understanding the relationships between production costs and commodities prices. Modigliani and Neisser focused on the implications for the terms of trade of changing prices of raw materials and manufacturing goods (during the interwar period); they investigated whether changes in the relationships between the two set of prices have a systematic character and which economic factors are responsible for these changes (Modigliani to Haberler: January 5, 1946, MP).[2] In a letter to Theodore Schultz, before accepting a fellowship at Chicago for the 1948 academic year, Modigliani asked for the possibility to continue his research with Neisser:

> I might undertake a study of the effects and properties of the world stabilization plans for foods and raw materials which were being discussed at that time. . . . This problem is definitely one that which interest me greatly and which I would like to take some time in investigating.

(Modigliani to Schultz: Jan. 20, 1948, MP)

Modigliani and Neisser also began to investigate empirically consumption and saving behavior, publishing a paper in the *U.S. Department of Commerce Bulletin* titled "Cyclical and Secular Factors in the Relationships between Income, Consumption and Savings (1946)", where they distinguished between cyclical and long-run savings behavior. Empirical research in this field was widespread in the postwar, both because of the increasing concern about stagnation with the end of the war and military expenditures and because postwar data did not conform to the received Keynesian consumption theory. Modigliani and Neisser's paper represented Modigliani's first step towards his work with Richard Brumberg on the life cycle hypothesis, in the beginning of 1950s, for which he was awarded the Nobel Prize in 1985.

Modigliani and American universities

In 1946 Haberler invited Modigliani for a seminar at Harvard on international trade, and soon after, he was offered to join the Economics Department.

According to Modigliani's autobiography, he rejected the offer after a meeting with the head of the department, Arnold Burbank, because of his anti-Semitic and xenophobe reputation (2001, pp. 53–54; also see Barnett and Solow 2000, pp. 226–227), a refusal Modigliani officially explained with the "difficult[y] in finding a house" (Modigliani to Burbank: April, 29, 1946, MP).[3]

A few months later, it was Marschak who wrote Modigliani asking to join the Cowles Commission at the University of Chicago to replace Leonid Hurwicz. Marschak clarified, however, that "it will probably be impossible for Chicago to make a satisfactory offer form the financial point of view", thus asking

> Whether your past enthusiasm for serious scientific research still exists and whether it will go to the extent of inducing you to financial sacrifices. . . . You are familiar with our progress: empirical [?] for policy use, applying [?] methods for statistical estimations. If you have maintain the [?] interest shown in your *Econometrica* article, it will be easy to fit your cooperation with our program. . . . Klein, Haavelmo and Koopman will continue on our staff.

(Marschak to Modigliani: May 6, 1946, MP)

This was an offer Modigliani refused because of the ranking of instructor:

> I must confess that I was frankly disappointed by this news, which was really unexpected. From our informal talks in Washington, I had gathered the impression that there would be no difficulty in granting me a rank equivalent to Assistant Professor. . . . Dr. Lowe had intended that if I decided to stay [at the New School] he would propose to the Faculty my candidature as Assistant Professor. . . . I still am ready . . . to make financial sacrifices . . . in order to work with you in subject of great interest to me. However, I must also think of my future.

(May 19, 1946, MP)

He decided to remain at the New School as assistant professor for the spring and fall terms. During 1947 Modigliani was asked to join the John Hopkins University as professor of statistics, and the University of Pennsylvania. He then received an offer from Schultz from the University of Chicago for a one-year academic fellowship.[4] Interesting enough, in the letter of proposal, professor Milton Singer, chairman of the Social Sciences, suggested to Modigliani that "to strength[en] considerably" his presentation at the Economics Department, it would have been worthwhile to have "something you may have written on the general political and social aspects of organization or related topics" (Milton Singer to Modigliani: February 17, 1947, MP).

In his reply, Modigliani claims to be somewhat puzzled by the request about an informal statement on his policy view because in their precedent conversation they already discussed "so many different problems on which I freely expressed my view". Then Modigliani referred to an article he wrote in Italian on the organization of a socialist economy: "I believe I mentioned you that about a year ago I finished an Italian manuscript on the economic theory of a socialist economy which I expected to be published in Italy shortly". Modigliani explained that the article was on a "technical nature" as economic theory is, an "essentially technical subject" but also acknowledging "the argument developed necessarily transcend purely technical considerations" (Modigliani to Singer: May 21, 1947 MP).[5]

This is at the beginning of the so-called McCarthyism campaign (see Chapter 4). A few months after the correspondence, in August 1947, the Illinois legislature created the Seditious Activities Investigation Commission, also known as the Broyles Commission (because it was chaired by the Republican Senator Paul Broyles) to investigate communist influence in the state. The commission identified the education system as the most vulnerable place for communist penetration. In 1949, the commission started hearing professors to investigate the presence of communists and subversive activities in public offices, including universities and colleges (www.encyclopedia.chicagohistory.org/pages/310. html). As Craufurd Goodwin (1998) explains, the attacks at Chicago University and Roosevelt College was a continuation of the 1930s with a new target represented by Keynesian macroeconomists. President of the University of Chicago Robert Hutchins had been already investigated in 1935 because on charges of indoctrinating a student. He then strongly reacted against the Broyles Commission, arguing that "the University of Chicago does not believe in the un-American doctrine of guilt association" and defined the commission the "greatest menace to the US since Hitler" (Hartman, pp. 76–77, see also Schrecker 1986, p. 25).

Modigliani decided to decline the invitation for that academic year because he had just been appointed associate professor at the New School, and "it would not be fair for me to leave the School before at least, one full academic year". Moreover, Modigliani remarked "one of the main attractions that Chicago held for me was the opportunity of working in closer contact with Marschak . . . but because lack of funds at the Cowles Commission and because . . . the kind of teaching at the college. . . . I would have very little opportunity for research work" (Modigliani to Singer: October 22, 1947, MP). Modigliani accepted Schultz's subsequent invitation for the 1948 academic year, moving to Chicago in September 1948.[6] However, he stayed only a couple of months because soon after he received and accepted an offer as associate professor at the University of Illinois.

Curiously enough, not only the Economics Department of the University of Chicago had asked Modigliani for a statement concerning his "non-economic background", but in November 1947 Modigliani also received a letter from the Office of Strategic Service of the War Department asking whether a "bound manuscript" that was found clearing the files at the office, titled "Organization and Direction of Socialist Economy", belonged to him. "If so, we will be pleased to mail it to you" (Colonel Knox P. Pruden to Modigliani: November 18, 1947, MP).[7] The title is the English translation of the essay Modigliani had just published in one of the most prominent Italian journals of economics, *Il Giornale degli economisti*: "*Organizzazione e direzione della produzione in una economia socialista*" (1947), that he mentioned in the letter to the chairman of the Social Sciences of the University of Chicago.

The organization of a socialist economy

Modigliani apparently began to work on a long essay on the organization of a socialist economy soon after the defense of his PhD dissertation, and it was completed already in the summer of 1945 (see Asso 2007, pp. 15–16). Modigliani mentioned this essay in his autobiography, however ascribing it a minor role:

> It had been an exercise in forcing myself to imagine how production was run efficiently in a socialist economy and how it handled the absence of a market so as to achieve the desired result. At that time, I was very interested in the theme of price controls, which was, in fact, a way of understanding how prices were formulated. Controls, rationing, and food cards were very commonly used in all Western countries immediately after the war. The question entailed understanding whether the market economy system was the only efficient way of formulating prices. . . . It was a classical theme [from Enrico Barone onwards]. . . . My conclusions, which were absolutely theoretical, did not paint a negative picture of socialism. . . . Of course, the long conversations I had with Bruno Pontecorvo in the café of Paris as the Nazi armies were taking up their positions along the Maginot Line had, in spite of everything, left me with some soft spots for socialism. . . . During my years in America I had been completely occupied with my studies of classical and the Keynesian revolution. That article has also been an attempt to interpret socialist economics in the light of classical economics. Perhaps it had been too enthusiastic.

(2001, pp. 165–167)

Both Lange (1936, 1937) and Lerner (1937, 1944) had already approached the analysis of a socialist system from the perspective of marginal economics, and both clearly shaped Modigliani's reasoning on the subject. In particular, Lerner's starting point in the *Economics of Control. Principles of Welfare Economics* (1944) was that "Liberalism and socialism can be reconciled in welfare economics", an idea Modigliani also developed in his essay. According to Lerner,

> pragmatic as contrasted with dogmatic collectivism is very close to the point of view of the liberal capitalist who is in favor of state activity whenever the ideal perfect competition does not work. . . . This rapprochement

also brings the orthodox theory into the picture as one of the main instrument to be utilized in the controlled economy.

(1944, p. 4)

As mentioned, in his autobiographical recollections, Modigliani referred to
the 1947 article on a socialist economy as a purely theoretical exercise. Nonetheless, this exercise was longer than seventy-seven pages (some parts were
cut in the published version), and it was not merely theoretical; rather, it was
conceived as a sort of guide for the government and managers of a socialized
economy, as it was Lerner's *Economics of Control*. Modigliani outlines the kind
of institutions, principles and practical rules to follow to implement a socialist economy, up to a detailed description of the eventual budget handled by
the government. From Modigliani's correspondence with Riccardo Bachi (his
mentor in Italy in the 1930s; see Chapter 1), it appears that the essay included
two more sections about *"Un tentativo di stabilire un bilancio approssimativo di
uno stato socialista italiano sulla base delle condizioni prevalenti nel 1936–37"* with
explicit reference to the applicability of the socialist system to Italy. Modigliani
and Bachi agreed to drop these sections from the published version because
they "had become meaningless" in the actual Italian situation (Modigliani to
Bachi: April 18, 1947, MP). Modigliani followed closely the publication of the
article. According to Asso's reconstruction (2007, pp. 18–19), the paper was
first sent to historical economist Gino Luzzato but, then, Modigliani lost trace
of it. Therefore, in 1947 Modigliani sent a couple of letters to Bachi asking
whether he was still interested in publishing his article: "I would be grateful if
could do the necessary" (April 13, 1947, MP).

Modigliani's aim was to demonstrate that the socialist system is not only economically possible but it would also work much better than the market system.
His reasoning does not seem a sporadic exercise. He begins the paper arguing
that the most relevant and promising developments in economics concern the
theory of a socialist state, adding, in the footnote, that his essay was part of
wider and unpublished research devoted to clarify the fundamental principles
of the modern economic theory of a socialist state (1947, p. 441). Like Lerner,
Modigliani also approached the analysis of the organization of a socialist economy as a branch of welfare economics.

Mongiovi (2015) read Modigliani's article in the context of Lange's and
Lerner's influence, with whom he had close relationships at that time. Nonetheless, the intellectual background can be enlarged to his Italian writings, particularly his 1939 thesis, in which he discussed the dynamic of the capitalistic
system from perfect competition towards a prevailing monopolist market structure. Modigliani opposed to the classical economics a system of state controls
supporting, in some cases, the socialization of large companies. The relationship between state interventions and market forms, the maximization of individual and social welfare and his reasoning about the allocative role of the price
system were the objects of his writing on economics in the 1930s. Modigliani

(1937) remarked, for example, that price control must be dynamic, that is, able to adapt continuously to changes in market conditions (see Chapter 1), arguing that price control must be able to replicate the behavior of market prices to reach an efficient resource allocation. Maybe Modigliani's disillusion with fascism and corporative economics led him to think about the alternative of a socialist economy organized within a "democratic way of life", as Lerner put it (1944, p. vii) and whose performance is analyzed through the tools of marginalist economics. As discussed in Chapter 2, although encouraging state interventions, the New School economists (not only Lerner but also Marschak, Lowe and Neisser) appreciated the formal and rigorous approach of marginalist economics and the general equilibrium framework to the examination of economic phenomena (see Mongiovi 2005, 2015).

Modigliani approached the study of a socialized economy from the perspective of efficient resources allocation and an equal income distribution to maximize social welfare.[8] He first explained that whereas efficiency responds to strictly economic criteria, income distribution involves ethics and political considerations, and the two issues are faced separately. In a socialist system (as it was in the corporative economics he discussed in the 1930s), the aim of individual profit maximization is replaced by social welfare, but the opposition between individual and social utility is now not taken for granted. There is no more an emphasis on the subordination of individual interests to the state or collective ones. The problem is that of protecting individuals (consumers and workers) from market power.

Modigliani then discussed the kind of incentives, other than "vague ethical principles", that will have to inform the economic decision process of the managers of socialized firms (1947, pp. 447–448). In the section "The Price Mechanism and the Four Fundamental Rules", Modigliani introduces the criteria to be followed to maximize social utility. These behavioral "rules" are all derived from marginal analysis. Modigliani acknowledged the indispensable role of market prices to coordinate the decision process, along with free-choice. Consumers have to be free on how to spend their income, leaving prices to exert their equilibrating function; each one must be free of choosing its own work, with price factors established by market forces (i.e., free labor market); the production techniques must be chosen to minimize the total production cost; the output level must ensure that market prices are equal to the marginal costs (Modigliani 1947, pp. 445–446; also see Mongiovi 2015, p. 11).[9] According to Modigliani, by following these rules the Pareto optimum conditions can be reached for a given income distribution. As already stated in his 1939 thesis, Modigliani pointed out that these rules are satisfied only under the hypotheses of perfect competition, where state interventions are not needed. Under imperfect competition and monopolies, that is, when firms have the power to set prices according to their own interests, the socialization of production becomes necessary, with managers of socialized firms that, however, must follow the same behavioral rules.[10] Modigliani's aim was to show that an efficient allocation is always possible independently from the individual profit maximization objective. He clearly defined not only the space for state interventions (under monopoly conditions) but also the method, i.e. the same behavioural rules of competitive markets. Although not formalized, his language is rigorous.

Next, Modigliani explained that while under a free-market system, prices respond to both allocative and distributive functions; in a socialized economy the organization of production is independent from income distribution. Indeed, it will not be necessary for prices to be effectively paid to the productive factors. They can be simply recorded in the firm's accounting as costs, with factor services that can be paid by distributing some kind of points according to any criterion. In other words, the prices of productive factors have an accounting function only as a measure of scarcity, of losses and profits.

Although profit incentives are not necessary for efficient allocation, they are still important for the dynamism of the economy. Modigliani acknowledged both the risk that "the one who administrates the social wealth will shrink from the novelty and remain stuck in the routine" and the "danger" that "using capital that is not his own, [the manager] embarks on senseless undertakings, wasting the resources of the community" (1947, p. 463). In this field, Modigliani remarked, "one should admit that . . . there is a serious danger that socialist system will prove to be considerably inferior to a private enterprise system" (1947, p. 463). Therefore Modigliani suggested assigning to research commissions the task of organizing, coordinating and stimulating technical-scientific research that must also indicate the optimal number of firms to minimize the total costs of all firms.[11]

After having outlined the rules for an efficient resources allocation and the one the commissions must follow to decide about new investments, Modigliani moved to the macroeconomics implications of a socialist economy and discussed the coordination problem of saving and investment decisions and economic fluctuations. To him the ignorance in which economic decisions are taken in a private economy makes firms much more subjected to cyclical demand fluctuations than in a socialized economy. He defined the lack of coordination among private savings and investment one of the most serious problem of a capitalist economy. Starting from a critique of the classical definition of savings in terms of renouncing consumption in exchange of an interest rate, Modigliani introduced the Keynesian concepts of demand for money to hold and unused capacity, ascribing to savings decisions a major role in economic fluctuations. Again, the problem is faced first by recognizing that people must be free to make consumption and saving decisions. On the other hand, to guarantee an adequate accumulation of capital, the government has to establish required savings on the basis of capital productivity and population growth, from which to deduce private voluntary saving to determine the amount of collective saving required for full employment. The task of coordinating savings and investment decisions is assigned to a central commission in collaboration with research commissions. The central commission also sets and periodically adjusts the rates of interest on the basis of the research commissions' requirements and of available liquid capital. According to Modigliani, once the interest rate had been established, an efficient allocation of capital among different branches of business will follow with firms that will receive the necessary credit from a socialized banking system. Discussing private and collective savings, Modigliani also analyzed how the balance sheet of a socialist state should be organized.

As in his PhD dissertation, Modigliani remarked that when aggregate demand is insufficient because of individual hoarding, the government must intervene by increasing its expenditure for an equal amount of hoarding to be financed through the creation of new money. Whilst in the 1944 dissertation this solution was discussed in the context of Keynesian economics, here the same policy recommendation was put forward for a socialized economy, introducing a last behavioral rule according to which "the state budget must be balanced if and only if the aggregate demand is equal to the aggregate supply, if the aggregate demand is lower, public expenditures must exceed revenues which will be financed by the creation of money" (1947, p. 499).

Modigliani concluded the first part of his essay with a critique of both the Soviet and the fascist systems (he refers to the Nazi and Japanese systems) for their centralization of the political and economic power in a social class that "gives rise to unprecedented exploitation of the working class" (1947, p. 480). Their aim, Modigliani claimed, was not social welfare but to strengthen the military power of the nation. By contrast, he emphasizes the advantages of the socialist system, which combines the benefits of the capitalistic and the communist systems: on the one hand, economic decentralization and consumer sovereignty are preserved, and on the other investment and production coordination are accomplished (1947, p. 480).

The second part of the essay was devoted to analyze income distribution. Modigliani agreed with differential incomes according to different kinds of jobs (skills, risk, endeavor, etc.), pointing out, instead, the importance of free choice in the labor market. This implies the right of equal access to all types of professions independently from possessing financial means (1947, p. 482). Labor unions still play a role although not in the determination of wages, established by the Minister of Labor to a level that guarantees the balance between demand for and supply of labor.

Finally, Modigliani discussed the transition towards a socialist system arguing that it not necessarily implied coercion. By repeating arguments already emphasized during the 1930s, he explained that the historical function of the capitalistic system has come to an end, producing "endless injustices and miseries" (1947, p. 512). Among the reasons explaining the overcoming of the capitalistic system, such as the advent of monopolies already discussed in the 1930s, Modigliani mentioned the problem of over savings as the result of increasing monopolists' profits and the unequal distribution of income. He also explained that government interventions, that is, public investments either to improve income distribution or devoted to control or eliminate the unemployment problem, are only temporary and palliative, not definite solutions. They interfere with private decisions, thus reducing further the courage and the will to assume new risks. Thus, for mature economies "the advent of a socialist system is urgent" (p. 512). In these countries, Modigliani concluded, the choice is among controlled private companies, or socialism, with the contradiction that controls require other controls, with increasing state interference with risks that remain individual. The capitalistic system, Modigliani remarked, "must be eradicated before the defense of already acquired interests generates new forms of fascism, and it is not necessary to remember that in Italy fascism was the most miserable and unsuccessful economic experiment that one can imagine" (p. 512). All arguments developed in the essay, Modigliani argued, are shared by "an increasing number of economists trained with the principles of the classical economics, and while remaining within its framework, believed that the transition from a private capitalistic system to a socialist system is necessary and urgent" (p. 512).

Modigliani remarked that an anti-capitalist party must act on the transformation with courage to avoid a counter-revolution, emphazising that when the capitalistic system does not work for economic or policy reasons "it must be suppressed with a brave single stroke" (p. 513). He concluded by quoting Lange (1937, p. 136): "There exists only one economic policy which the economist can indicate to a socialist government as likely to lead to success. This is a policy of revolutionary courage" (p. 514; also see Mongiovi 2015, p. 19).

Although Modigliani introduced this essay as part of wider research on the applicability of a socialist economy, he did not return to the topic in subsequent writings. According to Mongiovi (2015, p. 20), Modigliani moved on to other issues maybe because the article appeared when McCarthyism was beginning its anticommunist campaign within academia (on which I will return in Chapter 4). As mentioned, the Economics Department of Chicago asked Modigliani about his policy orientation, and in November 1947 Modigliani also received a letter from the Office of Strategic Service of the War Department apparently about his essay.

Modigliani did not stop searching for concrete solutions to economic problems whenever the market system failed. Thus, in 1947 in response to an increasing concern about shortage of food, Modigliani returned to thinking about price controls and efficient resource allocation.

Modigliani's Meat Plan

In October 1948, Modigliani moved from the New School to the University of Chicago, thanks to Schultz's fellowship on political economy, and joined the Cowles Commission as research assistant. Modigliani recalled having been welcomed by Milton Friedman, who was indignant about the letter Modigliani, with Neisser and Albert G. Hart from Columbia University, wrote to the *New York Times* on a plan to face the problem of a meat shortage: "[y]our suggestion in the *New York Times* is immoral, shame on you! It's a trick to make fun of the rules of the market. The rules of price formation must be allowed to work freely without any manipulation", Friedman apparently said (Modigliani 2001, p. 57).

In the 1947 article on a socialized economy, Modigliani acknowledged the fundamental role of price mechanisms and individual free-choice, defining the space and the conditions under which private and public enterprises may coexist and what they must accomplish to increase social welfare. With the so-called Meat Plan, on which Modigliani worked from September to the end of 1947, he moved a further step away from his reasoning in the 1930s about the relationships among the state, markets and individuals. While in the 1947 essay, following Lerner, Modigliani suggested "a third way" between the collective and the market systems, by applying the tools of the marginal analysis to a socialized economy, in the Meat Plan he attempted to outline a "third way" between the market system and price controls through only indirect state interventions. As stated by Alacevich et al. (2015), it was an attempt to bring socialist planning and Keynesian economics within the boundaries of neoclassical economics (p. 22).

Modigliani worked "rather frantically" on the plan during the fall of 1947, circulating it largely among economists and policy makers. The plan was aimed "to attack" the problem of meat shortages and of inflationary pressure due to the price and wage spiral (Modigliani to Marschak: October 6, 1947, MP). Modigliani's plan took part in the U.S. postwar debate over price controls and rationing, an issue he knew quite well having read and wrote about them during the 1930s in Italy. As reconstructed by Alacevich et al. (2015), the debate began at the July 1947 Congress committee in which the risk of an inflationary spiral was acknowledged, but it rapidly turned ideological by denouncing the perils of socialism. The control on meat prices and rationing had been released by President Truman in June 1946 even though since April the country was already experiencing a meat shortage, and meat and dairy prices began rising rapidly. In light of inflation pressure, Democrats supported some control measures, whereas Truman advocated credit restraint to induce voluntary savings and a return to price controls. All the others were contrary. The debate involved economists, policy makers and the public opinion on the eve of the 1948 presidential election (Alacevich et al. 2015, pp. 4, 14).

Modigliani began to think to a solution less coercive than price controls in which government intervention is only indirect. He outlined a system of "cost-of-leaving bonus" and excise tax on meat production (to finance the consumers' subsidies) aimed at avoiding the inflationary spiral without renouncing the market price system, that is, leaving meat prices to fluctuate to adjust to the demand and supply. Modigliani was detailed in explaining the functioning of his plan. A government agency should both establish the "standard" price of a "composite pound of meat", and to estimate the per-capita quantity of meat that should be made available. Consumers would receive coupons covering the cost of living that could be used for any kind of commodity (not only meat) to not interfere with consumers' preferences. Modigliani's idea was to face the price and wage spiral by referring to the substitution effect and the demand elasticity for meat:

> [a]s the market price of meat goes up, relative to other things, a growing number of consumers will be voluntarily induced to substitute other things for meat. . . . Further, since the consumer is already indemnitee for the rising cost of meat and since the plan will effectively tend to check the rise in prices of dairy products and will tend to eliminate the increase in the price of cereal, there will be no reasons for demanding wage increases.

(1947, pp. 5–6, MP)

As Modigliani wrote to Gerhard Colm from the New School, he hoped that "the plan be strongly supported and sponsored by labor groups. For, if the passage of the plan [by the CEA] is considered by organized labor as a victory, it will be easier to resist wage demands" (October 30, 1947, MP). In other words, the plan worked as a sort of income policy, easing industrial relations on the basis of major coordination by revising the value of the cost-of-living bonus in accordance with expected inflation. Indeed, in the 1970s, when the debate on price control, inflationary pressures and income policy resurged, Samuelson sent to Modigliani a draft on "Murphy Tax Incentive for National Energy Conservation" (by Alan R. Murphy) based on a system of incentives, asking: "Franco, is your name Murphy?" (quoted from Alacevich et al. 2015, p. 41).[12]

Behind the Meat Plan, there was Modigliani's fascination and confidence in the power of econometric tools because the plan could work only on the basis of estimates of the elasticity of substitution between meat and other foods, of the demand income elasticity, and the ability to forecast meat prices. The importance of these "technical" efforts clearly appears in Modigliani's correspondence, particularly with Marschak. He asked Marschak whether his study on "the demand for meat and related products ever been brought up to date" and whether "there is anything else outside Haavelmo's study which covers all foods and, is, therefore, not very useful?" (Modigliani to Marschak: October 6, 1947, MP). In sending his paper on "Money Illusion and Demand Analysis", where Marschak estimated the income elasticity and the price elasticity of meat, both from time series and family budgets data, he explained the number of complications involved in the estimates, especially to remove the bias due to the application of single equation regressions.[13] This attempt, Marschak wrote, "has given rise to the Girschick-Haavelmo article which you know". He agreed that the article did not help:

> [w]hen one is concerned with one particular type of food, like meat. We found that the substitution between various foods . . . make it necessary to increase the number of equations to an extent which makes the present available data insufficient. In other words, the difficulty which, as Theodore Schultz has pointed out, the administrative regulation of a meat market has necessary to face, namely the substitution between meat and other farm products.

(Marschak to Modigliani: November 13, 1947, MP)

Maybe for these reasons, Marschak did not fully endorse the plan, as Modigliani acknowledged: "Thank you for writing to [Paul] Douglas and, in general, for acting in connection with the Plan as a 'honest broker'. This implies, I take it, that you do not wish to be quoted as for or against the Plan" (Modigliani to Marschak: November 21, 1947, MP).[14] Marschak not only helped Modigliani with the econometric point of view, but he was instrumental in circulating the plan within the Cowles Commission and outside it by writing to Schultz and Douglas (at that time president of the American Economic Association), asking for the inclusion of the plan at the 1947 December meeting.[15]

Confident in the applicability of the plan were Albert G. Hart and Neisser, both contributing to a second draft and signing the *New York Times* op-ed of December 21, 1947, previously mentioned. It was Hart who also sent the plan to Schultz, to Chester Davis (Hart's former colleague at the Committee of Economic Development) and to D. Gale Johnson, who had written a similar plan. Among them, Schultz was the main critics of Modigliani's paln since he read the cost-of-living bonus as an incentive to consume meat.

Similarly, Maurice Clark argued that the income effect could induce a rapid spiral of meat prices; that is, the bonus could have inflationary effects and distortions on meat prices. Skepticism about the working of the model also referred to the distribution of the bonus independently from income and the practical complication in doing so. It was finally argued that the excise tax would be transferred upon the consumers, aggravating the problem of meat price increases. In November 1947 the plan was rejected by the Committee of Economic Development because it was not feasible.

After January 1948, public attention to the problem disappeared because the previous alarmism proved to be unfonded (see Alacevich et al. 2015, pp. 30–36). However, Modigliani continued to reason about it. In a letter to Marschak he complained that during the Chicago AEA Conference, he was unable to discuss with him such problems

> [w]hich were on my mind, especially concerning the use of your demand equation for meat to estimate the effect of our meat plan. I have tried to make use of your demand equation for this purpose. The main difficulty, however, is the following . . . the elasticity of demand estimated in your paper refers to the effect on demand of a proportional change in all income. What I need instead is the elasticity of demand with respect to an equal change in all income. Is there any way to estimate this elasticity from your material?

(January 6, 1948, MP)

A few days after, Marschak sent the regression, hoping that "your Chicago plan will materialize" (January 15, 1948, MP).

Modigliani's plan is a further example of his approach to economics in terms of an applied science that must provide practical solutions to economic problems. Moreover, as in his previous paper on a socialized economy, micro and macroeconomic analysis were entangled, moving from the price mechanism and the estimate of demand elasticities, to fiscal policy to influence aggregate consumption. And, while in the 1944 *Econometrica* article he distanced himself from the mainstream Keynesian theory by focusing on the role of money to support employment instead of fiscal policy, here fiscal policy was advocated not to raise aggregate demand but to influence its composition through income and substitution effects.

Towards more traditional studies: Modigliani's early writing on savings

In the introduction to his *Collected Papers* (vol. 1, 1980), Modigliani explained that his scientific concern over his academic career has been to "sorting out the lasting contribution of the Keynesian revolution" (p. xi) and that, "as it is well known", Keynesian economics "rests on four building blocks: the consumption function, the investment function, the demand and supply of money and other deposits, and the mechanism of determining wages and prices" (p. xii). Modigliani placed his study on savings behavior within these efforts.

He ascribed to Kuznets's (1946) results about the long-run propensity to save, which "challenges" Keynes's "fundamental psychological law" that consumption expenditure rises less proportionately than income increases, the departure point for his interest in savings behavior. Kuznets provided evidence on the long-run constancy of the savings ratio despite the large rise in per-capita income, and his results encouraged a great amount of further studies to solve the "puzzle" (see Modigliani 1986). The increasing attention was also encouraged by data availability and widespread concern about savings availability and investment opportunities, the so-called stagnationist debate (Modigliani 1986, p. 297 and especially 2001, p. 51).[16]

Dorothy Brady and Rose D. Friedman (1947) reconciled Schultz's empirical results with budget studies. Family data showed that the savings rate is not explained by the absolute income of the family but rather by its income relative to overall mean income. It is in this context that Modigliani placed his 1949 paper along with that of Duesenberry (1949) on savings secular trends and its cyclical fluctuations (see Modigliani 1986, pp. 297–299).

Modigliani had begun to study consumption and saving behavior already with Neisser at the Institute of Word Affairs, publishing an empirical paper on "Cyclical and Secular Factors in the Relationships between Income, Consumption and Savings" in the 1946 U.S. Department of Commerce Bulletin. Neisser had worked since the 1930s on economic fluctuations and structural growth (see Trautwein 2017), whereas Modigliani was probably stimulated by the previously mentioned postwar concerns about over savings (that also appears in Modigliani's 1947 essay on the socialist economy) as a source of both secular stagnation and short-run cyclical fluctuations. In the 1947 essay, Modigliani ascribed the lack of coordination of savings and investment decisions as the main problem of market economies. The solution he suggested was to estimate the amount of savings needed for full employment, then, by deducing private savings to establish the amount of government expenditures. To him, over savings created by monopolies, and by unequal income distribution, was the most important cause of "chronicle unemployment" (1947, p. 511). In other words, the crucial role he ascribed to savings and the possibility of its estimates explain his increasing interest in the field since the mid-1940s both under theoretical and empirical perspectives.

In 1946 Modigliani discussed a paper on "Fluctuations in the Savings Income-Ratio: A Problem in Economic Forecasting" at the December Econometric Society meeting that he submitted soon after to *Econometrica*. The paper is a first version of the 1949 National Bureau of Economic Research (NBER) article on the relative income hypothesis. The referee and the *Econometrica* editor, Ragnar Frisch were quite skeptical about the article (that was not re-submitted). According to the referee, the paper was not original because it merely "include[s] a variable lag which is supposed to account for trend/factors". An idea already suggested by Tinbergen and Klein among many others, also added that

> [t]hose who have worked with consumption function know of many alterations that can be made on it, yet do not write an 85-pages paper on each possible alternative. . . . [They] would not consider to write a paper every time they discovered some new empirical fact about data as Modigliani".

(Leavens to Modigliani: February 3, 1947, MP)

otherwise, it would be possible "to think up a new consumption function every week."

The referee also criticized the "the entire statistical analysis", because Modigliani did not examine the "residual variations" and finally defined the paper theoretically "very weak":

> What behavior patterns are assumed for households and firms in order to derive the savings equation that he obtains: it seems a very poor theory to assume consumers are influenced by their highest income of many years ago. . . . The procedure of this paper is the outmode one of looking at every observed point in a scatter plot and connecting an empirical equation that will fit data well. He does not start out with a sound economic model, but starts by playing with the data.

(Leavens to Modigliani: February 3, 1947, MP)[17]

Modigliani then discussed a revised version (with a section on economic theory and a section on statistical estimates) at the 1947 NBER conference on National Income.[18] Leontief refers to the paper as an "excellent piece of work", which "represents a most valuable contribution to the current discussion of statistical consumption function" (Leontief to Lillian Epstein: May 1,

1947, MP). The paper was published in the 1949 NBER issue and represents the departure point of Modigliani and Brumberg's life cycle hypothesis, on which he started work at the University of Illinois in the beginning of 1950s.

The purpose of the NBER essay was to analyze the "pronounced discrepancy between cyclical (short run) and secular (long run) consumption behavior, adding to absolute income, secular and cyclical movements, to explain the savings ratio" (Modigliani, 1949, p. 4). Modigliani's starting point was the dismissal of Smithies's (1945), Woytinsky's (1946) and Mosak's (1945) empirical studies and forecasts, particularly Smithies's hypothesis that consumption depends on current income plus a trend factor independent of income. Modigliani puts forward a counter-hypothesis according to which the apparent long-run stability of the saving income ratio is a structural property of the system, whereas the tendency of savings to fluctuate with and proportionately more than income is a cyclical phenomenon.[19] According to Modigliani, his empirical results suggested to distinguish between the short-run marginal propensity to save and the long-run average and marginal propensity, as already advanced by Woytinsky (1946). As long as income rises secularly, the savings income ratio depends only on the rate of change of income, rather than on its level, with the short-term ratio that tends to fluctuate with income during each cycle. Modigliani next explored whether his evidence was consistent with realistic assumptions of economic behavior, emphasizing that his confidence in his results "depends largely on the answer" (1949, p. 384). Modigliani points out that casual observations reveal that although it is true that rich people save more than the poor, "there is strong reason to suppose that as aggregate income increases, persons moving into progressively higher income brackets do not tend to acquire the savings habits of persons formerly in the income bracket, on the contrary they tend to save less" (p. 384). These results were supported by budget studies carried out by Dorothy Brady and Rose D. Friedman (1947) and explained by the "nature of economic progress" (1949, p. 385). To him, the rise in income accruing to each group of income receivers tends to be absorbed by the new commodities that gradually become available; thus, Modigliani remarked, the hypothesis that the savings income ratio tends to be relatively independent of the secular expansion of income is not unrealistic.

Regarding cyclical behavior, it is explained by several factors such as cyclical change of income distribution, consumption habits and changes in the level of unemployment. Modigliani also emphasized that profit earners and agricultural families, whose income is largely unstable, have on the whole a greater than average propensity to save: when incomes fall people try to maintain their consumption at the expense of savings.

In his conclusion, Modigliani underlined that his evidence shows that income seems less sensitive to fluctuations in the levels of investment than is usually supposed. The behavior of savers, especially corporate savings, "has tended to act and maybe therefore expected to act in the future as a power stabilizers"

(1949, p. 425). In particular, the relationship between the rate of investment and changes of real income is asymmetric; the effect of rising investment on economic growth is stronger than the effect of a fall of investment on a reduction of real income, partly because of consumption habits and, in the case of profits, because of the asymmetric behavior of overhead costs, which are largely fixed as long as output fluctuated downward.

Modigliani's paper along with that of Duesenberry (1949) contributed to devise the so-called relative income hypothesis and marked Modigliani's interest in the study of savings behavior that eventually led to the life cycle hypothesis with Brumberg. Modigliani and Duesenberry formulations are, then, brought to their logical conclusion by Brown (1952), who suggested to replace the highest previous income with the highest previous consumption, arguing that it is to the past consumption, rather than past income that consumption habit must refer (see Modigliani 1986, p. 152).

As Modigliani explained, "the Duesenberry-Modigliani consumption function tried to reconcile the cyclical variations of the savings ratio with its long run stability by postulating that current consumption was determined not just by current income but also by its highest previous peak, resulting in a ratchet-like upward creep in the short run consumption function" (1986, p. 289). He also recalled that the 1949 article was still unsatisfactory because it lacked a consistent theoretical framework (see Modigliani 1975, p. 5, 1986, p. 299). Modigliani and Brumberg as well, in their papers on the life cycle hypothesis claimed that most of the postwar studies on consumption were carried out on empirical level only, and that their work was aimed to provide this framework: "A person thinks of a new variable, dredges up the data, computes and announces a new high correlation. . . . Further empirical analysis is not likely to advance very far until the economic theorist has been able to provide a conceptual framework" (Modigliani and Brumberg 1953, p. 5, MP).

The two papers Modigliani wrote with Brumberg between 1952 and 1953 were not only a further development of a research line that distinguished between secular and cyclical savings behavior, but their intuition about the life cycle appears also influenced by the research Modigliani began at the University of Illinois, which he joined in November 1948, on firms' behavior planning under uncertainty (Chapter 4).

Notes

1 These suggested readings disappeared from the syllabus of the subsequent 1946–1947 academic year. Modigliani also began to teach Statistics with Alfred Kahler.
2 The mechanism of prices formation and the relationships with production factor costs already called Modigliani's attention in the 1930s discussing the advantages of price control, and in his 1939 thesis (see Chapter 1).
3 Modigliani recalled that Burbank "whom I later found out had a reputation of being xenophobic and anti-Semitic – worked very hard and successfully to persuade me to turn down the offer, which the Faculty had instructed him to make me. . . . I have never

regretted my decision. . . . My career progressed much faster than it would have, if I accepted the offer" (Barnett and Solow 2000, p. 227). In his interview with Camurri Solow provides a partly different explanation arguing that Modigliani was not hired at Harvard because he was not a native English speaker, because he was Keynesian, and because he was a Jew.

4 According to Young et al. (2004) it was Albert Hart who recommended Modigliani to Schultz for a postdoctoral fellowship. In his autobiography Modigliani referred, instead, to Friedman's recommendation; however there is any evidence on it in his Papers.

5 In his reply Singer explained that his request for "a written statement concerning your non-economic background" was part of the appointing procedure at the College which "involves eight or nine different people, and for the shake of the record, some of them who did not know you would have a written statement" (October 20, 1947, MP).

6 In 1947 Marschak again invited Modigliani to join the Cowles Commission as an external consultant, and he accepted.

7 Modigliani replied that if it belonged to him, he certainly would like to have the manuscript returned (November 24, 1947, MP).

8 Modigliani discussed the welfare economics of Hicks (1939) and Lange (1942) and the limits of the Pareto criteria by referring to compensation principle.

9 Also see Daniel B. Klein and Ryan Daza, with Viviana Di Giovinazzo (2013) in https:// econjwatch.org/file_download/750/ModiglianiIPEL.pdf (last accessed November 11, 2019).

10 Modigliani defined imperfect competition in accordance to the standard definition in terms of firms' ability to set prices. He then distinguished between the case of free entry, which guarantees only a normal profit but leads to an excessive number of firms with higher production costs.

11 Modigliani recognized that the optimal number and the firms' sizes cannot be closely satisfied either in a private or a socialist economy (1947, p. 467; also see Klein et al. 2013, p. 17).

12 Modigliani played an active role in the income policy debate of the 1970s, especially in Italy (see Rancan 2012).

13 The use of both time series and family budgets data is important as a route Modigliani also pursued in the study of savings in 1947–1949 and with Richard Brumberg to test the life cycle hypothesis on savings. An approach that became lost with the building of macroeconometric models that only concentrated on time series data (see Thomas 1992).

14 Both Marschak and Koopmans informed Modigliani that the atomic physicist Leo Szilard and Gale Johnson had similar ideas. Koopmans also recalled the he proposed a similar plan in 1943 for the distribution of durable consumers' goods during their scarcity (October 8, 1947, MP). Modigliani sent a copy to Michael Kalecki, at that time at the United Nations (October 7, 1947, MP), who was skeptical about its applicability, and to Lerner. He also wrote to the Italian economist Gustavo Del Vecchio because "it could be applied also elsewhere" (October 1947, MP).

15 In a letter on November 21, 1947, Marschak wrote Modigliani that Gale Johnson had undertaken to organize the breakfast meeting, along with Hart and Colm, "and to other people whom you suggest" (November 21, 1947, MP).

16 In his autobiography Modigliani recalled that his interest in savings began in 1946 "because it was held that national savings underpins the availability of capital", and that "saved income growth with income" on the one side, and on the other, there was Keynesian's fear that people might save too much (2001, p. 51).

17 The article was then rejected by Frisch as well. The referee eventually suggested he consider to reducing the article to four to five pages and to submit it as a note (Leavens to Modigliani: February 17, 1947, MP). The managing editor also asked Modigliani to send an abstract for the report of the 1946 meeting in which, however, Modigliani's paper does not appear.

18 Regarding methodology, Modigliani concludes with a section on "Another Method of Estimation", where he relies on Haavelmo (1943, 1944) and Koopmans's (1944, 1945) new method of estimates, the simultaneous equations method, as alternative to single equation estimates, which became largely applied in the 1950s and 1960s.

19 By secular movement of income Modigliani meant "a movement that carries real income per capita above the highest level reached in any preceding year; by cyclical any movement, whether up or downward, that leaves real income per capita below the highest previous peak" (1947, p. 379).

References

Alacevich, M., P. F. Asso, and S. Nerozzi. 2015. "The Shaping of Public Economic Discourse in Postwar America: The 1947 Meat Shortage and Franco Modigliani's Meat Plan", *Research in History of Economic Thought and Methodology*, 33 (1): 1–46.

Asso P. F., ed. 2007. *Franco Modigliani. L'impegno civile di un'economista*, Siena: Fondazione Monte dei Paschi.

Barnett, W. A., and R. Solow. 2000. "An Interview with Franco Modigliani November 5–1999", *Macroeconomic Dynamics*, 4: 222–256.

Brady, D., and R. D. Friedman. 1947. "Savings and the Income Distribution", *Studies in Income and Wealth*, National Bureau of Economic Research, 247–265.

Brown, T. M. 1952. "Habit Persistence and Lags in Consumer Behavior", *Econometrica*, 20 (July): 355–371.

Duesenberry, J. S. 1949. *Income, Saving and the Theory of Consumer Behavior*, Cambridge, MA: Harvard University Press.

Dunlop, J. T. 1938. "The movement of real and money wages". *The Economic Journal*, 48 (191), 413–433.

Goodwin, C. D. 1998. "The Patrons of Economics in a Time of Transformation, *From Interwar Pluralism to Postwar Neoclassicism: American Economics: The Character of Transformation*, ed. by M. M. Morgan and M. Rutherford", *History of Political Economy*, 30 (Issue Supplement): 53–81.

Haavelmo, T. 1943. "The Statistical Implications of a System of Simultaneous Equations", *Econometrica*, 11 (1): 1–12.

———. 1944. "The Probability Approach in Econometrics", *Econometrica,* 12 Supplement (July): 1–118.

Haberler, G. 1937. *Prosperity and Depression: A Theoretical Analysis of Cyclical Movements*, League of Nations.

Hicks, J. 1939. "The Foundations of Economics of Welfare", *Economic Journal*, 49: 696–712.

Kalecki, M. 1938. "The determinants of distribution of the national income". *Econometrica*, 6 (2): 97–112.

Keynes, J.M. 1939. "Relative movements of real wages and output". *Economic journal*, 49 (193): 34–51.

Klein, D. B., R. Daza, and V. D. Giovinazzo. 2013. "Franco Modigliani (Ideological Profile of Economics Laureates)", *Econ Journal Watch*, 10 (3), September. https://econjwatch. orgyModiglianiIPEL.

Kuznets, S. 1946. *National Income a Summary of Findings*, National Bureau of Economic Research, New York: Arno Press.

Lange, O. 1936. "On the Economic Theory of Socialism, Part One", *Review of Economic Studies*, 4: 53–71.

————. 1937. "On the Economic Theory of Socialism. Part Two", *Review of Economic Studies*, 4: 123–142.

————. 1942. "The Foundations of Welfare Economics", *Econometrica*, 10 (3): 215–228.

Lerner, A. P. 1937. "Statics and Dynamics in Socialist Economics", *Economic Journal*, 47 (186): 253–270.

————. 1944. *Economics of Control*, Oxford: Oxford University Press.

Modigliani (Franco) Papers. David M. Rubenstein Rare Book and Manuscript Library, Duke University.

Modigliani, F. 1937. "Concetti generali sul controllo dei prezzi", *Lo Stato. Rivista di Scienze Politiche, Giuridiche ed Economiche* (Aprile): 220–232.

————. 1944. "Liquidity Preference and the Theory of Interest and Money", *Econometrica*, 12 (January): 45–88.

————. 1947. "L'Organizzazione e la Direzione della Produzione in un'Economia Socialista", *Giornali degli Economisti e Annali di Economia*, 6, 441–514.

————. 1949. "Fluctuations in the Saving-Income Ratio: A Problem in Economic Forecasting", *Studies in Income and Wealth*, New York: National Bureau of Economic Research, no. 11, 371–441.

————. 1975. "The Life-Cycle Hypothesis of Savings Twenty Years Later" *Contemporary Issues in Economics*, ed. by M. Parkin and A. R. Nobay. Manchester: Manchester University Press.

————. 1980–1989. *The Collected Papers of Franco Modigliani* (voll. 5), ed. by A. Abel, Cambridge, MA: MIT Press.

————. 1986. "Life Cycle, Individual Thrift, and the Wealth of Nations", *American Economic Review*, 76 (3): 297–313.

————. 2001. *Adventure of an Economist*, New York and London: Texere.

————. Undated. "Plan to Meet the Problem of Rising Meat and Other Food Prices Without Bureaucratic Controls", Franco Modigliani Papers.

Modigliani, F., and R. Brumberg. 1953. "Utility Analysis and Aggregate Consumption Functions: An Attempt at Integrating", Franco Modigliani Papers); Box RW 43, David M. Rubenstein Rare Book and Manuscript, Duke University.

Mongiovi, G. 2005. "Emigré Economists and American Neoclassical Economics", *Journal of the History of Economic Thought*, 27 (4): 427–437.

————. 2015. "Franco Modigliani and the Socialist State", *Preliminary Draft*: 1–22. http://qcpages.qc.cuny.edu/~lussher/mongiovi05.pdfpp. Last access November 29, 2019.

Mosak, J. L. 1945. "Forecasting Postwar Demand III", *Econometrica*, 13 (1): 25–53.

Neisser, H., and F. Modigliani. 1946. "Cyclical and Secular Factors in the Relationships between Income, Consumption and Savings", U.S. Department of Commerce Bulletin.

————. 1953. *National Incomes and International Trade: A Quantitative Analysis*, Urbana: University of Illinois Press, xviii–396.

Rancan, A. 2012. "Politica dei redditi e spesa pubblica nella visione di Franco Modigliani", in *Saggi di Economia Pubblica*, Jovene Editore.

Schrecker, E. W. 1986. *No Ivory Tower: McCarthyism & the Universities*, Oxford: Oxford University Press.

Smithies, A. 1945. "Forecasting Postwar Demand I", *Econometrica*, 13 (1): 1–14.

Szenberg, M., and L. Ramrattan. 2008. *Franco Modigliani a Mind That Never Rests*, Palgrave Macmillan.

Thomas J. J. 1992. "Income Distribution and the Estimation of the Consumption Function: A Historical Analysis of the Early Arguments". In *History of Political Economy*, 24 (1): 153–181.

Tinbergen, J. 1939. *Business Cycles in the United States, 1919–1932 Statistical Testing of Business Cycles Theory*, vol. 2, Geneva: League of Nations.

Trautwein, H.-M. 2017. "Some International Aspects of Business Cycles: Neisser, Haberler, and Modern Open Economy Macroeconomics", *Journal of the History of Economic Thought*, 39 (Special issue 1) *Business Cycles and Economic Growth*: 47–67.

Woytinsky, W. S. 1946. "Relationships between Consumers' Expenditures, Savings, and Disposable Income", *Review of Economic Statistics*, 28 (21): 1–12.

Young, W., R. Leeson, and W. Darity, Jr. 2004. *Economics, Economists, and Expectations: Microfoundations to Macroapplications*, New York: Routledge.

4 Modigliani at the University of Illinois

"The Bowen war" and McCarthyism

Introduction

In the introduction to his 1947 article on "The Organization and Direction of Production in a Socialist Economy" (in *Il Giornale degli economisti*), Modigliani explained that it was part of wider research on the applicability of a socialist economy. Nonetheless, he did not return anymore to the topic. In his recollection Modigliani mentioned the article as the result of a sort of intellectual curiosity he had on a topic widely discussed at that time. Instead, according to Mongiovi (2015), Modigliani might have moved on from the subject because the article appeared when McCarthy was beginning his anticommunist campaign within academia. As mentioned in the previous chapter, already in May 1947 the head of the Economics Department of the University of Chicago asked Modigliani about his policy orientation. In November Modigliani also received a letter from the Office of Strategic Service of the War Department asking whether a "bound manuscript" that was found clearing the files at office, titled "Organization and Direction of Socialist Economy" belonged to him. "If so, we will be pleased to mail it to you" (Colonel Knox P. Pruden to Modigliani: November 18, 1947, MP).[1]

Between 1949 and 1951 Modigliani personally faced the political and intellectual climate of the McCarthy campaign in academia, although only indirectly, to which this chapter is mainly devoted. Soon after his moving to the University of Chicago, in September 1948, Modigliani received an offer from the University of Illinois as associate professor at the Bureau of Economic and Business Research directed by Lee Bassie, and research director of a two-year project on *Expectations and Business Fluctuations* sponsored by the Merrill Foundation and supervised by Clyde W. Hart from the University of Chicago and director of the National Opinion Research Center.

According to Young et al. (2004) Albert Hart recommended Modigliani to Howard Bowen, the new dean of the College of Commerce and Business Administration of the university, along with Schumpeter, who introduced Modigliani "as one of the ablest young theorists in the country" (Schumpeter to Bowen: October, 28, 1948, MP), and Marschak. Marschak refers to his former student as follows:

I do not think you could have made a better choice. I have known Modigliani for almost ten years and have not had reasons to change my first impression, to wit, that he is one of the most brilliant men of his generation. Certainly, he is the best pupil I have ever had. . . . He has a very profound way of thinking about economic problems, helped by quick intuition and, recently, by modern tools which he has learned to master. He is well aware of the necessity of combining theory and empirical research, and he has very good sense of proportion in doing so. He overflows with enthusiasm and energy and has a truly scholarly attitude toward the problems he tackles.

(Marschak to Bowen: October 27, 1948,
quoted from Hagemann 2005, p. 21)

The research project he was called to supervise was aimed to investigate the role of expectations and plans in economic activity. In his recollection and interviews, Modigliani remarked that this research represented the departure point of all innovative ideas he developed over the 1950s (2001, pp. 57–58). When Modigliani joined the University of Illinois, he was working on cyclical and secular trends of consumption and savings (see Chapter 3), a research interest largely shared in the department Bowen was setting up. In fact, as Modigliani recalled he had the opportunity to take advantage of Margaret Reid's "highly imaginative" studies on income and to benefit from "many unrecorded comments of Dorothy Brady" (Modigliani, *Collected Papers*, vol. 2, 1980, p. 129), who were also among Bowen's new appointees. Reid was researching household production and consumption, while Brady was working on personal income distribution and savings, both using family budget data.[2] In other words, the new Economics Department appeared promising to Modigliani.[3] However, the group of leading scholars Bowen brought together in 1948 left the department only few years later, between 1951 to 1952, as a consequence of Bowen's forced resignation.

Modigliani preserved a lot of material about the so-called Bowen war, a fight within the Economics Department for academic, ideological and political reasons began soon after Modigliani's arrival. Therefore, before discussing Modigliani's research at the University of Illinois, it is worthwhile to reconstruct the events that characterized that period to understand whether and how they influenced his research agenda.[4] Indeed, as he wrote to Patinkin, he found himself in "one of the most violent and dirtiest fights" he had "ever seen" in his life (Modigliani to Patinkin: November 1, 1950, MP). And, in a letter to Albert Hart, he claimed that his work was considerably undermined by the situation because "I have been so intensely absorbed by the local fight that I have hardly had time to think seriously of anything else" (Modigliani to Hart: October 3, 1950, MP).

Thanks to a number of factors, such as the 1944 G.I. Bill (The Servicemen Readjusted Act) devoted to assist WWII veterans, for example, in attending high schools and universities; to the baby boom; and to foundations' increasing financial support, in the postwar United States universities grew rapidly, opening a rising number of academic positions. As for economics, most professors came from governmental institutions, where they had been engaged during the New Deal and WWII, and most of them had a Keynesian background. This process accelerated the generational change in economics departments (see Bernstein 2001; Backhouse 2006; Bowen 1998; Jones 1972 among others). The 1946 Employment Act had "institutionalized" Keynesian economics and its stance for an active economic policy. According to Galbraith (1998), the Council of Economic Advisers became the platform for expounding the Keynesian view: "there was a strong feeling in Washington that key economic posts should be held by people who understood Keynesian ideas." Luachlin Currie, later victim of the McCarthy campaign, at the White House ran an informal "casting office in this regard," whereas the Center for Economic Development began to evangelize the business community (p. 14; also see Byrd 1972).

Most of Bowen's new appointee professors as well were "Keynesians", and in some cases they also were European émigrés. Thus, the problem of a rapid generational change became entangled with anti-Keynesians, anti-foreign and anti-Semitic sentiments.[5] These intertwined sentiments found in the McCarthyism campaign legitimation. At the University of Illinois, institutionalists, New Dealers and Keynesians were all identified with supporters of socialist and communist ideas and charged with disseminating collectivist ideas. The complexity of this situation was reconstructed by Solberg and Tomilson in a article on "Academic McCarthyism and Keynesian Economics: The Bowen Controversy at the University of Illinois" (1997) on which this chapter is partly based.

Bowen's Economics Department and the discipline turn

In 1942 the American Council of Education established a commission to investigate the University of Illinois and its administration because of the ineffectiveness of Arthur Cutts Willard's presidency. A year later the commission highlighted the negative influence of "conservative and sometimes reactionary senior professors and administrators" on the university (Commission of the American Council on Education 1943, pp. 70–71, quoted from Solberg and Tomilson 1997, p. 56). As a consequence in 1945 the Board of Trustees named George D. Stoddard the new president of the University of Illinois with the aim of transforming it into a world-class university (Solberg and Tomilson 1997, pp. 56–57). Stoddard was a professor of psychology from Iowa University with a national reputation as member of UNESCO. In 1946 President Truman made him member of the President's Commission on Higher Education, and in 1947 Stoddard appointed Bowen, his former colleague at Iowa University, new dean of the College of Commerce and Business, of which the Economics Department was part. Stoddard and Bowen fully shared the target of raising the level of excellence and to strengthen the position of social sciences within which economics had priority. Before then, the tone of the campus was practical: fields such as agriculture, engineering and business were dominant (see Bowen 1988). Bowen explained the reorganization of the economics department was an "intensive and exciting" task, spending much of 1947, 1948 and 1949 on recruitment of economists from the leading centers for economics in the United States: "I recruited both junior and senior faculty. Recruitment meant at that time persuasion because economists were in short supply. It also meant being competitive in salary and prerequisites, finding housing, providing research funds, and getting job for wives" (Bowen 1988, p. 29). He was greatly supported by Theodore Schultz, also a former colleague at the Iowa University: "Schultz was extremely helpful to me in identifying suitable people and in encouraging them to come to Urbana-Champaign" (Bowen 1988, p. 29).

Most of the new economists who joined the department were the higher expression of the new frontier of economic research: mathematicians, statisticians and econometricians such as Everet Hagen, Leonid Hurwicz, Modigliani and Patinkin.[6] Patinkin was among the first young economists to join the University of Illinois in September 1948, from the Cowles Commission. However, he accepted the position under the condition of leaving as soon as the Hebrew University called him to build a department of economics in Jerusalem, and left the University of Illinois already in February 1949 (Patinkin to Bowen: December 22, 1948, Patinkin Papers). Bowen and Patinkin maintained close a relationship, comparing their respective experiences in the organization of their new departments. Their correspondence shows Bowen's increasing satisfaction for the new shape the department was taking on:

> The Economics Department has been fully reorganized on a chairmanship basis with a new and highly effective executive committee. . . . We are still negotiating with your friend Hurwicz and hope that he will be with us. . . . We missed a couple of good boys from Chicago by a narrow margin.

(Bowen to Patinkin: May, 5, 1949, Patinkin Papers)

Bowen recalled that thanks to the G.I. Bill the University of Illinois "was booming. . . . It was saying . . . that the University of Illinois had more operating funds than any university in the previous history of the world". It was the ideal moment of "taking advantage of the unique post-war situation to raise by a quantum leap the stature of the university" (1988, p. 26). However, Bowen's ambitious project of attracting leading economists and introducing an innovative program was not welcome in a department where the 81 percent of the staff members of the rank of assistant professor or above had their terminal degrees from the University of Illinois (see *Harno Committee's Report*,

1950, p. 12, 1950, MP). In a letter to Patinkin, Reid described as follows the lively situation:

> We have a whole crop of new staff members this past fall so that Dorothy and I feel more like oldtimers with new staff to call on. The feeling of being old-timers is increased somewhat now that Everett [Hagen] has been made chairman of the department. His official appointment was announced only last week. Unofficially word has been around for some time. *We are wishing him luck since the department is still far from being unified.* Perhaps the seminars will help do the unifying.

(January 15, 1950, emphasis added, Patinkin Papers)

The McCarthyism campaign in the universities was in the beginning and it soon became a useful expedient to translate internal academic jealousies in ideological and political conflicts as it soon happened within the Bowen's department. Although he had the support of President Stoddard and Provost Coleman R. Griffith, Bowen had to resign in December 1950 because of the Executive Committee's charges of maladministration.[7] As a consequence, seventeen of the eighteen new leading economists he appointed left the University of Illinois.

In 1945 the House of Un-American Activity Commission (HUAC) set a permanent committee to respond to the "threats" of the Cold War, and in 1947 President Truman established the loyalty program for federal employees with the introduction of political tests for all jobs, allowing communists and suspected communists to be fired. According to Schrecker (1986, p. 9), the loyalty program opened the doors to McCarthyism. The political legitimation to denial civil rights to members of the Communist Party facilitated the more reactionary practitioners of the anti-communism battle to extend the denial to other types of political undesirables by claiming that they served the party's cause. American universities became one of the targets of the anti-communist campaign. In 1947 the Broyles Commission was set at Illinois, and the same year the University of Washington fired thee professors, two of them as communists. Since then, the number of professors involved in the McCarthy campaign increased rapidly.

Persecutions of economists within academia for ideological and political reasons were not new, as Goodwin (1998) recalled, nonetheless, in the 1950s, the attack was most intense because of economics's prominence in public opinion, its growing importance in higher education, its close relations with patrons and, finally, the new significance the Cold War attached to many economic issues.[8] The attacks came from legislators, trustees, alumni, the media, senior administrators and jealous, conservative colleagues. To these attacks universities and the American Economic Association (AEA) responded timidly. Among professors who were victims of McCarthyism, 20 percent were economists (Goodwin 1998); the most known were the Nobel Laureate Lawrence Klein at Michigan University, Paul Baran at Stanford University and Paul Sweezy at New Hampshire University.

The Bowen war is an example of the effects of McCarthyism, although it played only an indirect role in being the main argument to influence public opinion and the trustees about the perilous turn of the Economics Department under Bowen's directorship.

The "Bowen war"

Solberg and Tomilson (1997) reconstructed the controversy between senior professors and the economists appointed by Bowen, which rapidly turned into an ideological battle that involved the local media and public opinion. They referred to a couple of episodes that began the "anti-Bowen" campaign: Bowen's decision to restrict the graduate course in economics of the senior economist Ralph Blodgett to one semester and the substitution of his *Principles of Economics* with Samuelson's *Economics*. As a consequence Blodgett moved to the University of Florida, explaining the decision with the introduction of Bowen's new standards, which restrained his teaching activities and prevented the use of his textbook (see Solberg and Tomilson 1997, pp. 61–62).[9]

An ad hoc committee to investigate the infringement of academic freedom in the "Blodgett case" was appointed (Bowen to Griffith: May 17, 1950, MP). It was formed by senior faculty members from various departments of the university, with the aim of investigating whether the "honourable and traditional rights of a teacher . . . or of students to hear a diversity of viewpoints" had been infringed (*Harno's Committee Report* 1950, p. 2, MP). A few months later the report concluded that there was no infringement of academic freedom and that in the department there was neither "red" neither "radical" scholars: "There is perhaps a misapprehension as to the schools of thought typified in these groups [new appointed economists]" (*Harno Report* 1950, p. 7, MP). Presenting the report to the Executive Committee, Stoddard pointed out that the university aimed to meet standards unrelated to political boundaries.

However, local newspapers went on in the anti-Bowen campaign, reporting that Bowen "shifts the emphasis in basic courses from free enterprise to government control and deficit spending" (*News Gazette*, June 25, 1950, quoted from Solberg and Tomilson 1997). To reply to the ideological propaganda the so-called Bowen group wrote an open letter to faculty colleagues and to the editor of the journal to clarify the issues under dispute, showing that the department was aligning its standards to that of other departments all over the United States: "One piece of evidence is the supposed 'facts' presented to the public concerning the replacement of Blodgett's text by Samuelson's *Economics* . . . [giving] the impression that the course has changed, is dominated by 'national income analysis', that is no longer teaches the 'economic of free enterprise' and that it tends to indoctrinate students with belief in a controlled economy" (September 16, 1950, MP).[10] To confute the charges they especially referred to the results of an inquiry Hagen had sent to the members of three major groups of American university members of the Big Ten in the Midwest, of the Ivy League in the East and the Pacific Coast athletic association in the West to know the kind of textbooks in use. According to Hagen's inquiry, of the twenty-seven universities interviewed, only five did not teach national income analysis, eleven used Samuelson's textbook in their introductory courses, and only one of these major schools, the University of Iowa, used the Blodgett's textbook in special courses for pharmacy and engineering students (September 16, 1950, MP).

The Bowen group thus concluded that "[t]hese facts demonstrate that the change made was indeed overdue, to make our course comprehensive and to bring it up to the standard in this respect of other major American universities" (September 16, 1950, MP).[11]

The "censorship" of Keynesian textbooks was not a new episode. It had already happened with the publication of Lorie Tharshis's 1947 textbook *Elements of Economics*, which was charged with excessive sympathy towards communism. Soon after, the content of Samuelson's 1948 *Economics* was subjected to political negotiations with MIT officials, Samuleson's editors at McGraw-Hill and other economists. According to Giraud's detailed reconstruction, "Although Samuelson first intended to write a policy-oriented textbook with a strong Keynesian inclination, the changes he introduced, while keeping most of the substance, made it a more theoretically inclined text whose policy recommendations were presented in a softened fashion" (2014, p. 134).[12]

A memorandum titled "Analysis of the Actions of the Executive Committee" also denounced the pressure senior professors exercised upon the faculty members: "Repeated attempts [over the summer] were made to induce faculty members close to Bowen to suggest to him that he resign by using a mixture of reassurances and threats; reassurance that new people were indeed very much liked and esteemed, especially the Chairman Hagen, and the only trouble was Bowen . . . threats of outside pressures and legislative investigation" (undated, p. 15, MP).

Modigliani wrote to Albert Hart, asking to inform Paul Douglas, Patinkin and Jean Bronfenbrenner about the situation. To Hart he reported the "dirty fight of the old guard against Bowen, of which probably word has already reached you":

> What actually got me to sit at the typewriter is primarily the desire to acquaint you . . . with this affair, or I should say, dirty affair . . . [Blodgett's resignation] was accompanied and followed by a vicious press campaign . . . accusing Howard [Bowen] and Everett [Hagen] of being Keynesian pinks, of having brought in a group of Keynesian-Washington bureaucrats, Easterners, Californians, Government Interventionists . . . and of infringing academic freedom. . . . I can assure you that I have seldom felt as furious and as disgusted with humanity as after that meeting. . . . As a matter of fact you may already have heard of the pretty sad news that Dorothy Brady and Margaret Reid have already tendered their resignations . . . this

has been quite a shock to me for I consider them just about as fine a pair as I have ever met; and obviously if they and Howard [Bowen] should be liquidated, people like myself, Everett, Hurwicz, etc. would not stay much longer. This argument, I feel, is an important weapon in the hand of the President, especially with respect to the Board of Trustees, and this is perhaps the point where letters to the President from you and other top people in the profession might be of real help. . . . Furthermore what might be even more useful is to stress the rapid growth in the reputation of the College of Commerce since Howard [Bowen] took over, and the qualities of the group that he has been building up. . . . . If you feel there is any sense in it you might also pass this letter around to a few other people in your group.

(October 3, 1950, MP)

Hart immediately wrote to Stoddard and to Paul Douglas.[13] To Stoddard he pointed out the excellence the college had achieved under Bowen's deanship:

I am in a position to make a reasonably accurate evaluation of the effect of Dean Bowen's administration on the University's standing as a center of teaching and research in economics. To begin with, Dean Bowen himself is an economist of standing . . . in second place, the stature of Illinois as a center of economics has risen rapidly during his administration. A few years ago, it would never occurred to me to advise any young man to pursue graduate studies at Urbana . . . today Illinois is high. . . . Among state universities, I should rank Illinois in the top three (with California and Michigan) as a center of economics. . . . The economists who have joined the Illinois Faculty during these years are excellent standing. Margaret Reid and Dorothy Brady stand at the top. . . . Franco Modigliani and Leonid Hurwicz are among the leaders in the rising specialty of econometrics. . . . Hagen has done pioneer work on the application of national income techniques to policy problems. . . . I . . . Illinois has become an important center of economic research. The June meeting of the Conference on Research in National Income and Wealth at your conference center is a testimonial: previously, this conference has met only in New York and Washington, for the obvious reason that there was no focal concentration of workers in the field elsewhere. Dean Bowen's Merrill Foundation Project on research in business expectations is widely regarded as a crucial pioneer job . . . you cannot afford to resolve the conflict by methods which will lose you Dean Bowen and the strong economists he has added to the faculty. In a narrow sense, no issue of academic freedom is involved: these people are all so much in demand that all you have to do to remove them from the scene is to make it plain that the University has lost interest in being a first-rate center in economics. But in a broader sense, you can contribute to academic freedom by continuing to move ahead.

(Albert G. Hart to Stoddard: October 7, 1950, MP)

And, in his letter to Senator Paul Douglas (and 1947 President of American Economic Association), Hart denounced the increasing threats to academic freedom:

> This is to cover a letter of President Stoddard of the University of Illinois about the crisis in his Economics Department. The unavoidable tension between the "old guard" and the strong group of new economists brought in to build up the Department seems to have taken a very ugly form, with members of the "old-guard" attacking Dean Howard Bowen through the press, and efforts to exert political pressure to get rid Bowen. I gather that this affair is linked with the recent attacks on the University of Chicago . . . my file on the matter is somewhat incomplete. The "document stating and supporting the various charges of maladministration . . ." to which I refer seems not to exist. . . . Letters from members of the pro-Bowen faction indicate that a lot mischief has been done by unfair tactics on the part of an old guard executive committee [Hart also quoted two similar episodes at the University of Iowa . . . and California]. . . . I understood that two members of the Department of Economics have already submitted resignations [Brady and Reid], which if not reconsidered might disrupt the group seriously. . . . I presume attempts will be made . . . to influence the Trustees to bring about a change of Dean. If it happens, the rapidly rising Illinois Department of Economics will undoubtedly collapse.

(Albert G. Hart to Paul Douglas: October 7, 1950, MP)

As reconstructed by Solberg and Tomilson (1997), despite external support and evidence of the high standards reached by the department, the Advisory Committee explicitly embraced the ideological dimension of the conflict, pointing out in its report that Samuelson's textbook had been adversely reviewed by two national business groups. The committee also called "for the screening of future faculty appointees to determine not only their education and experience but also their personal economic and social-philosophy" (Solberg and Tomilson 1997). Bowen resigned in December 1950. In October 1951 Paul M. Green, a former faculty member, was appointed new dean of the college. In his correspondence with members of the board of trustees, he assured that "he would direct the college of commerce with the full cooperation of the businessmen of the state" (quoted from Solberg and Tomilson 1997, p. 78). Soon after Provost Griffith resigned, and in July 1953 the board of trustees fired Stoddard.

Bowen's resignation was followed by seventeen of the eighteen new economists he had appointed. Everett Hagen resigned in 1951, taking a position at MIT, Margaret Reid went to the University of Chicago, Dorothy S. Brady to the University of Pennsylvania, Robert Eisner to Northwestern University, Leonid Hurwicz to the University of Minnesota and Modigliani to the Carnegie Institute of Technology (now Carnegie Mellon). In his letter of resignation Modigliani denounced, once again, the abuse of power that accompanied the whole affair until and after Bowen's resignation:

> Mine is the seventeenth resignation in the Department of Economics since H. Bowen was forced out. . . . I believe that the University Administration and others in the Academic Community should be reminded of the reasons that lead me to join proudly a most distinguished group of economists in its exodus from the College of Commerce . . . during the past year and half . . . a clique of faculty members interested not in scholarship but in personal power, not in the welfare of the University but in the gratification of their vindictive impulses, has followed a policy calculated to wreck the Department of Economics. The success of this policy is clearly evident by seventeen resignations. . . . [T]he University may be pleased over the fact that it has almost succeeded in bringing peace to the strife-torn Department of Economics – but let us be clear about it, it is the peace of death. . . . I feel compelled to speak out for the few economists who are still left behind from that outstanding group assembled here under the deanship of H. Bowen. Those few are not free to speak out as I am now finally in a position to do. They have much to contribute to research and teaching, and they are entitled to academic freedom and to the exercise of the rights and privileges granted to them by the statues. These rights are being constantly disregarded by the Administration of the Department of Economics. . . . The University of Illinois is an outstanding institution. . . . If the University Administration and the University Senate want to sustain this reputation, it their urgent duty to investigate the circumstances which I have described and to put an end to these practices.

(Modigliani to Stoddard: August 29, 1952, MP)

Since April 1952 Modigliani had begun negotiations with the Carnegie Institute, which he would join in September 1952. In his autobiography Modigliani recalled his leaving as follows:

> There were only two ways for the dean to send me packing: either by showing there was no course I could teach at that university, or by proving me academically incompetent. . . . One day I was summoned by the dean, who greeted me with the following speech: "Dear Modigliani in the past you taught two subjects. One was macroeconomics, but you are evidently quite incompetent in that subject. There are plenty of professors here who can teach it better than you. The other subject . . . is mathematical economics. . . . But, you know . . . this subject . . . can no longer be taught because it doesn't agree with the trustees . . ."

Concluding: "this political threat, indirect as it was, remind me of Fascist times" (2001, p. 68)

The American Economics Association: committees on academic freedom

At the 1950 Annual Meeting of the American Economic Association (AEA), President Fritz Machlup introduced Bowen, two days after his resignation, as "the man who has just been fired from his job" and praised the high standards achieved by the Economics Department he had set up. The presentation was followed by an eight-minute ovation from the audience (*Champaign Urbana Courier*, December 31, 1950, quoted from Solberg and Tomilson 1997, p. 76). Despite the acknowledgment, the AEA did not actively intervene during the McCarthy campaign within the academia. The association chose to pursue a passive stance with the creation of ad hoc committees devoted to secure academic freedom that remained most of the time silent.

In 1947 the AEA voted on a resolution stating that universities and college teachers must be free to select textbooks and related materials, a copy of which was sent to the presidents and chairs of boards of trustees and chairs of economic departments (AER), May 1948). A committee formed by past AEA presidents was also established "to make public" the position of the association on academic freedom, to refer proper cases to the American Association of Universities Professors (AAUP) and to provide their own individual judgements on specific grievances. The statement refers only to the right of teachers of economics to select textbooks because, according to the committee, "it would be unwise, and beyond our mandate to concern ourselves with others aspects of academic freedom" (AER May 1950, p. 594). The committee should have intervened only when specific cases were submitted for full consideration. Therefore in 1950 and 1951 no actions were reported.[14] In April 1952 an ad hoc committee, *Freedom of Teaching, Research, and Publication in Economics*, replaced the former one with the aim of drawing up a statement formulating its functions, to explore a "pilot" case to test out operations and to submit a report at the December meeting. Again, the December 1952 and April 1953 reports did not denounce any case. The AEA was not alone in pursuing this kind of "passive" stance; most professional associations in the social sciences took the position that "cases involving academic tenure should be handled by the AAUP". The only exceptions were the American Historical Association, the American Political Science Association and the American Psychological Association, which instead pursued "a strong and independent line" (AER May 1954, p. 734). In 1954 a new ad hoc committee on the Status of the Profession was set up, and its chair, I. L. Sharfman, decided to maintain the previous line of conduct. According to the committee all matters were well covered in the *Statements of Freedom and Tenure* issued in 1925 and 1940 by the AAUP, and "if they have to be strengthened, it referred to all scholars" not only to economists (AER May 1955, p. 735).

Regarding investigations and reports upon specific cases, it would have implied a duplication of the AAUP activity. Nonetheless, the committee acknowledged the AAUP "lacking in vigour and effectiveness" because the "central office [was] virtually paralyzed" to the point that in 1953 its membership voted for an investigation of its inactivity (AER May 1955, p. 735). Indeed, from 1948 to 1956 the AAUP produced no reports (see Bahr 1967). Therefore, it was recognized that that AEA should act in the direction of a reinvigoration of AAUP activity also through a committee of leading economists that might offer its services on the objectivity of textbooks or the competence of its scholars. Alternatively, "and only if it is clear that it is impossible to reactive the AAUP", the AEA might propose to the other associations in the social sciences establish a joint secretariat to perform the function for which the AAUP was originally designed (AER May 1955, p. 736). The committee also recognized its lack of knowledge about the nature and dimension of the problem.[15]

It is only with the *Exploratory Committee on the Status of the Profession* Kuznets established in 1954 that for the first time two cases of infringement of freedom were reported. They were that of Horace Davis, who asked the association to take some action in favour of one of its members, and of Paul Sweezy's request for publication of a note about his case in the AER because of a "plain problem of communication" concerning attacks on economists' civil liberties (AER 1955, pp. 678–680).[16] From 1956 to 1957 no other cases were reported.

In 1958 the new ad hoc Committee on *Academic Freedom and Civil Liberties* (chaired by Machlup, with Bowen among its members) discussed the New Hampshire Supreme Court decision in favour of the Sweezy case because it recognized "an emphatic recognition of academic freedom as an essential liberty" (AER 1958, p. 651). Maybe encouraged by the court decision, the new committee also acknowledged the violation of academic freedom in the Davis case: the "one violation of academic-tenure regulations through the dismissal of an economist deserves notice here chiefly because of the principle involved . . . the case in point is that of Horace B. Davis" (AER 1958, p. 653). The committee concluded that this and similar cases seemed to lie in the "unwillingness of faculties to rally the support of a teacher who insists . . . on his right to be silent on political questions. . . . The faculty . . . fails to live up to the highest standards of academic freedom. It is difficult to expect university administrations and trustees to be more broadminded than their faculties, though, of course, this is exactly the 'ideal' university government ought to be" (AER 1958, p. 653).

The AEA political line towards violation of academic freedom found an explanation in its choice not to be involved in individual cases because its charter did not permit the association "to speak for its memberships". In other words, the association failed to perceive individual repressions as an attack towards the discipline (Coats 1960, p. 557; also see Coats 1985).[17] In addition, in 1950 the National Science Foundation was established; the scientific status of social sciences was under dispute until their inclusion in 1956. According to the literature this contributes to the explanation of the AEA's "neutral" stands towards ideological and political controversies (see among others Bernstein 2001; Goodwin 1998; Weintraub 2016).

McCarthyism and the economics research agenda

In *No Ivory Tower* (1986), Schrecker's asked to what extent academic research was influenced by political repression. Mary Morgan and Malcom Rutherford (1998) posed a similar question regarding economics. According to them, the McCarthy campaign contributed to the formalization of postwar social sciences and, in the case of economics, to the establishment of Keynesian ideas in the neoclassical synthesis version over more radical views, contributing to a redirection of academic work. Their reading, as most other interpretations of post war social sciences development, relied on Paul Lazarsfeld and Wagner Thielens's (1958) investigation about the situation within the academia. Through interviews with social sciences college and university professors, Lazarsfeld and Thielens showed how much apprehensive they became due to the increasing number of repressive incidents.[18] This apprehension would have found a professional refuge in a value-free neutral approach. According to the sociologist Daniel Bell (1982, p. 301), the intellectual quest for scientific objectivity and the professional advantage of such neutrality reinforced each other in the establishment of a new methodological consensus, moving social sciences from a qualitative to an empirical approach. Bell refers both to the case of philosophy that, with the formalist movement, essentially withdrew from the public realm and of political science's behaviorist revolution. Regardings economics, McCarthyism would have contributed to the rapid shift from interwar pluralism to postwar neoclassicism (Morgan and Ruthenford 1998; Goodwin 1998). According to Hodgson (2004) many neoclassical mathematical economists such as Lange, Marschak and Koopmans, who had socialist inclinations, found in formalism their professional refuge. Other schools of thought, such as institutionalism, which had no mathematics at their core, suffered a rapid decline, gradually losing their positions in leading departments. The refuge in mathematical economics represented not only an individual answer to a concrete threat but seemed to be encouraged by academic and research institutions seeking safe teachers and researchers (Lazarsfeld and Thielens 1958; Goodwin 1998).

Weintraub (2016) argued that this thesis has become standard reading, as his review of the literature on this topic shows. Although recognizing the persecution of radical economists in the 1940s and 1950s is true, he argued that the mathematization of economics already began during the inter-war period and involved other countries as well. He refers among others to Fisher, Evans, Frisch and Hotelling attempts to develop more rigorous modes of economic analysis.[19] To Weintraub, "they and their intellectual progeny – Charles Roos, Trygve Haavelmo, Kenneth Arrow – were to make significant contributions in the postwar years. Similarly important was the emigration to the U.S. of refugee European economists who had a mathematical and statistical background. The Econometric Society also played an important role, being active in holding meetings, publishing articles and naming meretricious fellows" (Weintraub 2016, p. 39; also see Weintraub 2002).

What about Modigliani's research agenda? Did the Bowen war add something about this historiography?

Modigliani's encounter with Marschak, Lowe, Neisser, Lange and Lerner influenced his approach to economics, particularly about the use of marginalist analysis and economic modeling. He joined the New School as a self-taught economist with no training in mathematical economics and statistics. His previous writings in economics lacked of any kind of formalized tools. It was his training at the New School that provided him mathematical, statistics and empirical sophistication. In other words, Modigliani's economic language was already shaped by the 1940s, that is, before the McCarthy campaign.[20]

Most of the young economists Bowen appointed were mathematical and quantitative economists like Hurwicz, Brady, Reid and Modigliani himself. The use of mathematical language did not prevent Modigliani and his colleagues to be labeled "reds" or "pinks" – quite the contrary. The Bowen controversy shows that to be mathematical economists (and European émigrés) meant, instead, to be identified with economic planners, Keynesians and Marxian economists. After Bowen's resignation, mathematical economics was no longer taught because, as Modigliani recalled, "it doesn't agree with the trustee" (Modigliani 2001, p. 68). In other words, the use of the mathematical language did not seem such a secure refuge for economists.

Another question the Bowen episode brings up is whether it influenced Modigliani's research agenda over the 1950s. Modigliani left Illinois to join the Carnegie Institute in 1952. He went on with his research on expectations and business fluctuations that began in 1948 and strengthened his collaboration with Herbert Simon, which was already initiated at the Cowles Commission. Differently from the 1940s, during the 1950s Modigliani apparently disregarded his research on Keynesian economics, focusing on microeconomics issues of firm's production planning, expectations and individual savings behavior in the context of the neoclassical intertemporal choice framework. Even if he still worked on Keynesian and classical economics, writing long notes on *The Theory of Money and Interest in the Framework of General Equilibrium Analysis*, they remained unpublished until the 1963 article "The Monetary Mechanism and Its Interaction with Real Phenomena", which summarized the results of these notes. In 1962 Modigliani had moved to MIT, explaining his decision with his desire to return to traditional Keynesian research (Modigliani to Pasinetti: January 31, 1960) and maybe also because the political climate had in the meantime changed. How much his prevailing work on microeconomics issues with any publication on Keynesian macroeconomics was the result of the political climate or simply the development of research agenda well established in the 1940s does not have a clear-cut answer.

Modigliani and Gaetano Salvemini

During the late 1940s Modigliani was also following the evolution of the political situation in Italy. Indeed, among the reasons that led Modigliani and his wife Serena Calabi to decide in 1946 to remain in the United States after the end of WWII – a possibility they had never considered until then, was their disillusion about the political climate that seemed to be established (see Modigliani 2001, pp. 49–51).

A couple of years after the publication of the article on the organization of a socialist economy (see Chapter 3), and in the beginning of the McCarthy campaign, Modigliani was indirectly engaged with the Italian political and economic situation through his encounter with Gaetano Salvemini. Salvemini was an academic historian and a leading antifascist since the 1920s, when he was member of the Italian parliament. He defined himself socialist in the aim of social justice and liberal in the method. In 1925 he emigrated to Paris, where in 1929 he founded with Carlo Rosselli and other prominent antifascists the political movement *Giustizia e Libertà*. Ten years later he emigrated to the United States to teach Italian history at the New School (where he met for few months Modigliani) before leaving for Harvard. Salvemini went back to Italy in September 1949.[21]

During his last year in the United States, Salvemini got in touch with Modigliani, apparently through the economist Paolo Sylos Labini, and met Modigliani in 1948 in Chicago. Sylos Labini was in the United States on a Fulbright research scholarship to study with Schumpeter, whereas Modigliani had moved to Chicago University and joined the Cowles Commission.[22] According to Modigliani's recollection (2001, pp. 165–167) Sylos Labini organized a meeting with Salvemini in 1946 to discuss Modigliani's paper on the socialist economy soon after Modigliani's refusal of Harvard's offer. However, Sylos Labini went to the United States in the 1948–1949 academic year, and he moved to Harvard only in the beginning of 1949. Therefore, Modigliani and Sylos Labini should have met Salvemini not before this date, that is, after the publication of Modigliani's 1947 Italian article.

As appears from their correspondence, Salvemini asked Modigliani to support his idea of founding an Italian journal he would have directed to challenge the actual policy situation and to support institutional and economic reforms in Italy (see Asso 2007, p. 16). In March 1949 Salvemini sent to Modigliani a memorandum about his plan in which he explained that the journal should be concerned with a critique of those Italian parties representing the left. It should have been especially devoted to a rigorous and continuous analysis of the still unsolved practical problems and to provide possible concrete solutions. Modigliani enthusiastically embraced the initiative. In the memorandum Salvemini sent him, he described the situation as follows:

> The former members of the Socialist party, of the Action party, of the Republican party and those Liberals of the Lefts who have flirted either with the Christian Democrats or with the Communists have actually

helped a situation which, if it persists, will inevitably wreck institutions of Italy, to replace them, not with fascist forms, but with clerical ones. And should the clerical dictatorship fail, there would remain nothing but the communists. . . . For all the problems of agrarian, educational, financial . . . there exist solutions which do not coincide with those applied or proposed by the clericals nor with those that might be adopted by the communists should they obtain the power.

(Salvemini 1949, MP)[23]

Prominent Italian intellectuals such as Ernesto Rossi, Gino Luzzatto, Piero Calamandrei and Riccardo Bauer were interested in collaborating with the journal (Salvemini 1949, MP).

Modigliani was actively involved in searching for financial support by attending Mazzini Society meetings in Chicago and trying to involve its member with the initiative. From his correspondence with Sylos Labini, it appears that he was quite familiar with the society (also see Camurri 2018).

Modigliani recalled that his conversations with Salvemini, and later the reading of his books, were crucial to distance himself, once for all, "whatever sympathy I had" from socialist theories and "led me to embrace democratic liberalism unreservedly" (2001, p. 167).

Modigliani came back to Italy for the first time in 1954 with a Fulbright fellowship and since then had strengthened his relationships with Italian economists, not only Sylos Labini but also Luigi Pasinetti, Giorgio Fuà and Siro Lomabardini, among others. He was actively engaged with the Italian economic and political situation since the late 1960s, starting from his collaboration with the Bank of Italy in building its first macroeconometric model (1966–1970) and the close relationships he established with its Research Department.[24]

Notes

1 Modigliani replied that if it supposedly belonged to him, he certainly would like to have the manuscript returned (November 24, 1947). The title is mentioned in English, so maybe there was an English translation that was circulating.

2 Margaret Reid was a researcher at Iowa University until 1945 where she was a colleague of Schultz. During 1943–1944 she served as an economic advisor to the Division of Statistical Standards and then she moved to Washington. After her resignation from the University of Illinois (in 1950), she joined the University of Chicago.

   Brady moved to the University of Illinois from the U.S. Department of Labor, where she was chief statistician from 1944 to 1948 of the Division of the Bureau of Labor Statistics.

3 Modigliani recalled as follows his acceptance of the offer: "A few months after my arrival at Chicago [having been awarded the prestigious Political Economy Fellowship of the University of Chicago, and to join the Cowles Commission] I was contacted by Howard Bowen, who had just been appointed dean. . . . Bowen asked me to come and work at his University on the project. . . . [T]he conditions offered were excellent, and the university was prestigious, full of brilliant young economists. I accepted. At the University of Illinois my career went much faster than it could have done at Harvard" (2001, p. 57).

4 There is extensive literature on the effects of the McCarthyism campaign on the development of social science and on economics, particularly about its postwar mathematization, to which I'll return in the next sections.

5 See "The Bowen War" in Franco Modigliani Papers.

6 Modigliani was a research consultant for the Cowles Commission from September 1948 to 1954. The director, Jacob Marschak, was his mentor at the New School for Social Research. Patinkin, who also had Marschak as a supervisor of his PhD dissertation, attended regularly the Cowles Commission seminars over his period at the University of Chicago (1947–1949); Hurwicz was a research associate for the Cowles Commission as well from 1942 to 1946. Patinkin left the university before the Bowen controversy; therefore, he was not among the distinguished economists who left Illinois in reaction to Bowen's resignation as reported instead in Solberg and Tomilson (1997, p. 80).

7 Griffith (1893–1966) was a psychologist who earned his PhD from the University of Illinois. He was promoted provost in 1944.

8 On the influence of patrons on postwar behavioral sciences, see Hunter Crowther-Heyck (2006).

9 Blodgett was an assistant professor of economics at the University of Illinois since 1937 whose contribution to the discipline mainly consisted of writing textbooks (see Solberg and Tomilson 1997).

10 The letter was signed by V. L. Bassie, D. S. Brady, E. C. Budd, R. Campbell, W. M. Capron, O. C. Herfindhal, L. Hurwicz, G. Kleiner, J. L. McConnell, F. Modigliani, D. W. Paden, M. G. Reid, D. B. Smith, P. N. Vukasin and E. T. Weiler. The letter was also sent to the editor of the *News Gazette* (in MP).

11 The letter also referred to the charge "specifically made that graduates from California, Chicago, Harvard and Columbia . . . are a selected group who believe in 'Keynesian' and dangerous ideas and could therefore be expected to indoctrinate students with these ideas. These schools are four of the most distinguished in the country – and therefore natural places to recruit able young faculty members. . . . [I]t simply happens to be a fact, which could have been ascertained, that the young faculty members in question have various liberal and conservative social and economic viewpoints. . . . One other example . . . is the charge that many 'bureaucrats' were brought into the faculty . . . [while] only two appointments were of persons working permanent" (September 16, 1950, MP).

12 Also see Colander and Landreth (1996) and Giraud (2014).

13 Hart also wrote to President Kisselgoff (New York, National Bureau of Economic Research), to Chair Williamson of the board of trustees (Letter from Albert G. Hart to Modigliani, October 19/1950, MP). Letters of support to Bowen were sent to Stoddard by a number of leading economists such as Jean Brofenbrenner and Avram Kisselgoff.

14 In the 1950s, thirty-six faculty members (more than half with tenure) were dismissed for their refusal to sign the loyalty oath as required by the university (see Gardner 1969; Slaughter 1980, p. 58; Schrecker 1986).

15 Scholar victims of McCarthyism, to avoid further complications in achieving new positions, often preferred not to publicize their cases. Nonetheless members of the AEA and ad hoc committees, such as Sharfman, were aware and directly involved in McCarthyism attacks. For example, in March 1955 Sharfman wrote to Gardner to support Klein's recommendation. However tenure was denied, and Klein went to Oxford for almost ten years (see Brazer 1981).

16 According to the committee, Davis's discharge "was not grounded on the fact that he was an economist. There is every reason to believe that the same result would have followed if he had been an astronomer. . . . The fact that he is an economist, and a member of the AEA, is purely coincidental" (AER 1955, p. 682, n 5). The AAUP published the findings of its investigating committee on Davis only in April 1957 and in December 1957 had not yet disposed the case.

17 In September 1951, Apel, chair of the Economics Department of Bridgeport University, wrote to James Washington Bell (secretary of the AEA) informing him of extramural suggestions to discontinue the use of some textbooks harming the proper education of students. In his reply Bell referred to the AEA's precedent refusal to take a stand on the use of Gemmill's and Blodgett's book (*Economic Principles and Problems*, 1936) as asked by the Army War Forces Institute's request. Bell explained that the AEA refused to do so "on the grounds that our charter does not permit any officers, representatives, or groups of the Association to speak for its memberships" (Bell to H. Apel: September 19, 1951, American Economic Association Papers). He also referred to the 1947 statement on textbooks and to the Committee on Academic Freedom. No references were made to the attacks suffered by Tarshis's and Samuelson's textbooks.

18 On Lazarsfeld and Thiels (1958) empirical study, see Weintraub's (2016) reading of their material (pp. 24–28).

19 Weintraub (2016) however acknowledged that the widespread professional apprehension and prudence may have discouraged scholars from radical interpretations of Keynes's ideas, thus contributing thanks to the lack of opposition to neoclassical synthesis, of its being dominant at the end of the 1950s.

20 On the shifts from literary to a formalist approach to economics, also see Solow (1997, p. 296).

21 According to Asso (2007, p. 14) it was Salvemini who suggested Modigliani publish his paper on the socialist economy in an Italian journal. But I found no evidence for it. Sylos Labini family was very close with Salvemini and he spent the last months at Harvard (until September 1949) living in the same house. Sylos Labini recalls Modigliani's encounter with Salvemini as follows: "For his part Franco revered Salvemini, and when he came to Harvard from Chicago on a brief visit I introduced them. From then on they kept up regular if not intensive correspondence. Franco was drawn to Salvemini not only on the intellectual plane, but also at the level of political and social commitment" (Sylos Labini 2005).

22 Modigliani and Sylos Labini maintained close correspondence and a lifelong relationship, sharing many intellectual interests. It was Sylos Labini who persuaded Modigliani to return for the first time to Italy in 1954.

On Sylos Labini's and Modigliani's biographical notes, see Modigliani (2001), Roncaglia (2006) and Sylos Labini (2005).

23 The memorandum is written both in Italian and in English, probably to circulate among non-Italians as well. For example, Salvemini suggested to Modigliani to get in touch with Paul Douglas because he knew Italy well and had similar opinions. He also asked about the availability of *Messagerie Italiane* (founded and directed by his father-in-law Calabi) for the eventual distribution of the journal.

24 About Modigliani's active involvement since the 1970s onward to the Italian economic and political debate, see in particular Asso's (2007) and Camurri's (2018) publications of Modigliani's journal articles.

References

American Economic Association Papers, David M. Rubenstein Rare Book and Manuscript Library, Duke University.

American Economic Association. 1950. "Report of the Secretary for the Year 1949", *The American Economic Review*, 40 (2): 588–602.

Asso, P. F. 2007. *Franco Modigliani. L'impegno civile di un'economista*, Siena: Fondazione Monte dei Paschi.

Backhouse, R. 2006. "Economics since the Second World War". http://www.lse.ac.uk/CPNSS/events/Abstracts/HIstoryofPoswarScience/Econsince1945.pdf.

Bahr, H. M. 1967. "Violation of Academic Freedom: Official Statistics and Personal Reports", *Social Problems*, 14 (3): 310–320.

Bell, D. 1982. *The Social Sciences since the Second World War*, New Brunswick, NJ: Transaction Books.

Bernstein, M. A. 2001. *A Perilous Progress: Economists and Public Purpose in Twenty–Century America*, Princeton: Princeton University Press.

Bowen, H. 1988. *Academic Recollection,* Washington, DC: American Association for Higher Educational.

Brazer, M. C. 1981. "The Economics Department of the University of Michigan: A Centennial Retrospective", in *Economics and the World Around It*, ed. by S. H. Hymans, Ann Arbor, MI: The University of Michigan Press, 133–275.

Byrd, L. J. 1972. "The Role of Keynesians in Wartime Policy and Postwar Planning, 1940–1946", *AER*, 62 (1–2), 125–133.

Camurri, R. 2018. *Franco Modigliani. Rischio Italia. L'economia italiana vista dall'America (1970–2003).* Rome: Donzelli Editore.

Coats, A. W. 1960. "The First Two Decades of the American Economic Association", *American Economic Review*, 50 (4): 556–574.

Coats, B. 1985. "The American Economic Association", *Journal of Economic Literature*, XXIII, December.

Colander, D. C., and H. Landreth, eds. 1996. *The Coming of Keynesianism to America: Conversations with the Founders of Keynesian Economics.* Brookfield, VT: Edward Elgar.

Don Patinkin Papers, David M. Rubenstein Rare Book and Manuscript Library, Duke University.

Galbraith, J. K. 1998. "How Keynes Came to America, in Keynesianism and the Keynesian Revolution in America", in *A Memorial Volume in Honour of Lorie Tarshis*, ed. by O. F. Hamouda and B. B. Price, Cheltenham: Edward Elgar.

Gardner, D. P. 1969. "By Oath and Association: The California Folly", *The Journal of Higher Education*, 40 (2): 122–134.

Giraud, Y. 2014. "Negotiating 'the Middle-of-the-Road' Position: Paul Samuelson, the MIT, and the Politics of Textbook Writing 1945–55", in *MIT and the Transformation of American Economics*, ed. by E. R. Weintraub, Durham, NC, Duke University Press, 134–152.

Goodwin, C. D. 1998. "The Patrons of Economics in a Time of Transformation," in *From Interwar Pluralism to Postwar Neoclassicism. American Economics: The Character of Transformation*, ed. Mary M. Morgan and M. Rutherford", *History of Political Economy* 30 (Supplement): 53–81.

Hunter, C.-H. 2006. *Patrons of the Revolution. Ideals and Institutions in Postwar Behavioral Science*, Chicago: University of Chicago Press.

Lazarsfeld, P. F., and W. Thielens, Jr. 1958. *The Academic Mind: Social Scientists in a Time of Crisis*, Glencoe IL: Free Press.

Machlup, F., H. Bowen, and R. B. Heflebower. 1958. "Report of the Committee on Academic Freedom and Civil Liberties", *American Economic Review*, 48 (2): 651–653.

Modigliani (Franco) Papers, David M. Rubenstein Rare Book and Manuscript Library, Duke University.

Modigliani, F. 1947. "L'Organizzazione e la Direzione della Produzione in un' Economia Socialista", *Giornali degli Economisti e Annali di Economia*, 6: 441–514.

———. 1980–1989. *The Collected Papers of Franco Modigliani* (voll. 5), ed. by Andrew Abel, Cambridge, MA: MIT Press.

———. 2001. *Adventure of an Economist*, New York: Texere.

Mongiovi, G. 2015. "Franco Modigliani and the Socialist State", *Preliminary Draft*: 1–22. http://qcpages.qc.cuny.edu/~lussher/mongiovi05.pdfpp. Last access November 29, 2019.

Morgan, M. S., and M. Rutherford, eds. 1998. "From Interwar Pluralism to Postwar Neoclassicism. American Economics: The Character of Transformation", *History of Political Economy*, 30 (Supplement): 53–81.

Roncaglia, A. 2006. "Paolo Sylos Labini, 1920–2005", *Moneta e Credito*, 59 (233): 4–21.

Schrecker, E. W. 1986. *No Ivory Tower. McCarthyism & The Universities*, New York: Oxford University Press.

Sharfman, I. L., and B. W. Lewis. 1955. "Report of the Exploratory Committee on the Status of the Profession", *The American Economic Review*, 45 (2): 677–684.

Slaughter, S. 1980. "The Danger Zone: Academic Freedom and Civil Liberties", *Annals of the American Academy of Political and Social Science*, March: 46–61.

Solberg W. U., and R. W. Tomilson. 1997. "Academic McCarthyism and Keynesian Economics: The Bowen Controversy at the University of Illinois", *History of Political Economy*, 29 (1): 55–81.

Solow, R., 1997. "How did Economics Get That Way and What Way Did It Get?", *Deadalus*, 126 (1), *American Academic Culture in Transformation: Fifty Years, Four Disciplines* (Winter), 39–58.

Sylos Labini, P. 2005. "Franco Modigliani and Oligopoly", *Banca Nazionale del Lavoro Quarterly Review*, 58 (233–234): 41–48.

Tarshis, L. 1947. *The Elements of Economics: An Introduction to the Theory of Price and Employment*, Boston: Houghton Mifflin Company.

Weintraub, E. R. 2002. *How Economics Became a Mathematical Science*. Durham, NC: Duke University Press.

———. 2014. "Mit's Openness to Jewish Economists" *History of Political Economy*, 46 (suppl. 1): 45–59.

———. 2016. "McCarthyism and the Mathematization of Economics", The Center for the History of Political Economy Working Paper Series 2016–18. Available at SSRN: https://ssrn.com/abstract=2736936 or http://dx.doi.org/10.2139/ssrn.2736936.

Wilcox, C., M. Newcomer, and P. M. O'Leary. 1954. "Report of the Ad Hoc Committee on Freedom of Teaching", *The American Economic Review*, 44 (2): 733–737.

5 Uncertainty and expectations
Modigliani at Carnegie Tech

Introduction

As mentioned in the previous chapter, Modigliani was asked to join the University of Illinois to supervise a large-scale research project, *Expectations and Business Fluctuations,* sponsored by the Merrill Foundation for the Advancement of Scientific Knowledge, and part of a research program carried out at the National Opinion Research Center.[1] The center was established in 1941 by Harry Hubert Field with the aim of collecting survey data on public opinion especially used by government departments and public agencies and of applying and testing new survey methods.[2] After Field's death in 1946, the center moved from the University of Denver to the University of Chicago under the new direction of Clyde W. Hart (see NORC Annual Report 1991).

Clyde Hart asked Howard Bowen to contribute to the research on expectations, and Bowen turned to Albert G. Hart of Columbia University and, then, to Modigliani.[3] The project explicitly stated that the research director would be an economist "selected because of his interest in the socio-psychological aspects of economic" (*Expectations and Business Fluctuations*, project outline, undated, p. 6, MP). Its aim was to investigate the role of expectations in economic activity by analyzing a systematic body of data collected through interviews and surveys. The data about expectations formation were to be analyzed for an understanding of economic behavior and to verify their ability to forecast economic activity (see Modigliani and Cohen 1961, p. 3).

As explained in the previous chapter, Modigliani remained at the University of Illinois only few years, from November 1948 to 1952 then moved to the Carnegie Institute of Technology. However, he continued to work on the project, which closely overlapped with the research agenda of the newly created Graduate School of Industrial Administration (GSIA).

The expectations and business fluctuations project

In the paper "Assets, Liquidity, and Investment", presented at the December 1948 American Economic Association meeting, Albert Hart discussed the problem of firms' investment decisions and economic fluctuations with reference in particular to the role of expectations. Hart emphasized the need of a theory of firms' behavior in which the problem of expectations formation was explicitly addressed, abandoning the "arbitrary assumption that plans and estimates are not 'observable', and setting out to observe them systematically" (Hart 1949, p. 171). Next, he suggested a research agenda based on interviews to businessmen about expectations formation and their role in the decision process, explaining that this was the kind of investigation "now being launched by the University of Illinois" (p. 171). Hart also remarked that similar research could succeed only through an interdisciplinary approach:

> Our central hypothesis that business maximizes something gives us a method of deriving plans from estimates. But the link in the chain which takes us from experience to estimates is not pure economics. We need to find out how estimates are made . . . [by] building up teams which include both economists and specialists in attitude studies.

(pp. 176–177)

Discussing Hart's paper Modigliani explained that the project concerned the study of factors governing investment decisions, particularly expectations and the firms' financial positions (such as current and prospective liquidity) through an empirical microeconomic investigation. An analysis of time series of individual firms combined with a survey of firms' management through personal interviews and/or self-administrated questionnaires to understand firms' decision-making under uncertainty. Modigliani emphasized both the novelty of their approach and that the University of Illinois project originated from dissatisfaction with the traditional postulate of rationality, which was of little or no application under uncertainty conditions:

> There obviously cannot be any rational theory of attitude toward risk taking; and there hardly is a rational theory of deriving expectations from current data. . . . On these types of problems the prospective investigation might help to supply the needed *factual background* and enable us to test the possible relevance of the psychological factors in the business cycles. Second, even in those cases where the theory of rational behaviour exists, or can be elaborated, we frequently suspect that actual behaviour follows a different pattern, and that this pattern is not an erratic one. *This pattern may be simply irrational . . . or it may be rational, or close to it, though in a sense not fitting our postulate of rationality. For instance, the cost of making the best decision, both psychological and material, is hardly taken into account in our theorizing, though it may in fact be a very important factor in explaining rule of thumb and non-optimal decisions.*

(Modigliani 1949a, p. 203; emphasis added)

At the 1949 Annual Conference of the American Association for Public Opinion Research, Modigliani remarked, once again, on the dominant role of expectations in firms' investment plans and, therefore, on an understanding economic fluctuations. He also acknowledged that proper analytical tools must be searched outside the boundaries of economics: "there is hardly any doubt that . . . we will have to rely heavily on methods of collection of information and analysis which are being developed and employed in opinion and attitude research" (1949b, p. 770). Modigliani concluded by emphasizing the practical as well as the purely theoretical purpose of the project, believing in the possibility of conjugating an empirical approach to uncertainty with rigorous behavioral models.[4]

The methodology underlying the research is that learned from Marschak, which will represent a constant of his contributions to economics where theory and empirical evidence are closely linked: "in this field . . . the inquiry should help to check our theoretical schemes against reality, indicate systematic biases and help perhaps to construct more useful schemes of analysis". In other words, the research on uncertainty would have contributed to further development of the theory of rational behavior, looking at the "institutional setup that effectively confronts the decision makers" (1949a, pp. 202–203).[5]

This approach would fit with the research agenda pursuits at Carnegie Tech with the building of the GSIA by Lee Bach, Herbert Simon and William Cooper. In fact, the GSIA had to be characterized by a strong interdisciplinary and empirical approach to the study of firms' behavior with the aim of establishing a modern management science.[6]

Modigliani's *Expectations and Business Fluctuations* project formally ended in 1952 with his moving to the Carnegie Institute of Technology. Nonetheless, Modigliani continued to work on the project, taking advantage of its similarity with the research carried out at the GSIA, which overlapped with the University of Illinois research under many respects. In fact, still on April 1959 Modigliani submitted to the GSIA research committee "a request of assistance for continuation of empirical and theoretical research on business expectations and plans and their influence on economic behaviour".[7]

Uncertainty and planning horizon

Modigliani faced the problem of decision-making under uncertainty under two different perspectives: from an applied one, by looking at how firms design their production and investment plans, and a highly theoretical perspective analyzing the effects of the hypothesis of perfect foresight for economic activity. In his recollection Modigliani referred to his reasoning about uncertainty and to the University of Illinois project as the starting point for his most innovative contributions to economics in the 1950s, such as his intuition and study with Richard Brumberg about the life cycle hypothesis and the Modigliani–Miller theory on corporate finance he developed with his Carnegie colleague Merton H. Miller.[8] To Modigliani both research lines, for which he was awarded the

Nobel Prize in 1985, were a direct and indirect outgrowth of the project about expectations and plans.

As for the first line of research, based on an empirically grounded theory, the way out of the problem of uncertainty was to have a model reducing as much as possible its effects on planning decisions. Modigliani suggested subdividing firms' production planning into a sequence of single decisions, each related to a single period of time. He explained that the idea was the result of evidence collected through interviews and case studies from 1950 to 1952, from which he figured out the convenience of a firm of producing at a constant pace, reducing fluctuations in production.[9] According to Modigliani, production planning should follow a step-by-step procedure depending only on sales in a single period of time rather than expectations for the entire seasonal production cycle. The subdivision of complex problems into a sequence of single decisions (and thus collapsing an infinite future into one step forward in time) was a procedure also followed in game theory to which Modigliani was partly exposed at the Cowles Commission in the late 1940s, (see Düppe and Weintraub 2013).[10]

The same idea was at the basis of Modigliani and Brumberg's intuition about the life cycle hypothesis, on which they began to work in the same period. Indeed, they translated firms' convenience of reducing fluctuations in production into a representation of individual saving behavior aimed at maintaining average consumption stable over the entire life span, to which I'll return in the next chapter. In their essays Modigliani and Brumberg explicitly refer to the analogy between "consumption, assets, income expectations and the life cycle of income . . . and . . . production, inventories, sales expectations, and the seasonal cycle of sales" (1954, p. 338fn).[11]

One of the first results of the University of Illinois research was a paper Modigliani wrote with his colleague Franz Hohn from the Department of Mathematics, devoted to analyze firms' optimal production plans. Their departure point was the divergence between firms' observed behavior and existing theories based on the assumption of rational behavior, a divergence arising from the recognition that acquiring information was a costly activity. Because of that firms must distinguish between relevant and irrelevant information. Modigliani and Hohn's main target was Hicks's "classical" theory of entrepreneurial planning according to which firms' decision depends on expectations regarding the parameters of every future constraint (Hicks 1939, Chapters. 10–11). Instead, Modigliani and Hohn suggested that in setting plans, the horizon of the anticipations may well be different for different phases of the operation and for different types of anticipations: "It may be sufficient to form anticipations and make plans with respect to only certain aspects of the future . . . the anticipations . . . may be but a small subset of all future parameters and moves which finally determine the outcome of the entire 'game' " (1952, p. 5).

Thus, the system of equations that maximize the outcome, involving all future parameters and moves, can be solved with respect to the first move only – the move that can be implemented currently – under the hypothesis that the system of equations may be partitioned in such a way that the solution for the first move may be obtained from a subset of the entire system (1952, p. 3). According to Modigliani and Hohn, the actions that need to be solved to decide the first move may be explicitly planned as "by-products" of the solution for the first one. Contrary to traditional theories, these plans were not to be considered as final decisions on later moves because such decisions would be reached at the right time on the basis of information available later on. That is to say, they could be replanned in response to new information.[12]

Their crucial point was that taking into account the cost of forming expectations and planning, rational behavior suggested not devoting scarce resources to ascertaining parameters that are irrelevant at a specific point of time. Thus, the approach was valid under conditions of both perfect and imperfect knowledge of the future.

In the mathematical appendix, Modigliani and Hohn showed that a firm's optimal production plan (in terms of lowest costs) could be obtained both with a backward-looking approach, starting at the horizon and moving towards the present, and through a forward-looking procedure. They also introduced the case of seasonal cycles to demonstrate that the optimum plan does not extend over the entire first seasonal cycle, except in the presence of a rapid overall trend (1952, p. 21). These issues were further developed in Modigliani's and Hohn's (1955) *Econometrica* article, in which they also pointed out that they referred to the "best possible" course of actions only with regard to the immediate future rather than to the entire horizon.

Modigliani and Hohn discussed their paper at the 1952 Cowles Commission seminar. Their approach to the concept of rational behavior under uncertainty called the attention of Herbert Simon, a nonresident consultant of the Cowles Commission, who was working on similar problems.

The Cowles Commission was a prominent place for exchanges among scholars.[13] Simon was in close relationships with Marschak and Koopmans, confronting them about their common research interests, whereas Bach invited Koopmans, Marschak and Hurwicz to visit the graduate school in 1951 to discuss their research on administration, economics and programming (Koopmans to Bach: May 9, 1951, Simon Collection).[14] Modigliani had already illustrated the University of Illinois project to the Economics Department at Carnegie in 1949, and in spring 1952 he organized the Cowles Commission seminar to discuss with Simon the results of their research groups.

Simon was working with Cooper and Holt on the application of the servomechanism theory for the determination of firms' optimal production planning, a research sponsored by the RAND Corporation.[15] Modigliani's focus on the shortness of the planning horizon, the flexibility of future plans, and the distinction between relevant and irrelevant costly information was not far from Simon's definition of rationality as strictly connected to the ability of entrepreneurs to obtain and use information relevant to the decision-making process under uncertainty. In fact, as he wrote to Marschak, he was developing a model of rational choice in the case of incomplete information whose departure point was close to that of Modigliani and Hohn: "rules for optimal decision making, if they are to be of any real use, must be 'optimal' in relation to the information possessed by the decision-maker and the size of the computational problems he can handle" (Simon to Marschak: April 11, 1953, Simon Collection).

Neoclassical and behavioral economics at the GSIA

Lee Bach asked Modigliani to join the GSIA in 1952 to contribute to the new graduate school by improving the mathematical studies in economics and participating extensively in the closely related areas of economics and social statistics. The GISA program was partially financed by the Office of Naval Research (ONR) and the Air Force: "One big part of the job is to develop cooperatively with Simon, Cooper, Charnes, Henderson and the others here, an optimal graduate program in this broad area, standing in close relationship to the Industrial Administration program already under way" (Bach to Modigliani: March 31, 1952, MP).[16]

In a subsequent letter, Bach asked Modigliani to take a leading role in their project, Intra-Firm Behavior research, that overlaps with Modigliani's study on expectations because the underlying approaches were close (April 28, 1952, MP).[17] Both research projects were aimed to find a more realistic and "useful" definition of rationality in terms of a "rational adaptation" to uncertainty, with uncertainty considered a problem of scarce and costly information. They shared the idea that the best decision should be defined in relation to the cost of determining it.

As from the early 1950s Simon was working with Cooper and Holt on the application of servomechanism theory (now labeled control theory) to inventory production planning because, to them, it had the advantage of considering uncertainty in terms of adjustments (that is learning) rather than forecasting.[18] The research began in 1951 under Cooper's leadership (within the Intra-Firm Behavior Project) and was later transferred (as from 1953) to the Inventory-Planning Project under Holt's leadership with contributions from graduate students, among them John Muth.

As mentioned, the exchanges between Modigliani and Simon started before Modigliani's arrival at Carnegie. Both believed in fertile combination of their models. As appears from their correspondence, Modigliani was convinced of the convergence of the maximization assumption with Simon's satisficing behavior:

> The one thing I would like to have discussed with you [Simon] is the relation of your servo-mechanism to other approaches to uncertainty, including mine. *You have suggested that the behavior you are describing is adapted rather than maximizing. I frankly am not sure as to the meaning of this distinction.* While I had played around a good deal with the notion of choosing actions on the basis of forecasts it seems to me that to some extent *your servo-mechanism also imply adaptation to forecast,* excepts that the forecast is made

by the mechanism itself. Furthermore, *I wonder to what extent the difference between our maximizing and your adaptation behavior reduces to the problem of certainty equivalents. I have a feeling that your adapted behavior is equivalent to a maximizing behavior when you don't have certain equivalents and your decision is, therefore not maximizing with respect to any specific possible state of environment, but with respect to several possible mutual exclusive possibilities.*

(Modigliani to Simon: January 16, 1952,
emphasis added, MP)

In the summer of 1952 Holt discussed a research report on "Rational Decision Making in Business, Single Person" at a joint conference with the Cowles Commission, the University of Illinois Bureau of Business Research and the USDAF-CIT Research Project on Intra-Firm Behavior (see "Intra-Firm Planning and Behavior, Final Report", July 1953, Simon Collection). A few months later Simon sent Marschak a discussion paper on production planning, "Notes on Two Approaches to the Production Rate Problem" (Cowles Commission Discussion Paper on Economics no 2057, November 1952), which represented the outcome of his discussions with Modigliani: "I am enclosing the manuscript of a paper that will indicate one direction of thinking about 'uncertainty' over the past several months. *As you will see it was stimulated by a restudy of the Modigliani-Hohn paper and by Franco's presence on the campus here*" (Simon to Marschak: November 11, 1952, emphasis added, Simon Collection).

In this paper, Simon worked on the possibility of combining his learning model with Modigliani and Hohn's forecasting method to determine the optimal rate of production. Simon referred to Modigliani's and Hohn's approach as the "certainty method" because it forecasts future sales for the relevant time period and behaves *as if* these were the actual future sales.[19] Simon explained that despite the different methods they applied (respectively, calculus of variations and the Laplace transform methods), the two approaches led to the same solution. In both cases, under the condition of a quadratic cost function (to be minimized), the optimal production path would be represented by the same linear differential equations with constant coefficients. According to Simon, the dynamically unstable solution of the forecasting method – without the assumption of perfect foresight – and the time lag in his servomechanism theory, suggested an attempt to integrate these two procedures, that is, to combine a good forecasting technique with a relatively simple feedback rule to take care of the forecasting errors:

> what we have called the forecasting method involves feedback, and what we called the feedback method involves at least implicit short-run forecasting. That is to say, w*hichever alternative we take, we are led in the direction of combining forecasting methods with dynamically stable feedback to correct forecasting errors.* What seems to me hopeful about this combined approach is that it still leaves room for genuine uncertainty and does not require, for its application, assumptions about the probability distribution of estimated future

sales. Finally, it proceeds on the very human assumption that, whatever procedure is adopted, errors of forecast, planning, and implementation of plans will be made, and that these errors must be corrected without introducing into the system sources of dynamic instability.

(1952, p. 8, emphasis added, Simon Collection)

This possible combination was further investigated in Simon and Holt's (1954) paper in which they refer to the servomechanism approach and to the perfect foresight approach as complementary methods.[20] Nonetheless, Simon was critical of the use of the maximization assumption under the hypothesis of uncertainty: "It is not clear in what sense a path so determined [through the first move approach] will be optimal ex-post, simply because such segment of it is optimal ex ante" (Simon 1952, p. 7, Simon Collection).

Following Simon's suggestion Modigliani, in a 1955 National Bureau of Economic Research paper with Owen H. Sauerlender (Modigliani's graduate student at the University of Illinois), explicitly discussed the servomechanism analogy and the combination of feedback and feed-forward procedures to determine the optimal production plan. Modigliani and Sauerlender introduced a "feed-in coefficient" in the production plan equation to measure whether expectations were useful for forecasting and whether production responds to these psychological variables. According to them, the extent to which new information about the actual level of sales and revised expectations influences production for the same period must depend on two main factors, namely, the accuracy of the initial forecasts and the extent to which the firms find it advantageous to adjust their production to conform with their revised expectations (1955, p. 316).

As acknowledged by Cooper and Simon in their comments on the paper, it represented the first successful attempt to introduce a control system into industrial analysis.[21] However, they criticized Modigliani and Sauerlender once again for not developing the basic implication of the model, that is, for not recognizing the distinction suggested by the servomechanism analogy between rational (maximizing) and adaptive (step-by-step) behavior:

> The traditional model of economic man has been that of a being who continually strives to attain optimal positions. . . . Servomechanism theory suggests . . . the model of an organism that continually adjusts its behavior so that it gets along "well enough" – it adjusts to changes in external conditions rapidly enough and successfully enough to avoid trouble, but it does not in any precise sense maximize or optimize.

(1955, p. 357)

According to Cooper and Simon, because human behavior exhibits elements of both, the question of optimality should be rephrased, asking *what is the optimal combination of rational and adaptive behavior rules* that should be designed into the model. In other words, "the advantages to be gained from eliminating or reducing errors can thus be matched against the cost of securing this greater precision" (1955, p. 358).

Simon developed further the notion of rational adaptation – which must rely as much upon correction of past errors as upon accurate anticipation of the future – in the paper he presented at the 1955 Symposium on *Expectations, Uncertainty and Business Behavior* organized at Carnegie, where he also explained that plans should not depend sensitively on forecasts that peer into the future beyond a modest planning horizon (1958, p. 53).

A similar approach, based on the distinction between relevant and irrelevant information and the costs of acquiring them, was once again pursued by Modigliani and A. J. Cohen in the paper they also discussed at the symposium: "The Significance and Uses of Ex Ante Data" (1955 (1958)) and in Modigliani and Cohen (1961), a monograph summarizing the main achievements of the University of Illinois research.[22] Their departure point was a definition of decision-making under uncertainty as a problem of choosing the best first move that is best in the "limited" sense of first component *of an optimal complete course of action* (1961, p. 153). In particular, they substitute the use of a behavioral function, which implies perfect information concerning anticipations and environmental behavior, with a "realization function", which simply measures the extent to which decisions fail to be realized as a result of anticipation errors.[23] They went back to the interdisciplinary philosophy of the project: "the problem of how anticipations are formed and revised which falls on the borderline of traditional economics, and it may well be that advances in this area will require closer cooperation between economists, psychologists, and other social scientists" (1961, p. 152).[24]

Towards more certain horizon

At the beginning of the 1960s, the main achievements of the Office of Naval Research (ONR) study on inventory planning by Holt, Modigliani, Muth and Simon (the HMMS model) were published. The implementation of the quadratic cost function, which generated linear decision rules and limited the amount of information required to solve decision-making problems, represented the formalization of their early definition of rationality in terms of the agent's ability to economize on scarce and costly information. They demonstrated that under this condition, the certainty equivalence property led to the same decision as would be the case with complete information about the distribution function (1960, p. 125). According to Simon, the model represented an example of "satisficing behavior" because it substituted complete optimization for a more limited search for the best policy or best decision defined on the basis of the information currently available.[25]

It had already been demonstrated in Holt et al. (1955, 1956) and Simon (1956b) that dynamic programming under uncertainty could be reduced for the case of certainty simply by replacing in the computation for the optimal first-period action the unconditional expected values of the relevant variables, assuming that they are the (unknown) certain values (see Simon 1956b, p. 74). The decision-making process described by Simon (1956b) followed a procedure close to Modigliani's "first move" approach: "the initial task of the decision-maker is to determine his course of action for the first time period. At the end of that period, and on the basis of the new information then available to him, he chooses a course of action for the second period, and so on" (p. 75). In his reconstruction of the genesis of the certainty equivalent argument, Simon recalled the similarity of his own and Modigliani's models and their shared dissatisfaction with the classical definition of rationality:

> It is only in the past five years . . . that *attention has been given to theories of rational decision-making under uncertainty that place in the forefront of concern the amount of information required by the decision-maker.* One such line of inquiry begins with my paper on the application of servomechanisms to production control, where the servomechanism analogy was suggested by the fact that these instruments make decisions about an uncertain future without forecasting. *A continuation of this work with Charles Holt led to the idea that even if the decision-maker has correct forecasts, a "natural" horizon limits the relevance of future events to present decisions. The same idea was reached independently, and in somewhat different context, by Modigliani and Hohn. . . . It is not an accident that most of the work just mentioned was motivated by contact with actual decision-making situations in firms. . . .* It is only when one tries to understand the actual mechanism of decision-making – as distinguished from the classical concern with what a man would do if he shared God's omniscience – that one appreciates that the central problem in this kind of rational behavior is to obtain information and to use that information in computations; and that the entire mechanism of decision is modeled by information-processing considerations.

(Simon, 1956a, pp. 4–5, emphasis added)

It is worth noting that not only did the certainty equivalent argument emerge from a combination of two opposite approaches to uncertainty, that is, backward- and forward-looking procedures, but that the father of the rational expectations theory (RET) also defined Simon's (1956b) article as the "foundation of [his] paper on rational expectations" and the quadratic cost function a fundamental step for the subsequent development of rational expectations (Muth 2004, in Augier and March ed., p. 379).[26]

Thus, the model carried out by Holt, Modigliani, Muth and Simon was a quite uncommon example of collaboration among economists who embraced different ideas about the limits of rational decision-making. As recalled by Jacques Drèze: "the ONR project was a beautiful example of joint work. They were all excited about the project and eager to contribute. They met, mostly informally, all the time and were competing with each other for contributing new ideas or results". Drèze also underlined that "Modigliani held Simon in very high esteem, and conversely. I think that *both regarded as positive the fact that alternative approaches were developed in parallel* (Drèze to the author: September 3, 2009, emphasis added).[27]

How this rich combination of different versions of rationality had been possible is especially explained, in retrospect, by one of the authors of the model. According to Holt, in fact, the HMMS model serves as an example that behavioral economics and rational expectations were not mutually exclusive:

> Muth's analysis of an exponentially weighted moving average showed that it could be as a feedback system in which the expected value of forecast is adjusted in response to error, the adjustment being a certain fraction of the error. That is a pretty crude forecasting model, and one quite consistent with Simon bounded rationality. . . . However, any rational consideration of the forecast problem immediately suggests that the forecasted variable has multiple components – not just level but often trend and seasonal as well. Why not apply the error feedback adjustment to each of the components, and then combine them into an integrated forecast? . . . There you have the HMMS forecast system – partially crude and bounded-rational and partially rational-expectational based on an analysis of components.

(Holt 2004, pp. 359–360)

In the HMMS model, "the relevant time series were infinite backward and forward in time. The known past time series were readily accessible and so were consistent with bounded rationality, and the future time series to be forecast called for rational expectations. Because the first order conditions were linear, past sales and forecasts of future sales entered simply as weighted average" (2004, pp. 359–360).[28] On the contrary, Simon read Muth's expectations model as a challenge to his theory of bounded rationality (see Simon 1991, p. 250). According to Simon (1979), "Muth imaginatively saw in this special case [the HMMS model] a paradigm for rational behavior under uncertainty. What to some of us in the Holt, Modigliani, Muth, Simon research team was an approximating, satisficing simplification, serves for him as a major line of defence for perfect rationality" (p. 486).[29]

Thus, further developments emphasized different goals and implications of the learning and the foresight approaches to uncertainty. As they became successively more formalized and the proponents of behavioral economics and rational expectations theory became ever more confident that their answers to the problem were the keys to a new paradigm for economics, the divergent positions became relevant and more prominent than their commonalities.

Modigliani and Simon were both interested in the analysis of how uncertainty influences economic behavior. They believed in the possible combination of their models to obtain a concrete decision rule. However, Simon was interested in the analysis of the dynamic process by which decisions are made and revised in uncertainty dynamic contexts, taking account of ignorance. His focus was on the agents' limited knowledge as opposed to the neoclassical postulates, whereas economists such as Modigliani concentrated on *the optimal outcome* of revised expectations. He focused on the ability to foresee both through anticipations data and the shortness of the planning horizon and saw in the study of the formation (and revision) of expectations a way for removing, or at least reducing, the effects of uncertainty. Despite his early emphasis on the inadequacy of the traditional rational assumption, his assertion of the relevance of psychological variables, and indeed the attention he dedicated to scarce and costly information, he never abandoned the neoclassical postulate as it was necessary to obtain a uniquely determined (optimal) solution. In his interview with Arjo Klamer, Modigliani made it clear that he "took [Simon's] arguments seriously", but the question was "whether Simon's hypothesis of satisficing behavior was more helpful than the neoclassical hypothesis of optimizing behavior". Starting from a definition of the basic postulates of economic analysis as tools rather than an exact description of an agent's behavior, Modigliani concluded that the optimization assumption presents a great advantage of a unique answer (1983, p. 119).

Modigliani's approach to rationality, moving in between the neoclassical and Simon's meanings, recalls under some respect the one of his mentor Marschak. As Cherrier (2010) noticed, Marschak's definition of economics as "the science of optimizing" did not coincide with the neoclassical definition, but it is conceived as a normative concept, as economics is, and still relevant to empirical explanations (pp. 5–6). A rational organization of the economic activity is a necessary premise to plan state interventions. In other words, a rational approach to economics is something to be implemented through planning.

At the end of the 1950s, not only were both the University of Illinois and ONR projects coming to an end, but also the stimulating and highly profitable interactions among different economic perspectives ("the golden age" of the GSIA) were coming to an end. Simon explained the tensions between economists and behavioral scientists at the GSIA as originating from both his increasing dissatisfaction with mainstream economics – the economists "viewed [him] as the main obstacle to building 'real' economics in the school" – and the ambivalent character of the GSIA:

> Keeping the balance of the scientific and professional, of the economic and the behavioral, was an arduous job. . . . Organizing a professional school . . . is very much like mixing oil with water: . . . [l]eft to themselves, the oil and water will separate again. So also will the disciplines and the professions.

(Simon 1967, quoted by Simon 1991, pp. 144, 147)

Modigliani, like other leading economists at the school,[30] decided to leave because of a divergent position on the role played by economics within the GSIA:

> *The unhappy prospect of your leaving has been made more unhappy for me personally by the knowledge that you have felt that you and I have different pictures of the future of the GSIA and the economics in it.* I believed and I believe that these

differences didn't really exist. . . . . We will try very hard to maintain the excellence in economics that you represented here, so that you will continue to be proud of GSIA and of your part in building it.

(Simon to Modigliani: January 7, 1960, emphasis added, MP).

In 1960 Modigliani went to Northwestern University and in 1962 he moved to MIT.[31]

Modigliani's contribution to the study of expectations during his period at Carnegie Tech is also closely connected with his paper with Emil Grunberg on the fulfilment of public predictions, which anticipated Muth's rational expectations hypothesis.[32] The paper represented Modigliani's most famous attempt to reconcile the maximization assumption with decision-making under uncertainty through a definition of rationality in terms of individual behavior consistent with correct public predictions.

Grunberg and Modigliani's study on perfect foresight

In 1954 Modigliani published with his Carnegie colleague Emil Grunberg a paper on the effects of correct public predictions, also an outgrowth of the University of Illinois project, which anticipated Muth's rational expectations hypothesis.[33] Although Modigliani referred to this paper as a joke, "written with tongue in cheek, to really make fun of my colleagues" (Klamer 1983, p. 125), by looking at Modigliani's study of expectations over the 1950s, it does not appear an isolated reasoning. Instead, the article can be read as a further attempt to face the uncertainty problem. While in his work on firms' rational behavior, the effect of uncertainty on decision-making was neutralized, as far as possible, by focusing on relevant information and shortening the planning horizon; in the paper with Grunberg, rational behavior is taken to mean that people behave according to correct public predictions. As Modigliani recalled:

> We both developed an interest in the effect of forecasts on changing behavior. I showed him some examples of what I had worked out, and we decided to pursue them more formally. Our work made a great step forward when Herbert Simon suggested that our results could be generalized by means of Brouwer's Fixed Point Theorem.

(quoted from Young et al. 2004, pp. 36–37, September 16, 1991)[34]

In 1953 Modigliani wrote to Carl Christ asking for a copy of the paper he presented at the Chicago meeting of the American Economic Association dealing with the effect of forecasts on their fulfilment because he was interested in writing a brief note on the subject with Brumberg (Modigliani to Christ: February 18, 1953, MP).[35] This comment was, however, never written. Instead, a critique to of Christ's argument represented the departure point of Grunberg and Modigliani's (1954) article. From their correspondence it emerges that they were also working from 1956 to 1959 on a second paper, which would represent a further development of the earlier one. Their aim was to provide empirical groundwork for their previous article, which had been conceived as an essay on methodology and, especially, to address the issue of the effects of public predictions on the stability of equilibrium, a problem Robert Dorfman brought up in his comment to the 1954 article. This second paper, titled "Further Remarks on the Prediction of Social Events", was submitted after lengthy discussions to the *Southern Economic Journal*.[36] However, due to the cold reaction of the referees (Grunberg and Modigliani received in April 1959) and, most important, to the circulation of Muth's paper on rational expectations, Modigliani decided to withdraw their article. Grunberg and Modigliani published only a short comments responding to criticisms on their previous article in the 1963 issue of the American Economic Review.[37]

The 1954 article, "The Predictability of Social Events", showed that under two weak conditions – economic variables have upper and inferior bounds, and the reaction function is continuous over the relevant range – correct public prediction is possible even if the agent does react to it, contrary to Christ's argument. Their proof was based on a generalization of the Brouwer Fixed-Point Theorem and the use of a reaction function such as $x_{t+1} = R(x^*_t)$, which relates the actually observed value of a variable (x_{t+1}) to the previously predicted value x^*_t. The hypothesized agent's reaction function – they remarked to be merely theoretical – was derived from the assumption that it is possible to ascertain how the agent's expectations are formed, how they change as a result of given information and how the agent acts in response to given expectations.

According to Grunberg, "as long as we believe that there are any observable regularities in the agents' behavior (reaction to expectations) . . . this particular reaction function must always *conceptually* be knowable. . . . If people do act in a certain way, then we must be able to find out how they behave".[38] He also remarked that to assume that people react randomly implied "the impossibility of any social science because of the complete absence of any regularity in human behavior" (Grunberg to Modigliani: January 31, 1956, MP). It was on this ground that Grunberg and Modigliani rejected Knight's (1947) argument that private prediction reacted in a completely random fashion so that no regularity could be identified, as well as Morgenstern's (1935) denial that a predictive model incorporating the reaction function would yield at least one meaningful solution.[39]

Grunberg and Modigliani's aim was to demonstrate both that correct public prediction was always possible in principle, and that its effect was precisely that of removing unwarranted expectations by providing agents with the relevant information that was previously unknown to them. Therefore, correct public predictions coincided with the equilibrium position of the system in terms of an efficient resources allocation (1954, p. 477). They also suggested that "[b]y substituting knowledge for exaggerated fears, correct public prediction would [in the case of economic depression], make the community better off than it would have been otherwise" (1954, p. 477), having, in other words,

a stabilizing effect – an implication they did not develop, and that was criticized by Dorfman in a letter to Modigliani. Dorfman claimed that Grunberg
and Modigliani did not investigate properly the implication of their model on
stabilization, which was not merely an "academic question", on the contrary:
"people in Washington sweat over it every time they are about to release a forecast". To him, Grunberg and Modigliani minimized the destabilizing effects of
correct public predictions of broad economic aggregates:

> Suppose you are to predict change in national income and that this changes
> depends on public expectation of the change [E]. . . . The self-confirming
> prediction is the level at which the E-line and the delta – Y-curve cross
> and, in the situation drawn, is a considerably greater decline than K, which
> would be expected without a prediction or with a purposely inaccurate
> one. . . . Since the public generally underestimates the strength of the
> forces making for change in either direction, self-confirming predictions
> will generally be destabilizing ones. This yields a nice dilemma, a one
> which has baffled the CEA for years.

(Dorfman to Modigliani: January 2, 1957, MP)

In 1956 Grunberg, whose tenure at Carnegie Tech was denied, moved to
Akron University and began an intense correspondence with Modigliani over
the writing of the second article. He was especially stimulated by the manuscript Martin Bronfenbrenner sent to him, which according to Grunberg, had
completely misunderstood the significance of their work.[40] Bronfenbrenner's
criticisms were on empirical grounds, particularly with regard to the possibility
of correct prediction, whereas the main point of their paper rested on its conceptual possibility (Grunberg to Modigliani: January 31, 1956, MP).

From the correspondence between Grunberg and Modigliani, it emerges that
their second paper was to deal in depth with the relation between correct public predictions and the stability of the equilibrium in the context of the cobweb
analysis and would further develop the section devoted to "Welfare Aspects
of Public Predictions" (criticized by Dorfman). Their goal was to move from
static to dynamic expectations, introducing "learning, and the effect of changing belief in the public prediction on the expectation-function of the agent"
(Grunberg to Modigliani: January 31, 1956, MP). Grunberg and Modigliani
were aware of the limits of their previous model, as Grunberg acknowledged in
his response to Bronfenbrenner:

> There is, however, a real conceptual difficulty which we pointed out
> without doing much about it . . . namely the expectation-function. The
> reaction-function, like a demand – or supply-function simply states how
> the agent will act *given certain expectations*. The expectations-function states
> what the agent will expect given certain observations available to them.
> Clearly, this is an animal quite different from all other functions with which
> we deal in economics. Let me return for a minute to the idea of equilibrium.

It is quite possible that the correctly predicted set of values actually may constitute either an unstable equilibrium or a disequilibrium. . . . Since these situations do occur in the real world, why should they not be correctly and publicly predicted? Of course, if an unstable equilibrium (or a disequilibrium) is predicted for any specified amount in time, there will be further change. Even if we had predicted a stable equilibrium, we would still expect the situation to change after a while, due to random shocks or what have you. Nothing in the problem of prediction puts any restriction on the actual course of events, which is not stable.

(Grunberg to Modigliani: January 31, 1956, MP)

Even if they were well aware of the problem, they decided to confine the analysis to static prediction, that is, "for *one point in time*":

This was a result of a deliberate decision after lengthy discussion: We just wanted to clear up the basic *conceptual* point, leaving for later elaboration all the fascinating implications and developments. Thus, for example we have fully written (chiefly by Franco) a beautiful section on "*conditional predictions*" (cf. p. 467, footnote 11) which we finally did not use. So, we did not attack the fascinating problem of predicting publicly and correctly *successive situations*, where one grows out of the preceding one. . . . Whatever a situation is one of stable or unstable equilibrium maybe of greatest interest to the policymaker. . . . We have deliberately neglected the [practical application and the empirical content of our argument] because we felt that we should *first* establish our point conceptually: namely that the difficulty of correct prediction is that of private prediction alone. And that therefore our efforts should be concentrated on improving our faculties of private prediction (which would include finding reaction-function).

(Grunberg to Modigliani: January 31, 1956, pp. 5–6, MP)

Starting from Brofenbrenner's and, later, Dorfman's unpublished criticisms Grunberg insisted with Modigliani to go ahead with their work, dealing with both continuous expectations and the distortive effects of public predictions (on equilibrium) to investigate whether they may lead to a less desirable welfare position – a line of reasoning close the one Muth was also pursuing. They would have focused on a precise definition of perfect foresight, excluding the possibility of distorting effects and shifting attention from discrete to continuous expectations, specifying the sequence of values of the relevant variables that define the agent's decision horizon.[41] Their analysis was carried out within the cobweb model, so their results had a more limited value than that of Muth.

Grunberg and Modigliani's departure point seemed to be the passage omitted in the 1954 article on "conditional prediction", acknowledging that "a correct public prediction can not be satisfied with merely giving the values of the relevant variables for a specified point in time. It is rather necessary *to give a sequence (continuous?) of such values for all the relevant variables referring* to a whole interval. This interval . . . may coincide with the agent's decision horizon" (Grunberg to Modigliani: May 14, 1957; see also Grunberg to Modigliani: July 2, 1958, MP).

The writing of the second paper was further stimulated by Harvey J. Levin's critique to some implications of Grunberg and Modigliani's model that appeared in the *Southern Economic Journal* in the July 1958 issue. Levin addressed the questions of whether public prediction can adequately anticipate the effects of its prediction on public expectations "so as to make an accurate one" and, again, whether public prediction may lead the market to reach a (stable) equilibrium position by providing agents with relevant information.

Levin remarked that a determinate solution requires the knowledge of the degree of public confidence on the authority forecast. In other words, this latter has to ascertain whether expectations will change, and how, after public prediction, which to him, meant to consider social and cultural factors like the level of economic education and sophistication in the community (an argument later applied to the rational expectations hypothesis). Indeed, Levin concluded that the theory of public prediction might be relevant to real-world forecasting and stabilization policy, as already acknowledged by Grunberg and Modigliani (1954).

In their second article Grunberg and Modigliani analyzed the effect of public prediction on market stability under the conditions of locally linear demand and supply functions and an expectation function that took into account the degree of belief in the public prediction to establish how stability is affected by this confidence degree.[42]

Grunberg and Modigliani submitted the paper to the *Southern Economic Journal*, but it was received with skepticism. According to one referee, some of its implications appeared "strange and paradoxical" because the assumed government's omniscience would deprive the market exchange process of any significance (Grunberg to Modigliani: April 21, 1959, MP) – an implication Levin (1958) had already emphasized arguing that "if the impact on expectations can be estimated", the forecaster would necessarily control the market outcome. In other words, "public forecasts would enable suppliers to act on warranted expectations even though they were competitively organized" (1958, p. 342).

As the referee also pointed out,

> [t]he crucial assumption [of the model] is . . . that public policy predictions are always fulfilled. Consider now the first model. The public predicted price must equal the actual price in period t. This price is the one found on the demand curve at the quantity produced in (t-1) and supplied in (t). . . . After the publicly predicted price has been set, supply is determined. As under pure monopoly, this determines a price-quantity point lying on the demand curve. The nature of this process and its dependence on government all omniscience-knowledge of demand, modified supply, and the price found at the intersection-should be mentioned. . . . *Here an equilibrating process is carried out by the government, imposed by the necessity of validating*

its prediction in advance. . . . Some discussions of the assumptions and their implications is essential. Otherwise this article would seem strange and paradoxical.

(G. T. Sohwening, managing editor, April 15, 1959, MP;
Grunberg to Modigliani: April 21 1959, emphasis added)[43]

Although Modigliani's handwritten comments on the passage about the government's imposition of the equilibrating process were "so what?", Modigliani appeared increasingly discouraged with their work, especially because the results he had by extending the analysis to inventory cycles and his difficulties in defining the expectations horizon:

> The real trouble is that these results seemed to me to raise more questions than they settled. In particular, is it meaningful to extend the prediction just one period ahead when presumably behaviour is based on the longer horizon? On the other hand, the problem of making correct predictions for more than one period ahead seems to be quite messy though I have hardly tried.

(Modigliani to Grunberg: May 11, 1959, MP)

Most important, Modigliani felt uncomfortable because the circulating of Muth's paper on rational expectations, whose analysis was close to theirs but extended beyond the cobweb theorem. He sent a copy of Muth's paper to Grunberg in September, anticipating some of his concerns and doubts: "I haven't had the time *to read this last version, although I am generally familiar with its content from conversations with Jack and a seminar he gave.* If, after having read it, you feel that it affects in some way our paper, it might be good for you to drop me a line about it before you come" (Modigliani to Grunberg: September 14, 1959, emphasis added, MP). Soon after, he suggested to revise their submitted paper simply in the form of a reply to Levin's article, showing how the problem must be handled for the "limiting case" of the cobweb, finding a justification for not having enlarge the perspective, "[t]hus to turn the disadvantage into advantage", making Levin "the excuse for the paper" (Modigliani to Grunberg: September 29, 1959, MP). In this letter Modigliani explained his decision:

> On Monday I also carried out the experiment of asking a few people to sit in for a couple of hours to listen to what we had to say, and advise us whether it was worth the effort. The people were Joseph [presumably Myron], [Merton] Miller and [Kalman] Cohen and they tried hard to be helpful. The outcome was mixed. . . . [T]here was argument that the analysis was ingenious, even quite cute and the results not obvious. However there was on the whole also considerable misgivings as to whether the paper would have any useful content. Though there were different shades of opinion expressed *on the whole people did echo our doubt as to whether an*

analysis which leads to conclusions only for cobwebs and then under some more restrictive conditions is really a worthwhile exercise. These views were of course unavoidably colored by Muth's recent paper which in a sense is "sweeping the cob-webs out of economics". Even our ability to prove that under fairly mild conditions perfect (and within limits also incorrect) public prediction leads to an outcome closer to the warranted expectation, turns out on further reflection to be of uncertain significance unless we can somehow specify what is good or bad about a "warranted expectation"; this unfortunately we can do at least at the moment only for cobweb where we can interpret the expectation as the long run equilibrium position. It may well be that further thought on the matter might yield more interesting proposition, but this means investing additional effort into an uncertain enterprise.

(Modigliani to Grunberg: September 29, 1959,
emphasis added, MP)

Apparently, the revised version of the paper was not submitted. Grunberg insisted in subsequent letters on the relevance and validity of their approach and results. And, after the publication of Devletoglou's paper "Correct Public Prediction and the Stability of Equilibrium" (1961),[44] he regretted Modigliani's decision to abandon their project. According to him, Devletoglou's analysis of inventory cycles was similar to that sketched by Modigliani and went beyond their paper only "in arguing successfully both, that cobweb and inventory cycles, really represent a sufficiently important portion of economic phenom-ena" (Grunberg to Modigliani: May 15, 1961, MP).

Grunberg and Modigliani published a short note to respond to some com-ments on their first article. In the1963 *American Economic Review*'s note, Modi-gliani and Grunberg explicitly refer to the inconsistency of their findings on the relation between correct public prediction and the stability of the economic system because perfect foresight may cause or increase oscillatory disturbances. However they are now able to offer a possible explanation of such results:

We suspect that the reported mathematical results may arise from the fact that macroeconomic models from which they derived fail to take prop-erly into account relevant aspect of economic behavior of the individual units. . . . In short we suggest that before we can reach a sensible conclusion on this complex issue we need to learn to construct a macroeconomic model whose behavior equations are more directly tied to optimizing behavior and embodied less preposterous assumption about the nature of anticipations.

(1963 p. 736)[45]

Modigliani and Grunberg referred to Muth (1961), Holt and Modigliani (1961)[46] and Modigliani and Ando (1963) on the life cycle hypothesis as works that were going in the right direction to solve this inconsistency.

Finally, Modigliani was among the first to test empirically Muth's ratio-nal expectations hypothesis, in particular its consistency with regressive expectations. In the Bosson and Modigliani papers (1960, 1963, 1966), they demonstrated that regressive individual anticipations are consistent with rational forecasts and that business expectations reported in public surveys (such as the Employment Forecast and the Dun and Bradstreet surveys) behave in accordance with the rational expectations hypothesis.

However, they also noted that this regressivity should disappear when the forecasts are aggregated. Bosson and Modigliani explained the "non-rational" persistence of regressivity on aggregates both by a "pattern-seeking behavior" of individual firms that relied on "adaptive rationality" as opposed to the attempt to "correct" forecasts" to make them unbiased (1963, p. 69) and, especially, by the wide diversity of individual firms' experiences. They concluded that it is "easier to predict change in an aggregate variable from an equation expressed in terms of aggregate variables than from the aggregated composite prediction of a set of micro-equations" (1963, p. 70).[47] Thus, the appropriate application of the data on business people's anticipations should be only indirect through incorporation into business planning and decision-making models that could be used to derive macro-predictions.

Modigliani's rejection of rational expectation as the microfoundation of macroeconomic expectations models went in the opposite direction of the 1970s' application of Muth's hypothesis and explained his skepticism long before Lucas's (policy) neutrality assumption (he had already acknowledged in the 1954 paper with Grunberg).

Modigliani returned in the late 1960s and the early 1970s on expectations formation when working on building the Federal Reserve–MIT–University of Pennsylvania macroeconometric model (1966–1975). In a couple of papers with Richard Sutch (1966–1967) and especially in a paper with Robert J. Shiller (1973) on long-term interest rates, they analyzed the role of adaptive expectations in the determination of real interest rates focusing on the problem of measuring expectations. In the paper with Shiller they demonstrated that adaptive and rational expectations led to similar results. According to Modigliani and Shiller, evidence showed that the distributed lags of their term structure equation were consistent with rational expectations (1973, p. 34). The relation between the long rates and the past short rates and prices estimated in the process of fitting the term structure equation was in fact similar to the relation that would hold if the long rates were an average of expected future rates. Moreover, because their term structure equation fitted the current long term closely, it was also demonstrated that past rates and prices were the two major variables on which markets based their forecasts of the future course of short-term interest rates – a conclusion that recalled the idea developed with GSIA group at Carnegie.

Notes

1 The chapter is largely based on Rancan (2013).
    See NORC Social Research 1941–1964, and F. Modigliani and J. J. Feldman, *Expectations and Business Fluctuations: First Progress Report to the Advisory Committee*, 1949, 25–26, www.norc.org/PDFs/publications/NORCSocRes_1941_1964.pdf, last access 12 November 2019.

2 See https://academic.oup.com/poq/article/10/3/399/1835002; last accessed November 2019.

3 Albert Hart recalled that Bowen consulted him as a possible director of a center for research on the expectational field and that he recommended Modigliani (whom he had placed earlier as a postdoctoral fellow with Schultz at the University of Chicago) (see Young et al. 2004). It was Hart who later recommended Modigliani to Lee Bach (Young et al. 2004).

4 The session was chaired by Colonel Paul D. Guernsey (US Army); the other participants were an anthropologist and a political scientist. Harrod Domar wrote to Modigliani to compliment him on his "first Progress Report on March 1949 regarding your study of 'Expectations and Business Fluctuations'. I think the work you are undertaking is extremely worth-while, to say the least" (May 31, 1949, MP). Modigliani complained to Domar the difficulties he met: "I must confess that the problem is so terribly vast and difficult to come to grasp with, that I frequently feel somewhat discouraged" (June 6, 1949, MP).

5 The use of questionnaires to investigate investment behavior is criticized by Friedman (1949): "I doubt any reasonably simple answers to many of Hart's questions exist; or that if the answer exist, businessmen know them; or that if they do know the answers, they will give them in response to questioning" (p. 199).

6 The interdisciplinary and analytical approach to social sciences was supported over the 1950s by a patronage system formed by public (especially military) and private institutions (foremost the Ford Foundation). Thanks to Simon's involvement in numerous projects and committees, the GSIA represented one of the main beneficiaries, becoming the most important protagonist in the "behavioral revolution".

7 I wish to thank Professor Warren Young for sending me a copy of the document.

8 Merton Miller also won the Nobel Prize in 1990 with Harry R. Markowitz and William F. Sharpe in 1990; see www.nobelprize.org/prizes/economic-sciences/1990/miller/biographical/.

9 On this interviews see Robert Eisner's (1957) NBER paper on "Interviews and Other Survey Techniques and the Theory of Investment", pp. 513–601.

10 However, in Modigliani there was no reference to the notion of strategy interpreted as a complete plan of actions or as a rule for choosing future actions in response to later information. His focus was on the consequences for the entire "game" of a step-by-step decision rule in which adjustment of later actions to earlier ones represented his crucial point. The same intellectual influence can be found in Simon as well. Regarding Simon's attitude towards game theory, see among others; see also Sent (2001, 2004).

11 See also Modigliani's autobiography at http://nobelprize.org/nobel_prizes/economics/laureates/1985/modigliani-autobio.html) and Hartley (2004, p. 433).

12 Modigliani pointed out that the relevance of the "first move" had already been recognized by A. G. Hart (1942, 1951), H. Markowitz (1952), G. Tintner (1941) and Marschak (1949), among others. According to him, however, the plan did not represent a decision as to the actual level of future activity, and it had no implications at all with the respect to future operations: "It seems possible to find many economic instances . . . in which later actions can be adjusted with no loss of efficiency to earlier ones, whatever these might have been, so that these earlier actions may be chosen without regard to later ones" (Modigliani 1952a, p. 20).

13 On the Cowles Commission attitude towards scholars' interchanges, see Düppe and Weintraub (2013). As for the GSIA, Jacque Drèze recalled that "Carnegie in the mid and late fifties was a tremendous place. The permanent staff had constant interchanges. Visitors were entirely welcome. Seminars by outsiders were organized regularly, well attended by the Carnegie Faculty, and the occasion of lively debates. The 'organization of research' looked spontaneous, and graduate students were part of it. Contacts with other departments of the university were not systematic, however, with the exception of

the notable Charnes-Cooper association. Later on, close ties with statistics developed" (email to the author: September 3, 2009).

14 In a letter to Marschak, Simon pointed out that what he valued "more than anything else in my association with the Cowles Commission has been the opportunities it has provided for interchange of ideas – this has been immensely stimulating to me" and claimed that "the communications lines have been somewhat weak during the past year, although the problems we are jointly working on are closer than ever to my central interests" (June 22, 1953, Simon Collection).

15 Regarding the RAND research project, see Simon (1991) and Mirowski (2002).

16 See Klein (2019).

17 Before accepting the position at the GSIA, Modigliani asked Albert Hart about the possibility of joining him at the Economic Department of Columbia University to carry on his research on expectations, (Hart to Modigliani: March 31, 1952, MP). In a letter dated July 25 1952, Hart was congratulatory about Modigliani's decision to accept the Carnegie offer: "Carnegie Tech . . . is a place where you can strike up constructive relationships with colleagues, and be secure under decent working conditions for a reasonable period. The market will undoubtedly offer you several good spots in the next few years" (July 25, 1952, MP).

18 According to Simon, the production system presented a feedback loop similar to that of a servomechanism (such as a thermostat) by means of which output (actual behavior) is compared with input (the norm) and the difference is fed back into the system to alter the output in the direction of reducing the error (Simon 1955, p. 357). In his autobiography Simon recalled that his father, an engineer, had been a significant contributor to the development of feedback devices, influencing his own approach to the dynamic behavior of economic systems and organizations (Simon, 1991, p. 108).

19 On the other hand, Simon's feedback method first restricted the class of decision rules to those that are dynamically stable then found a rule that was optimal in the sense that it did not depend on forecasts of sales (Simon 1952, p. 7).

20 H. Simon and C. Holt, "The Control of Inventories and Production Rates: A Survey", *Journal of the Operations Research Society of America*, 2 (3), August 1954. The paper was presented at the Operations Research Conference in Boston, November 1953, and benefited from suggestions by Modigliani and R. Culbertson. According to Simon and Holt, a forecast was good not if the forecast error was small but if the forecast, combined with the decision rule, resulted in low production and inventory costs. It might be that refinement of the forecast beyond a certain point was not terribly important (Simon and Holt 1954, p. 296).

21 "As a matter of fact there is no reason why adjustment and prediction cannot be combined, why the servomechanism cannot encompass both 'feed-back' (or adjustive) and 'feed-forward' (or predictive) control. Indeed, Modigliani and Sauerlender have implicitly recognized this by introducing a feed-forward device in their model of production and inventory behavior (Cooper and Simon 1955, p. 356).

22 The similarity between Simon's and Modigliani's analyses of production planning under uncertainty was stressed both by the editor of the conference proceedings, Mary J. Bowman (1958, p. 7), and A. Hart in his comment on Simon's paper: "For each moves there are several possible responses; for each combination of move-and-response, several moves we may consider making next. As in analyzing chess, we slough off some contingencies as resting on extremely unlikely responses, or as falling into patterns we know from experience we can handle" to conclude that "[t]his summarizes an underlying theme of much of the paper by Modigliani and Cohen . . . and indicates the underlying links between that paper and Simon's analysis" (1955b (1958), p. 7).

23 The realization function established a relation between the actual course of action, the planned course, the anticipated and actual behavior of the environment and certain initial conditions. According to Modigliani and Cohen, once we know the decision X_{t-1} (t), knowledge of the realization function can replace knowledge of the "very complex"

general behavior function (in Modigliani and Cohen 1955b (1958), p. 160). The realization function approach had already been suggested in Modigliani (1952b). Empirical investigations, to derive the realization function, were carried out by Friend and Bronfenbrenner, Eisner, Jean Bronfenbrenner Crockett, Modigliani and Weingartner, and Ferber and Sauerlender.

Modigliani and Cohen also introduced the distinction between parameters that are practically relevant and practically irrelevant taking into account costs and benefits of acquiring information. To analyze whether information is worth acquiring, they refer to Savage's expected utility theory as "the best available tool" for decision making under uncertainty (1955b (1958), pp. 155–156).

24 In his review of the book, Hicks (1963) acknowledged that one of the main results of the study was the distinction between relevant and irrelevant expectations thanks to linear theory. Nonetheless, the recognition that acquiring information is a costly activity and thus decisions may be made without acquiring it still leaves room for the uncertainty problem.

25 When the criterion function is quadratic, the only information required is about the expected values of the variables under consideration (expected sales values) rather than the whole joint probability distribution. On the notion of optimality in the terms of economizing information, see Duarte (2009).

26 As pointed out by Sent (2001), certainty equivalence enabled separation of the optimization problem into two steps: optimization and forecasting. This is the line of reasoning followed by Muth, who first solved the deterministic version of the model and then added uncertainty (pp. 299–300); see also Sheffrin (1996), Lovell (1986) and Lucas and Sargent (1981) among others.

27 In 1958, in a letter to Luigi Pasinetti, Modigliani still showed his enthusiasm for the GSIA's environment: "Coming back to Pittsburgh I have again been impressed by the high quality of the School and by the fervor and passion for research of my old and new colleagues. . . . With the addition of Marschak . . . the team is really 'out of this world' and impressively vibrant in respect to the old Harvard composure" (Modigliani to Pasinetti: November 18, 1958, MP, translation by the author).

28 Muth, too, argued that his rational expectations model allowed for both cognitive limits and cognitive biases (2004, in Augier and March ed., 379).

29 Discussing the origin of his paper, Muth denied that it was motivated by the challenge launched by Simon's bounded rationality and recalled: "when Franco Modigliani assigned a problem in class to explain executive salaries. Herbert Simon presented a model to explain that phenomenon. As a member of Modigliani's class, I tried to develop one too, but I wasn't very good" (Young and Darity 2001, p. 783). See also Muth's comments on Grunberg and Modigliani's paper (Young and Darity 2001, p. 788).

30 At the beginning of the 1960s, along with Modigliani Charles Holt, Merton Miller and Lee Bach also left the GSIA. In a letter to Modigliani Miller wrote: "As you can imagine, this has been a very sad week around here [Carnegie Tech], full of the sorrows of parting. Both Charlie and I made our formal announcements of departure this week. Allan Meltzer has also pretty well decided now to take at least a year off. . . . Ed Mansfield going off to Yale for a year and Dick Nelson going to Council in Washington, the economics group is . . . going to be pretty well decimated for a while" (April 12, 1961, MP).

31 In his autobiography Modigliani recalled that at the end of 1959, he was invited to be visiting professor at MIT, but the administration at the Carnegie Institute was against it. He also added, "In that period I felt rather annoyed by the university, for I had the impression that the administration did not intend to invest resources in the economics sector. . . . To my dismay, they decided not to replace an excellent economist, Alexander Henderson, who had worked alongside me" (2001, p. 91). Furthermore, in a letter to Luigi Pasinetti, Modigliani explained that his decision was motivated by his desire to come back to more traditional researches: "it's been a while I felt the desire of being

again part of wider department of economics, more traditional in its interests, and to be more free in the courses to offer and the researches to carry out" (Modigliani to Pasinetti: January 31, 1960, MP, translation by the author). Finally, Drèze recalled that his impression, at the time, was simply "that Modigliani wanted to pursue his career in a department of economics (hopefully MIT) rather than a business school" (September 3, 2010).

32   Muth acknowledged his debt to Modigliani. Modigliani was his teacher of microeconomics, general equilibrium and macroeconomic theory and, partially, statistic, as well as his PhD dissertation advisor (Sent 2002, p. 292).

33   Emile Grunberg was an Austrian economist who emigrated to the United States during WWII. He was an empirical economist with a Marxian education he had in Germany, where he conducted statistical studies on the progressive proletarization of artisans and small-scale industry. In the United States he especially worked in the field of economic methodology and philosophy of science. In a letter of recommendation for Ernest Manheim for a position in the Economics Department of the University of Kansas City, Gherard Mayer presented Grunberg as follows: "[Grunberg] has overcome his somewhat narrow Marxian bias, is a very able empirical research worker and has improved his theoretical knowledge very considerably by studying here [at the University of Chicago] under [Frank Hyneman] Knight, [Jacob] Viner, [Oskar] Lange, [Paul Howard] Douglas and [John Ulric] Nef" (Gherard E. O. Mayer to Ernest Manheim: August 24 1942; see Brief von Gerhard E. O. Meyer and Ernest Manheim in Kansas City, Mo. Chicago, Ill., August 24, 1942; translation and comment by Reinhard Mülle: http://agso.unigraz.at/manheim/dt/4_gb/meyer.htm#8a). Grunberg taught at the University of Akron from 1946 to 1948 and at Carnegie Institute of Technology from 1948 to 1956. He returned to teach at the University of Akron in 1956 until his retirement in 1973.

34   At the same time Simon published a paper on the same topic: "Bandwagon and Underdog Effects and the Possibility of Election Predictions" (1954). Modigliani and Grunberg refer to Simon's suggestion; thus, they were probably still unacquainted with Nash (1950). I wish to thank Nicola Giocoli for drawing my attention to this point.
      It is worth noting, however, that Modigliani and Simon were, in the same year, publishing posthumously a paper of a colleague who applied Nash's equilibrium (A. Henderson, *The Theory of Duopoly*, vol. 68, no 4, Quarterly Journal of Economics). A colleague who, Modigliani recalled in his autobiography, worked alongside him (2001, p. 91).

35   See Christ 1953, "Discussion (Development of Economics Thought)", *American Economic Review*, 43 (2): 271–274, 1953.

36   I was unable to locate a copy of the paper in the Modigliani papers.

37   Grunberg and Modigliani "Economic Forecasting When the Subject of the Forecast Is Influenced by the Forecast: Comment (to Kemp), 1962".

38   Grunberg's comment to Martin Brofenbenner's manuscript about the 1954 article Grunberg sent to Modigliani; see Grunberg to Modigliani: January 31, 1956, MP.

39   Regarding the debate in the 1930s on the recursive argument, see Giocoli (2003) and Young et al. (2004) among others.

40   M. Bronfenbrenner replaced Modigliani at Carnegie for the 1955 semester, when Modigliani went to visit Italy on a Fulbright grant.

41   The mathematical part of both papers was mainly constructed by Modigliani (see Grunberg and Modigliani correspondence).

42   Modigliani developed the equation system in an appendix sent separately from the letter, which I am unable to locate.

43   Modigliani also suggested to Grunberg, in revising the paper, to not "change spirit" (April 21, 1959).

44   The paper was part of research carried out in connection with the Columbia University Seminar-Workshop in Expectational Economics, under the direction of Hart. It deals

with the effects of correct public forecasting on the stability of the equilibrium using the cobweb and the inventory cycle models as in both cases the conditions for stability around the equilibrium point depend on the foresight of the agents (1961, p. 142).

45 "Furthermore, perfect foresight may have to be defined as perfect foresight of the future time path of the relevant variables and not merely as knowledge of their standing at an arbitrary chosen nearby point of time" (1963, p. 736).

46 Modigliani referred to Holt, Modigliani: "firms' cost structures and the dynamic responses of inventory, production, workforce" in "Inventory Fluctuations and Economic Stabilization, Pt. II", Joint Economic Committee, Washington 1961; on this see Duarte (2009).

47 They refer to the work of Y. Grunfeld and Z. Griliches, "Is Aggregation Necessarily Bad?", *Review of Economics and Statistics*, 42, 1960: 1–13.

References

Augier, M., and G. March. *Models of Man: Essays in Memory of Herbert A. Simon*, Carnegie, MA: MIT Press.

Bosson, J., and F. Modigliani. 1960. "The Source of Regressiveness in Surveys of Businessmen's Short-Run Expectations", in *The Quality and Economic Significance of Anticipation Data*, ed. by A. Hart, G. H. Orcutt, and F. Modigliani, Princeton, NJ: NBER and Princeton University Press, 239–263.

———. 1963. "On the Reasonableness of Regressive Expectations", *MIT's Library*, (10–63), March 11: 1–73, mimeo.

———. 1966. "Statistical vs. Structural Explanations of Understatement and Regressivity in 'Rational Expectations'", *Econometrica*, 34 (2): 347–353.

Bowman, M., ed. 1958. *Expectations, Uncertainty, and Business Behavior, a Conference Held at CIT, 20–27 October, 1955, under the Auspices of the Committee on Business Enterprise Research*, New York: SSRC.

Cherrier, B. 2010. "Rationalizing Human Organization in an Uncertain World: Jacob Marschak from Ukrainian Prisons to Behavioral Science Laboratories", *History of Political Economy*, 42 (3): 443–467.

Cooper, W. W., and H. A. Simon. 1955. "Comment on Modigliani and Sauerlender" *Short-Term Economic Forecasting*. Studies in Income and Wealth, vol. 17, Princeton: Princeton University Press, 352–359.

Crowther-Heyck, H. 2006. "Herbert Simon and the GSIA: Building an Interdisciplinary Community", *Journal of the History of the Behavioral Science*, 42 (4), Fall: 311–334.

Devletoglou, E. A. 1961. "Correct Public Prediction and the Stability of Equilibrium", *Journal of Political Economy*, 69, April: 142–169.

Duarte, P. G. 2009. "A Feasible and Objective Concept of Optimality: The Quadratic Loss Function and U.S. Monetary Policy in the 1960s and the 1970s", *History of Political Economy*, (suppl. 1), 41: 1–55.

Düppe, T., and E. R. Weintraub. 2013. "Siting the New Economic Science: The Cowles Commission's Activity Analysis Conference of June 1949", *Science in Context*, 27 (3): 453–483.

Eisner, R. 1957. "Interviews and Other Survey Techniques and the Theory of Investment", *National Bureau of Economic Research*: 513–601.

Friedman, M. 1949. "Discussion." *American Economic Review* 39 (3): 196–199.

Giocoli, N. 2003. *Modeling Rational Agents: From Interwar Economics to Early Modern Game Theory*, Cheltenham, UK and Northampton, MA, USA: Edward Elgar.

Grunberg, E., and F. Modigliani. 1954. "The Predictability of Social Events", *Journal of Political Economy*, 62 (6): 465–478.

————. 1963. "Economic Forecasting When the Subject of the Forecast Is Influenced by the Forecast: Comment to Kemp 1962", *American Economic Review*: 734–736.

Grunfeld, Y., and Z. Griliches. 1960. "Is Aggregation Necessarily Bad?", *Review of Economics and Statistics*, 42: 1–13.

Hart, A. G. 1942. "Risk, Uncertainty and the Unpredictability of Compounding Probabilities", *Studies in Mathematical Economics and Econometrics in Memory of Henry Schultz*, ed. by H. Schultz, O. Lange, F. Mcintyre, and T. O. Yntema, Chicago: University of Chicago Press.

————. 1949. "Assets, Liquidity and Investment", *American Economic Review*, 39 (3): 171–181.

————. 1951. *Anticipations, Uncertainty and Dynamic Planning*, New York: M. Kelley, August.

Hartley, J. E. 2004. "Modigliani's Expectations", *Eastern Economic Journal*, 30 (3): 427–440.

Hicks, J. 1939. *Value and Capital: An Inquiry into the Fundamental Principles of Economic Theory*, Oxford: Clarendon Press.

————. 1963. "Reviewed Work: The Role of Anticipations and Plans in Economic Behaviour and Their Use in Economic Analysis and Forecasting by F. Modigliani; K. J. Cohen", *Economic Journal*, 73 (289): 99–101.

Holt C. C. 2004. "Rational Forecasting, Learning, and Decision Making" in Models of Man. *Essays in memory of Herbert H. Simon*: 355–364.

Holt, C. C., and F. Modigliani. 1960. "Firms' Cost Structures and the Dynamic Responses of Inventory, Production, Workforce", *Inventory Fluctuations and Economic Stabilization*, Pt. II, Joint Economic Committee, Washington.

Holt, C. C., F. Modigliani, and J. F. Muth. 1956. "Derivation of a Linear Decision Rule for Production and Employment", *Management Science*, 2 (2): 159–177.

Holt, C. C., F. Modigliani, J. F. Muth, and H. Simon. 1961. *Planning Production, Inventories and Work Forces*, Prentice-Hall.

Holt, C. C., F. Modigliani, and H. Simon. 1955. "*A Linear Decision Rule for Production and Employment Scheduling*", ONR Research Memorandum no. 30, May, 1–53.

Klamer, A. 1983. *The New Classical Macroeconomics: Conversations with the New Classical Economists and Their Opponents*, Harvester Press.

Klein, J. 2019. "The Cold War Hot House for Modeling Strategies at the Carnegie Institute of Technology", Working Paper No 19, Institute for New Economic Thinking, 1–69.

Knight, F. H. 1947. *Freedom and Reform: Essays in Economics and Social Philosophy*. New York: Harper.

Levin, H. J. 1958. "Public Prediction in Theory and Facts", *Southern Economic Journal* 24 (3): 338–352.

Lovell, M. C. 1986. "Tests of the Rational Expectations Hypothesis", *American Economic Review*, 76 (1): 110–124.

Lucas, R. E., Jr., and T. Sargent. 1981. *Rational Expectations and Econometric Practice*, vol. 1, Minneapolis: University of Minnesota Press.

Markowitz, H. M. 1950. "On the Certainty Equivalence and Risk Discount Hypothesis", *Cowles Commission Discussion Papers Economics*. https://cowles.yale.edu/sites/default/files/files/pub/cdp/e-0295.pdf.

Marschak, J. 1949. "Role of Liquidity Under Complete and Incomplete Information", *American Economic Review*, 39 (3): 182–195.

Modigliani (Franco) Papers, David M. Rubenstein Rare Book and Manuscript Library, Duke University.

Mirowski, P. 2002. *Machine Dreams*, Cambridge: Cambridge University Press.

Modigliani, F. 1949a. "Discussion", *American Economic Review*, 39 (3): 201–208.

————. 1949b. "New Areas of Opinion Research: in other social sciences", *Public Opinion Quarterly*, 13 (4): 770–771.

————. 1952a. "Some Considerations on the Expectations and Planning Horizon Relevant to Entrepreneurial Decisions", Cowles Commission Paper, Economics No 2038, April.

————. 1952b. "The Measurement of Expectations: Abstract of Paper Presented at the Boston Meeting December 1951", *Econometrica*, 20 (3): 481–482.

————. 2001. *Adventures of an Economist*. Texere.

Modigliani, F., and A. Ando. 1963. "The Life Cycle Hypothesis of Saving Behavior: Aggregate Implications and Tests", *American Economic Review*, 53 (1 part 1): 55–84.

Modigliani, F., and R. Brumberg. 1954. "Utility Analysis and the Consumption Function: An Interpretation of Cross-Section Data", in *Post-Keynesian Economics*, ed. by K. Kuhihara, New Brunswick, NJ: Rutgers University Press, 388–436.

————. 1955 (1958). "The Significance and Uses of Ex Ante Data: A Summary View", *Proceeding of the Conference on Expectations, Uncertainty and Business Behavior, Social Science Research Council*, October, 27–29.

————. 1961. *The Role of Anticipations and Plans in Economic Behavior and Their Use in Economic Analysis and Forecasting*, Studies in Business Expectations and Planning No. 4, Bureau of Economic and Business Research, University of Illinois.

Modigliani, F., and F. E. Hohn. 1952. "Solutions to Certain Problems of Production Planning over Time Illustrating the Effect of Inventory Constraints", Appendix to Cowles Commission Paper: Economics no. 2038, April.

————. 1955. "Planning Over Time and the Nature of the Expectations and Planning Horizon", *Econometrica*, 23 (1): 46–66.

Modigliani, F., and O. H. Sauerlender. 1955. "Economic Expectations and Plans of Firms in Relation to Short-Term Forecasting, Short-Term Economic Forecasting", in *Studies in Income and Wealth*, vol. 17, Princeton, NJ: Princeton University Press for the NBER, 299–303.

Modigliani, F., and R. J. Shiller. 1973. "Inflation, Rational Expectations and the Term Structure on Interest Rate", *Economica, New Series*, 40 (157): 12–43.

Modigliani, F., and R. Sutch. 1966. "Innovations in Interests Rate Policy", *American Economic Review*, 56 (1/2): 178–197.

————. 1967. "Debt Management and the Term Structure of Interest Rates: An Empirical Analysis", *Journal of Political Economy*, 75: 569–589.

Morgenstern, O. 1935 (1976). "Perfect Foresight and Economic Equilibrium", in *Selected Economic Writings of Oskar Morgenstern*, ed. by A. Schotter, 151–167, New York: New York University Press.

Muth, J. 1961. "Rational Expectations and the Theory of Price Movements", *Econometrica*, 29 (3): 315–335.

Nash, J. 1950. "Equilibrium Points in n-Person Games", *Proceedings of the National Academy of Sciences*, 36: 48–49.

Rancan, A. 2013. "Modigliani's and Simon's Early Contribution to Uncertainty (1952–1960)", *History of Political Economy*, 45 (1): 1–38.

Research Project Under Task Order 358(01). 1953. *Decision Making Project under Uncertainty*, Eight Progress Report.

Sent, E. M. 2001. "Game Theorists versus Herbert Simon: Playing Games with Bounded Rationality", *Journal of Economic Behavior and Organization*, 44: 129–143.

————. 2002. "How (Not) to Influence People: The Contrary Tale of John F. Muth", *History of Political Economy*, 34 (2): 291–319.

Sheffrin, S. M. 1996. *Rational Expectations*. Cambridge: Cambridge University Press.

Simon, H. 1945. "Review of *Theory of Games and Economic Behavior*, by John von Neumann and Oskar Morgenstern", *American Journal of Sociology*, 50: 558–60.

Simon, H. 1952, "Notes on Two Approaches to the Production Rate Problem", Cowles Commission Discussion Paper: Economics no. 2057, November.

———. 1954. "Bandwagon and Underdog Effects and the Possibility of Election Predictions", *The Public Opinion Quarterly*, 18 (3): 245–253.

———. 1955. "A Behavioral Model of Rational Choice", *Quarterly Journal of Economics*, 69: 99–118.

———. 1955 (1958). "The Role of Expectations in an Adaptive or Behavioristic Model", in *Expectations, Uncertainty, and Business Behavior: Social Science Research Council, October 27–29*, ed. by M. J. Bowman, New York: Social Science Research Council, 49–73.

———. 1956a. "Reply: Surrogates for Uncertain Decision Problems", *ONR Research Memorandum* (38): 1–22.

———. 1956b. "Dynamic Programming under Uncertainty with a Quadratic Criterion Function", *Econometrica*, 24: 74–81.

———. 1958. "Review of Games and Decisions: Introduction and Critical Survey", *American Sociological Review*, 23: 342–43.

———. 1979. "Rational Decision Making in Business Organizations", *American Economic Review*, 69 (4): 493–513.

———. 1991. *Models of My Life*, New York: Basic Books.

———. 2000. *An Economy of Markets or Organizations?*, Akron University, April.

Simon, H., and C. Holt. 1954. "The Control of Inventories and Production Rates: A Survey", *Journal of the Operations Research Society of America*, 2 (3): 289–301.

Tintner, G. 1941. "The Theory of Choice under Subjective Risk and Uncertainty." *Econometrica*, 9 (July–October): 298–304.

Young, W., and W. Darity, Jr. 2001. "The Early History of Rational and Implicit Expectations", *History of Political Economy*, 33 (4): 773–812.

Young, W., R. Leeson, and W. Darity, Jr. 2004. *Economics, Economists, and Expectations: Microfoundations to Macroapplications*, New York: Routledge.

6 The life cycle savings in an unstable economy

Introduction

In a letter to Modigliani for the Nobel Prize assigned to Merton Miller (with Harry Markowitz and William Sharpe), Herbert Simon commented the higher standards of the Graduate School of Industrial Administration (GSIA):

> I expect you were considerably cheered by the award of the Nobel to Merton, which was, in a real sense, a second award to you also. GSIA of the 1950s already have produced three awards, we have left only two more sets of first line candidates: Dick Cyert and Jim March for the behavioral theory of the firms, and Jack Muth, Bob Lucas and Tom Sargent for rational expectations (however wrong-headed that idea may be, it is important). . . . (I think the Committee is embarrassed about what to do with Jim – who is not an economist – and with Jack – who has done nothing since 1961) but whether or not it is an amazing record for the little school.

(Simon to Modigliani: October 22, 1990, MP)

In his reply, Modigliani recalled with nostalgia the

> glorious GSIA days. . . . [N]o matter how many awards we pile up, I certainly agree that GSIA was an exciting place: we felt at the center of the universe and, as you point out, maybe we were. And, most important, we had a lot of fun working hard together, and arguing even harder.

(November 29, 1990, MP)

Modigliani spent almost eight years at Carnegie Tech, where he worked on different models of individual behavior from which the life cycle hypothesis, an outgrowth of the University of Illinois project on uncertainty, and the Modigliani and Miller theorem on corporate finance, partly emerged. The idea about firms' convenience to produce at a constant pace, reducing fluctuations in production, and that firms' production planning should depend on expectations for the entire seasonal cycle rather than on the sales of the period, was the departure point for Modigliani and Richard Brumberg's intuition about savings behavior (see Modigliani 2001, pp. 57–58).

This chapter is largely devoted to Brumberg, Modigliani and Albert Ando's contributions to the theory of savings, and to Modigliani's unpublished writings on the theory of money in a general equilibrium framework, which he used for his classes, in which he further developed the content of the 1944 article, partly to answer to the so-called Patinkin controversy on the real balance effect. Modigliani's notes were at the basis of the 1963 article on the "Monetary Mechanisms and Its Interactions with Real Phenomena". His development of the IS LM model, along with Ando and Modigliani's 1959 growth and fluctuations model, served as a theoretical framework in the building of the Federal Reserve–MIT–University of Pennsylvania macroeconometric model (1966–1970) that marked Modigliani's Keynesianism (Chapter 7).

Savings and consumption planning

As discussed in Chapter 3, Modigliani began to work on savings at the Institute of Word Affairs, publishing with Neisser an article in which they distinguished between secular and cyclical savings behavior. The crucial role Modigliani ascribed to savings and its coordination with investment decisions, along with the possibility of measuring and forecasting it, which already appeared in his article on the working of a socialist economy (Modigliani 1947), contributes to explain his early interest in this subject. The project on *Expectations and Business Fluctuations* he then supervised at the University of Illinois also added important stimulus to Modigliani and Brumberg's approach to the problem. Their starting point was the idea behind the relative income hypothesis (Modigliani 1949) that the variable to observe for understanding savings behavior is not the absolute income but the normal income that a person could expect. To them savings was not affected "by one who is rich (or poor) but by one who is transitory rich (or poor)", retaining the idea of cyclical influence beside absolute income to explain savings. They further developed the intuition that income is high or low relative to a person's lifetime income with current income that can be lower or higher than lifetime income for transitory reasons such as temporary unemployment (see Szenberg and Ramrattan 2008, Chapter 4, pp. 85–86).

Moreover, as Modigliani argues in his recollection, the motive behind saving is not to acquire wealth as an end in itself but to accumulate resources to spend later on with the aim of a guarantee of a stable average consumption over the entire life.[1] Their shift of attention from current income to lifetime resources (including expected average income and initial assets) and to savings as aimed at smoothing fluctuations in consumption over the life cycle clearly reflects the approach to firms' production planning on which Modigliani was also working. Within the project on *Expectations and Business Fluctuations*, Modigliani and his research team collected evidence, through interviews and case studies from 1950 to 1952, about firms' producing at constant rate to avoid fluctuations in production – an idea he formalized in a couple of papers with his colleague at the University of Illinois, Franz Hohn (1952, 1955; see Chapter 3).[2] Modigliani and Brumberg explicitly mentioned the analogy between "consumption, assets, income expectations and the life cycle of income . . . and production, inventories, sales expectations, and the seasonal cycle of sales" (1954, p. 338n). To them, there was no close and simple relation between consumption in a given period and income in the same period because it is a "plan which extends over the balance of the individual's life, while the income accruing within the same period is but one element which contributes to the shaping of such plan" (1954, p. 392). Like for firms' production planning, in which the problem of uncertainty was omitted through the distinction between relevant and irrelevant information and expectations, also in the life cycle model Modigliani and Brumberg abstracted from uncertainty, arguing that it does not affect the savings behavior. To them, uncertainty simply adds further motives such as the precautionary motive but not the logic behind the model (1954, p. 392):

> even under uncertainty there are sufficient incentives for the households to accumulate assets at a rapid rate during the early years of the life . . . [uncertainty] does not seem essential . . . for the development of a useful theory of the factors controlling the overall rate of saving.

(1954, p. 428)

Other important sources of inspiration in devising the life cycle hypothesis were Dorothy Brady's and Margaret's Reid's studies on family budgets. When Modigliani met Brady and Reid at the University of Illinois, they were working on cross-sectional data to estimate the impact of the standard of living on consumptions and savings habits of families. Modigliani always acknowledged the important role of Reid's "highly imaginative" work and Brady's "many unrecorded comments" (Modigliani 1980, pp. 2, 129, 1986, p. 299). As Reid wrote to Patinkin, who had left the University of Illinois to go to Jerusalem:

> There is now an official economics seminar that meets once a week. There have been several meeting already. I think that we had the largest crowd when Dorothy presented the preliminary findings of her project on savings. She got some very interesting and consistent relation out of the family data which includes all the studies that have been made between 1889 and 1947.

(January 15, 1950, Patinkin Papers)

Brumberg and Modigliani's life cycle theory was entirely developed within the neoclassical economics framework. Their departure point was the Fisherian intertemporal choice and the individual theory of utility maximization. The cornerstone of their model is the explanation of household savings behavior in terms of choice between present and future consumption, with utility as the objective function to maximize and current and expected average income, wealth, and age as constraints (1954, pp. 398–400). Their life cycle model, according to which people save during their work life to maintain constant consumption when they retire, was built and tested at microeconomic and macroeconomic levels in two pioneer contributions they wrote between 1952 and 1953. The "Utility Analysis and the Consumption Function: An Interpretation of Cross-Section Data" (1954) was primarily concerned with individual behavior; the second article, "Utility Analysis and Aggregate Consumption Functions: An Attempt at integrating" based on time-series data examined the macroeconomic implications of the model. This latter paper remained unpublished until Modigliani's *Collected Papers* (1980, vol. 2) mainly because of Brumberg's premature death in the summer of 1954. Modigliani recalled he lost interest in the topic, and it was only with his Ph.D student at Carnegie Tech, in the late 1950s that he returned to work again on the aggregate consumption function.

Modigliani and Brumberg's first essay was published in a volume edited by Kenneth K. Kuriara and devoted to post-Keynesian economics. In the introduction he emphasized that all the contributions collected represented in some way an extension of Keynes's *General Theory*, also acknowledging that "many would now consider his analysis less than adequate for meeting such special problems as cyclical forecasts and control, persistent inflation, the maintenance of full employment booms, secular growth, nonlinear structural relations, and macrofoundational distribution" (1954, p. vii), as Modigliani and Brumberg's neoclassical framework and empirical approach well testify.

Modigliani and Richard Brumberg's life cycle models

Brumberg and Modigliani met in 1952 at the University of Illinois when Brumberg was a first-year graduate student and Modigliani was moving to Carnegie Tech. The same year Brumberg went to the John Hopkins University to carry out his PhD dissertation under Carl Christ supervision. After the dissertation, he joined the Department of Applied Economics at Cambridge (UK) for a research period, working with Michael Farrell and Richard Stone on the life cycle model.

While the article on individual savings was published in the Kurihara volume (1954), Modigliani submitted the essay on the aggregate consumption function to *Econometrica* in 1953. The managing editor informs Modigliani that the length of the paper (99 pages) "certainly presents a formidable problem", asking for a list of people who had already red the manuscript and to whom he could have asked for the reports (Stroz to Modigliani: October 5, 1953, MP).[3] Soon after, they decided that the manuscript could be published as the first volume of an "Occasional Paper Series" *Econometrica* wanted to launch (Stroz to Modigliani: December 15, 1953, MP). Unfortunately, the initiative found many obstacles, and in March 1954 Stroz wrote to Modigliani that the Council of the Econometric Society had not yet approved the monograph series. A few months later, in August 1954, Christ wrote to Modigliani about Brumberg's illness and premature death at Cambridge. He asked Modigliani about the possibility of publishing Brumberg's works: the PhD dissertation, a couple of articles and the manuscript with Modigliani. In a letter to Farrell, Modigliani explains that he had already submitted the paper to *Econometrica* and was waiting for news about that (September 13, 1954, MP). Only in November the managing editor sent to Modigliani the reports, while Modigliani was returning for the first time to Italy with a Fulbright grant. In April 1955 Stroz asked Modigliani's about the revised version of the paper, also adding that there was no news about the approval of the monograph series. Therefore, he added, the paper could be published in full in *Econometrica*, and he asked whether Modigliani had any preference between the two options. Modigliani remarked his preference for "the Special Publication form also because it could have an introduction devoted to Brumberg and written if possible by Stone".[4] This is the last correspondence concerning the paper that finally as mentioned, remained unpublished until Modigliani's *Collected Papers* (1980, vol. 2).

In the "Utility Analysis and the Consumption Function" (1954), Modigliani and Brumberg developed a model of individual consumption and savings behavior that served to provide a theory able to explain the large amount of data available and as a departure point for the building of an aggregate consumption function for an understanding of the determinants of national savings. Under this perspective, the life cycle hypothesis represented one of the earlier attempts of microfoundation of macroeconomics (see Fisher 1988, p. 315; also on post-war microfoundational programs see Duarte and Lima 2012).

In the beginning of the paper, Modigliani and Brumberg discussed the "impressive" amount of "empirical facts" that had been collected without a theory to explain them. A lacuna they aimed to fulfill:

> We seem to be in imminent danger of being mothered under them. What is, however, still conspicuously missing is a general analytical framework which will link together these facts, reconcile the apparent contradictions and provides a satisfactory bridge between cross-sectional findings and the fluctuations of aggregative time series analysis. It is our purpose to attempt to provide such an analytical framework through the use of the well-developed tools of marginal analysis.

(1954, p. 389)

Modigliani and Brumberg's savings model was built on a number of restrictive assumptions such as constant prices, no interest rates, absence of the estate motive, the hypothesis that agents allocate their additional income to increase consumption "roughly" in the same proportion and, finally, that everybody consumes in the same way. The resulting consumption function was a linear and homogenous function of current and expected average income, net worth and the age of households. Brumberg and Modigliani justified their restrictive assumptions arguing that in the face of the complexity of the real world, "the question of just which aspects of reality are essential to the construction of a theory is primarily a pragmatic one". If the resulting theory "is useful in explaining the essential feature of the phenomena under consideration in spite of the simplifications assumed, then these simplifications are thereby justified" (1954, p. 394).

Since the 1940s, numerous attempts had been made to estimate marginal and average propensities to save, thanks to the increasing availability of data. In 1946 Kuznets provided evidence on the long-run constancy of the savings ratio despite the large increase in per-capita income in contrast with the Keynesian short-run consumption function. Brady and Friedman (1947) reconciled Kuznets's results by looking at budget families' data and observing that the savings rate was not explained by the absolute income of the family but rather by its income relative to overall mean income. As mentioned in Chapter 3, Duesenberry (1949) and Modigliani (1949) elaborated such empirical finding in the relative income hypothesis. This approach is then further developed by Modigliani and Brumberg's life cycle consumption function.

In the 1954 essay Modigliani and Brumberg distinguished between two situations: one of equilibrium in which household is in a stationary position, that is, with no short-run fluctuations of income, and expectations are, therefore, always fulfilled, and a situation in which an individual's current income can differ from the expected one. While in equilibrium, the proportion of income saved is the same independently from the income level, with this proportion that rises with age up to retirement; in the latter situation the nonpermanent component of income makes short-run savings fluctuate.

With the life cycle hypothesis, Modigliani and Brumberg were challenging the "generally accepted" view that the proportion of income saved rises with the economic status of the household, whereas to them it was only a temporary (cyclical) phenomenon. However, as they recognized, the standard reading and their own interpretation were both consistent with budget studies about the relationships among income, consumption and savings. Therefore, further tests were needed to discriminate between the two theories. It was in this context that Reid's study became crucial because, according to them, she provided the kind of empirical tests they were searching for.[5] They had in mind the possibility of measuring the elasticity of consumption to current income in the alternative situations of households that earned a stable or unstable income. Modigliani and Brumberg's starting point was a household's behavior in a stationary position, in which the correlation between current and expected income is unity; that is, income expectations are always fulfilled, and income perceived is stable. To them, if the life cycle hypothesis were correct, budget data had to show that also the elasticity of consumption with respect to current income was unity. In other words, consumption is a constant proportion of current income. They refer to an hypothetical sample formed either by governors' employers and college professors, for which short-run fluctuations of income were of relative minor importance and, on the other extreme, by farmers whose income was highly unstable, for which the correlation between consumption and current income was, therefore, low, as should have been the elasticity of consumption with respect to current income.

The implication about elasticity appeared to Modigliani and Brumberg crucial because it provided evidence that long-run saving is independent from current income and that short-run fluctuations of savings are relative to variations in the nonpermanent component of income. In other words, they read the correlation as an indirect, approximate measure of the degree to which the current income of each household is close to the normal level. When the correlation is high, the elasticity must be close to unity; when the correlation is low, thus showing the presence of pronounced short-term income fluctuations, the elasticity must be well below unity:

> According to our model the typical findings of budget studies as to the relation between consumption and income are basically due to the fact that in the presence of short term fluctuations, income over a short interval is a poor *and seriously biased* measure of the accustomed level. The extent of this bias is measured by the correlation. . . . . [T]he higher the correlation the smaller the bias and therefore the higher the elasticity of consumption on income. Reid and few others have suggested and tested alternative methods of getting a more reliable index of the accustomed level than current income and, invariably, it is found that when consumption is related to such a measure, the elasticity of consumption with respect to it rises markedly above the consumption-current income elasticity, and comes close, frequently remarkably close, to unity.

(Modigliani and Brumberg 1954, pp. 421–422)

They finally remarked, with some ambiguity, that their model confirms Keynes's propositions – they do not say which ones, but:

> At the same time, we take some satisfaction in having be able to tie this aspect of his analysis into the mainstream of economic theory: by replacing his mysterious psychological law with the principle that men are disposed as a rule and on the average, to be forward-looking animals. . . . We depart from Keynes, however, on his contention of a "greater proportion of income being saved as real income increases". We claim that the proportion of income saved is essentially independent on income, and that systematic deviations of the savings ratio from the normal level are largely accounted for by short run fluctuations of income around the basic earning capacity of the household. . . . The common sense of our claims rests largely on two propositions: (a) that the major purpose of savings is to provide a cushion against major variations in income that occur during the life cycle; (b) that the provision household makes for retirement and for emergencies are basically proportional on the average to its basic earning capacity while the N of years over which these provisions can be made is largely independent of income level.

(1954, p. 430)

Although Modigliani and Brumberg's paper was not concerned with the model's policy implications, they also concluded that their "new" understanding of the determinant of savings led to a "a very skeptical view of the effectiveness of a Keynesian policy of income redistribution for the purpose of reducing the average propensity to save" (1954, p. 431).[6] The connection between income distribution and savings was discussed, especially on aggregate level and regarding capital accumulation and growth, by Ando and Modigliani in opposition to the Kaldorian double propensity to save assumption (see the next section).

Finally, the implications of the life cycle model for the Keynesian income multiplier, and the effectiveness of monetary policy, was investigated through the building of the Fed–MIT–Penn macroeconometric model in the late 1960s.

Modigliani and Brumberg's aggregate consumption function

Modigliani and Brumberg concluded the essay on the individual consumption function arguing that the life cycle model was consistent with both cross-section and time-series data, thus: "we seem to be near to the ultimate goal of a unified and yet simple theory of consumption function" (1954, p. 430). They placed their study on aggregate consumption within the lines traced by Duesenberry's (1949) and Modigliani's (1949) relative income hypothesis but especially by the "pioneer contribution" of Tibor de Scitovszky (1941): "The present writers owed a great debt to these authors, especially Reid and Scitovsky, and hope that this paper successfully integrates their major ideas" (1953 (1980), p. 129).[7]

In the 1941 article on "Capital Accumulation, Employment and Price Rigidity", de Scitovsky analyzed the implications of the hypotheses of flexible and rigid prices for full employment in the framework of a theory of long-run capital accumulation (i.e., cycle free). The main connections between Modigliani and Brumberg's study and de Scitovsky refer to his analysis of the effects of price level on aggregate demand through change of wealth, by which he acknowledged its importance in the consumption function. According to Modigliani (1955) de Scitovsky anticipated the Pigou effect, Modigliani discussed with Brumberg in relation to the implications of their aggregate model.

de Scitovsky distinguished between the working of a noncapitalist and a capitalist economy (defined as the economy in which the quantity of a production factor, namely, capital, can change) under flexible and rigid prices. As for a capitalist economy his long-run analysis, under price rigidity, moved in a direction similar to that Modigliani and Brumberg's research should have taken and would later take with Ando (see Ando and Modigliani 1959). Starting from a situation of full employment equilibrium, de Scitovsky showed that as time goes on, the accumulation of capital depresses its marginal productivity, whereas the corresponding increases in the demand for securities will rise interest rates, thus decreasing the rate of investment. On the other hand, the propensity to save increases with the increase of real income (due to the rise of equipment) and of interest rates although partly offset by the rise of wealth. Because of the rise of savings and the fall of investment, the employment levels must decline to ensure the equality between the two variables, concluding that the "secular accumulation of capital equipment and of securities is likely to lead to increasing unemployment even if prices are not perfectly rigid . . . there need be no inherent tendency in the economic system towards the full (optimum) employment" (1941, p. 88). de Scitovsky also connected price flexibility with the system instability and price rigidity with stability, as Modigliani did in his preliminary notes on the theory of money and interest (discussed later), concluding that the criticism of the Keynesian theory because of the assumption of wage rigidity is totally "unwarranted; not only because this assumption is probably less unrealistic than the classical assumption . . . but also because the model of rigid wages – fulfilling the condition of stability – is unlikely to differ significantly from the real economy in its essential features" (1941, p. 88).

In Part 3 of the manuscript, Modigliani and Brumberg relaxed the assumption of constant prices to discuss the Pigou effect. According to them, a once-for-all fall in price does not reduce savings permanently because the temporary increases in consumption are not accompanied by a permanent increase of income; thus the Pigou effect "wears off" (1953 (1980), vol. 2, p. 152). For savings to remain at the lower level, "prices would have to continue to fall endlessly" (1953 (1980), vol. 2, p. 152) with the system becoming unstable. In this sense, they argued, the Keynesian conclusion is vindicated although admittedly at a more complex level of analysis.

Price flexibility, the Pigou effect and system instability were also the main object of Modigliani's (1955) notes on monetary economics.

Modigliani and Ando's macroeconomics implication of the life cycle theory

In a letter to Michael Farrell concerning the publication of the memorial volume for Brumberg, Modigliani referred to the reading of his (Farrell's) paper apparently titled "Misery and Bliss", asking whether it would be published somewhere. Modigliani explained that the paper precisely pursued the kind of development he had in mind for the life cycle model and that he hoped Brumberg would have undertaken

> [n]amely, to embed our Consumption Function into business cycles models and models of economic growth. I had indented to write an extensive comment on your paper for Dick's [Brumberg] benefit in carrying this line of inquire further. However, as you can understand, I lost interest in doing so.

(Modigliani to Farrell: September 13, 1954)

This will be the research line Modigliani pursued few years later with another PhD student, Albert Ando, whose dissertation "A Contribution to the Theory of Economic Fluctuations and Growth" (1959) was devoted to the building of a macroeconometric model based on the multiplier and accelerator mechanism, in which the implications of the life cycle hypothesis were developed and tested.[8]

Ando's growth model (derived from Solow's 1956 neoclassical model) should be microfounded, having the consumers' expenditures and firms' investment behavior as its building blocks. His aim was to analyze theoretically and empirically the role of the price mechanism, especially of interest rates, in the determination of growth and fluctuations, by modeling individual and aggregate consumption and investment behavior in the context of the maximization principle. Starting from analyzing the characteristics of the individual's utility function and the age structure of population, Ando aggregated consumption within each age group and, then, over the age groups (Ando 1959; Ando and Modigliani 1963, pp. 56–58). From the aggregate consumption function, he derived the aggregate supply of assets, which plays a crucial role in the growth model developed in the last part of the dissertation (Ando 1959, Chapter 3, p. 28).

Ando's most important conclusion was the explanation of fluctuations through time needs to households and entrepreneurs to adjust their savings and investment decisions to changes of prices (i.e., by lags and rigidities).

His model was further developed in a paper with Modigliani they presented at the 1958 American Economic Association conference and published in the 1959 proceeding under the title "Growth, Fluctuations and Stability". As in Ando's dissertation, their departure point was a modified Solow's growth model, emphasizing that their aim was to demonstrate the crucial role of the price mechanism on economic behavior neglected by post-Keynesian growth models. They criticized in particular the explanation of the long-run stability of the capital-output ratio in terms of a fixed technological datum rather than the result of demand for and supply of capital funds in response to changes in interest rates (Ando and Modigliani 1959, p. 502).

Ando and Modigliani pursued this research line in contrast with the Harrod–Domar and the Kaldorian growth and distribution models in a series of subsequent papers (Ando and Modigliani 1963; Modigliani 1964, 1966 among others). Their explanation of the capital output coefficient through the life cycle model denied any role of income distribution in economic growth arguing that savings behavior is independent from different classes of income perceivers.

As Modigliani (1964) remarked, one significant macroeconomic implication of the life cycle model was both to demonstrate that the growth trend of income was independent from the marginal propensity to save and consume (these quantities determine only the equilibrium capital output) and to reveal "the central importance of the much neglected supply side of the capital market for an understanding of the behaviour of the capital-output ratio and of the capital–labour ratio and the phenomena associated with growth" (Modigliani 1964, pp. 49–50). To him the capital-output ratio did not merely reflect rigid technical capital requirements, but the adjustment of capital to the supply of wealth resulting from consumption and savings behavior as formalized by the life cycle model (Modigliani 1966). Starting from a definition of wealth in terms of labor income accumulated over time, and saving as an increasing function of income and a decreasing function of the stock of wealth, Modigliani read the long-term stability of the capital output ratio as the result of the stability of the wealth income ratio inverting, with respect to Harrod, the causal link. According to Modigliani, the capital output ratio might be understood as a long-term relationship that reflects the adjustment of the amount of capital in use to the supply of wealth that results from consumption and savings behavior as theorized by the life cycle hypothesis. Under the hypothesis of a constant rate of growth, both aggregate private savings and aggregate private wealth tend to rise at the same rate, and therefore, the saving and wealth income ratios tend to remain constant. Both ratios depend on the growth rate of income, and their constancy would explain the long-term stability of the capital output ratio.

Modigliani, Brumberg and Ando's life cycle hypothesis was at the basis of the specification of the consumption sector of the Fed–MIT–Penn macro-econometric model. The presence of wealth in the consumption function led to relevant implications in terms of the working of the monetary and fiscal stabilization policies. As Modigliani and Ando explained, the life cycle hypothesis provided a direct channel of influence from monetary policy to consumption that moved from the short-term interest rate to the long-term rate, the market value of shares and hence to wealth, with important consequence in terms of stabilization actions. The resulting impact on aggregate output was estimated of the same order of magnitude as that resulting from the response of the components of gross investment but relatively faster (Modigliani 1975, pp. 249–250). On the other hand, because current consumption depended on expected resources over the entire life span, short-run variations in income caused by shock, appeared largely absorbed into savings. In other words, the life cycle hypothesis reduced the magnitude of the multiplier and the impact of transitory fiscal actions through the distinction between permanent and transitory changes in income.[9]

Returning to Keynesian economics

By looking at Modigliani's research lines from his arrival at the New School in 1939 to the years he spent at Carnegie Tech, it would seem, from first glance, that his study of Keynesian and classical economics, the subject of his dissertation and the 1944 *Econometrica* article, had been quite an exception. Soon after he began to work with Neisser on a macroeconometric model of international trade, on savings behavior within the neoclassical framework, on firms' production planning under uncertainty and price-setting behavior in oligopolistic markets (Modigliani 1958). The study of aggregate consumption was devoted only marginally to verify the validity of the so-called Pigou effect, which should have undermined Keynes's theory. The life cycle model, as Brumberg and Modigliani 1953 concluded, vindicated empirically the Keynesian conclusion on the ineffectiveness of price flexibility (in practice) to restore full employment (through change in real balances of wealth).

The place where Modigliani especially developed his Keynesian economics were instead his classes on macroeconomics, mathematical economics, monetary economics and advanced economics which dealt with wage and price rigidity and the role of money in a general equilibrium framework. They represented the departure point for working in the mid–1950s to a lengthy typewritten manuscript, "The Preliminary Notes on the Theory of Money and Interest in the Framework of General Equilibrium Analysis" (Modigliani 1955, MP), which would have become the subject of a monograph. In a letter to Sylos Labini, he referred to them as a "General Treatise on the Theory of Money and Interest" of which he also wanted an Italian translation (see Modigliani to Sylos Labini: September 14, 1956 in MP; Rancan 2014).[10]

Modigliani's "Preliminary Notes" were especially stimulated by the so-called Patinkin controversy about the real balance (or Pigou) effect, as Modigliani wrote to his student Jaques Drèze:[11]

> My latest absorbing occupation has been monetary theory and the famous Patinkin controversy. The whole issue was kindled by three factors: 1) A very sharp attack on my liquidity preference paper written by Hahn, in the Economic Journal, last year; 2) Visit and lecture here by Patinkin who is visiting professor at John Hopkins on leave from Jerusalem; and 3) the preparation of my course in monetary theory, which I am giving this spring. I have made some very remarkable progress and have finally established the result that the whole Patinkin controversy was basically a red herring in which all people have made a large number of mistakes and I, myself, am by no means above blame. I am now in the process of writing some preliminary notes with the help of Ando.

(January 30, 1956)

Modigliani dealt with the dichotomy and neutrality issues, wage and price rigidity, effective demand and unemployment. These first parts of the analysis should have been followed by the study of the same problems under uncertainty, on which there are some handwritten notes, and with reference to different market forms.[12] Modigliani did not end the work and the "Preliminary Notes" remained unpublished, with most of Modigliani's results summarized in the 1963 article on "The Monetary Mechanism and its Interaction with Real Phenomena".

With respect to the 1944 article, Modigliani enlarged the perspective, analyzing the classical and Keynesian theory in a more elaborated general equilibrium framework in which the role of changing expectations is also discussed. Maybe influenced by his contemporary working on uncertainty, in these notes the existence and the stability of the equilibrium depend crucially on the elasticity of price expectations. Moreover, while the 1963 article also investigated the policy implications of the classical and Keynesian models (particulary with reference to Friedman's counterattack), the monetary notes were mostly theoretical.

Preliminary notes on money in a general equilibrium framework

The postwar economic debate was characterized by attempts, led by Patinkin, to integrate Walrasian and Keynesian economics through the introduction of money in a general equilibrium system of equations and to demonstrate the so-called wealth or real balance effect. Modigliani's "Preliminary Notes" were partly concerned with this debate, establishing the conditions under which money is neutral and the classical dichotomy holds. Most important, as pointed out by Béraud (2018), he also defined the conditions for the existence and stability of an equilibrium position under wage and price flexibility and rigidity, static and dynamic expectations.

With respect to the 1944 model, in the 1955, 1963 models Modigliani relied explicitly on the general equilibrium framework, where all markets are analyzed in the same way, with explicit reference to the bonds market and its relation with the money market and the banking system. He also underlined his improvement in the analysis of the labor market, with a different definition of wage rigidity (no more in terms of a horizontal labor supply), of the consumption function (through the life cycle theory) and the investment function (a variant of the acceleration principle) and about the homogeneity assumption: of zero degree of the individual demand and supply equations in money income, wealth and prices (see Modigliani 1963, pp. 22–23, 81–82; also see Béraud 2018, pp. 2, 15).

Modigliani started from static analysis of a classical system without money, whose existence and uniqueness of solution relied on Arrow and Debreu's (1954) model. Next, he introduced money, thus facing the dichotomy and neutrality issues and the so-called Patinkin controversy. In this context Modigliani also discussed the case of an elasticity of price expectations different from unity, only mentioned in the 1944 dissertation, and the indeterminacy of price level in Hicks's (1939) and Mosak's (1944) models.

The second part of Modigliani's notes is entirely devoted to the system dynamics under the hypothesis of rigid and flexible wages and prices where the Pigou effect and the non-unit elasticity of expectations are analyzed.

Modigliani acknowledged that in the long-run equilibrium the price ratios are determined by the agents' preferences and the quantity and distribution of physical resources, whereas the general level of price is determined by the quantity of money. He also added that these propositions hold for the short run as well if the effects on the aggregate demand of a redistribution of initial cash balances cancel out. Otherwise, as already demonstrated by Patinkin (1948), "prices and price ratios will be affected also by the distribution of cash balances and cannot be determined exclusively from the real equations of the system" (1955, p. 21, also see Béraud 2018, p. 5). In other words, Modigliani remarked that Patinkin's introduction of money in the general equilibrium system rested on the assumption that changes in the redistribution of initial cash balances, due to arbitrary changes in money supply, affects the aggregate demand for commodities. By contrast, "if we are willing to assume enough similarity of tastes" of all individuals, the redistribution effects cancel out: "those who loose reduce their consumption as much as those who gain increase it". Consequently, the equilibrium price ratios are still determined exclusively by the real equations of the system, and the classical dichotomy still holds.

After having "fully vindicated" the validity of the classical theory, Modigliani began the discussion of the cases in which it is not confirmed. He first introduced the distinction between money bank only, non-money bank only, and of a mixed economy partly anticipating Gurley and Shaw's inside and outside money analysis (1960; also see Mehrling 2011, Chapter 3 and 4), under the hypothesis of price flexibility and unit elasticity of expectations, to assess the Pigou effect and the conditions for the existence and stability of the equilibrium.[13]

Modigliani showed that with pure banking money only and no government, both neutrality and dichotomy are valid, and the only role of the monetary part of the system is to determine the price level. Moreover, the Keynesian contention that the system might not possess a position of equilibrium is also valid when the equilibrium interest rate is negative or below the interest floor (1955, pp. 20–27, also see 1963, pp. 84–87).

If the money supply consists entirely of non-bank money and there is no other form of national debt, then money is neutral, but the dichotomy breaks down; that is, the equilibrium value of real variables is independent of the money supply but not of the demand for money, in accordance with Patinkin's conclusions (1955, pp. 27–33; also see 1963, p. 87).

Finally, in a mixed money supply economy, neither the dichotomy nor the neutrality hold, with the price level that affects demand through wealth (the Pigou effect), and real variables are also influenced by the composition of the money stock (between bank and non-bank), as recognized by L. Metzler (1951). However, both appear to Modigliani "shaky" concepts that can be of some interest "from the standpoint of the history of economic controversies" (1963, p. 88). Indeed Modigliani concluded the dichotomy and neutrality discussion arguing that "despite the unquestioned logical significance, from a more practical point of view one cannot escape the feeling that the Pigou effect is a mere technicality", and hence

for those situations in which the traditional Keynesian analysis neglecting the Pigou effect suggests the necessity of outside interventions in order to prevent the system from breaking down, such outside interventions would still appear desirable to prevent extreme fluctuations in the price level; and this is especially true if the elasticity of expectations of interest rates is close to zero or if prices expectations are elastic. . . . In conclusion, under normal conditions, the Pigou effect plays an insignificant role in the determination of equilibrium either in the short or in the long run. Under the pathological conditions where it is effective, it is foolish to rely on the Pigou effect for the determination of equilibrium.

(1955, p. 39)

Along with the validity of the classical analysis under the hypothesis of flexible prices, unit elastic expectations, Modigliani also discussed the case in which the equilibrium prices require a negative interest rate, or below the interest floor, and analyzed in depth the role of expectations for the existence and stability of equilibrium (1955, pp. 33–39).

Already in the 1944 article, Modigliani discussed the Keynesian case (i.e., the liquidity trap), and in the dissertation, he mentioned the case of elastic price expectations in which an initial fall in prices may lead to the expectations of further reduction with cumulative and depressive effects on profit expectations and, thus, on investment – an argument he used against wage reduction policy (see Chapter 2). In the "Preliminary Notes", both arguments are further developed. While in 1944, Modigliani defined the Keynesian case a situation in which the system is overdetermined, in 1955 the problem became that of the existence of equilibrium (on this different perspective see Béraud 2018, pp. 10–13).

Modigliani remarked that the system solution requires "one very important qualification", namely, that the elasticity of expectations must not exceed unity or equivalently the equilibrium rate of interest must be nonnegative (1955, pp. 23–24). If this condition is not satisfied, "the overall system will have no solution at all because a negative value of interest rate is inconsistent with the money equation" (p. 24). As prices fall (approaching zero), the real cash balances rise absolutely and relatively to the unchanged volume of real transaction, and the rate of interest falls. However, "no matter how large the liquidity of the economy the rate of interest can never become negative . . . for owners of wealth will prefer to hold wealth in the form of cash rather than in a form that is less safe and less liquid unless it yields some income" (pp. 25–26).

The nonexistence of a solution is deeply analyzed in a section concerning "[S]ome remarks in the behavior of the system with elasticity of expectations of prices different from unity" (1955, p. 40). Modigliani showed that in the case of bank money only and zero elasticity of interest rate expectations, if the elasticity of price expectations is minor than one unit – that is, people believe that price change is only temporary – there will be one and only one solution. A rise in current prices tends to reduce the excess demand through the substitution effect (people postpone their consumption). However, as Béraud noticed, Modigliani did not demonstrate such a proposition (see Béraud 2018, p. 26).

When the elasticity of expectations is unity – that is, price change is perceived as permanent – the substitution effect disappears, as in Hicks's (1939) temporary equilibrium.[14] Thus, according to Modigliani, the only stabilizing force is "the very roundabout mechanism through the discount rate" (p. 41). Modigliani acknowledged that under this situation

> one of the important mechanism that are supposed to equate the current demand with the current supply, namely the mechanism of substitution over time via the ratio of current to future discount prices, must rely entirely for its functioning on variation in the rate of interest. Under this condition it is quite conceivable that a *negative* rate of interest might be required in order to clear all the current markets. But from the point of view of the money and bond market, it is impossible to have negative rate of interest. . . . Hence, if *r* is negative, this system will have no solution.

(1955, p. 64)

Modigliani remarked that the difficult disappears only if: a) the elasticity of price expectations is less than unity or b) if there exists fiat money . . . which gives rise to the Pigou effect and the elasticity of price expectations is not too large (p. 66).

Under price expectations larger than one unit, a rise in price that is expected will continue in the future lead to a rise of the actual demand, and the system becomes unstable. Modigliani specified the system dynamics through a graphical analysis showing that it depends on the prices-discount rate relationship (with the latter inversely related to interest rate). To reach an equilibrium position, the interest rate should rise (and the discount rate to fall), and the system may not have an equilibrium solution:

> We can have situations in which there is no equilibrium position to reach . . . or even if it exists the initial conditions prevent the system to reach it, rather it will move away from it and the result is a continuous fall in prices.

(1955, p. 48)

Modigliani's conclusion goes, next, in the direction of de Scitovszky (1941) on the stability role of price rigidity as he had already mentioned in 1944, in the correspondence with Patinkin, and his classes on mathematical economics in which he pointed out that a wage deflation policy would worsen the situation because a corresponding decline in consumption and, thus, in entrepreneurs' expectations and, therefore, investments:

> If changes in the wage rate are allowed . . . you can have full employment. Let wages fall. Then income will fall and less money will be needed for

transaction. More money will then be available for investment, the interest rate will fall, and investment will increase. The proposal that might be made on the basis of the preceding paragraph is that wages should be lowered in the time of downturn. This lowering of wages, however, cause a decline in consumption which may affect the expectations of potential investors. . . . A policy of lowering wages to fight recession must be seriously questioned.

(1952, "Notes in Mathematical Economics, III",
by W. Hartigan, W. Holter, MP)

Wage and price rigidity: unemployment and system stability

Modigliani introduced and discussed the case of price rigidity with reference either to Keynesian unemployment equilibrium and the existence of the system's solution, making clear the meaning and the role he ascribed to wage rigidity assumption that is of stabilizing the economy, also enlarging the perspective from nominal to real wage and price rigidity.

First, he defined downward price rigidity as a situation in which "the price is not permitted to fall below the level p even though at this price there exists an excess supply in the market for the *ith* commodity" (1955, p. 68). According to him, it follows that $f_0{}^j$ represents the quantity the $j'th$ individual actually succeeded in selling "*which may be less than the quantity he intends to sell, because there is excess supply in the labor market*", with "current demand that depends on current employment" (1955, pp. 70–71, emphasis added). With this definition of price rigidity, Modigliani seems to anticipate Robert Clower's (1965) dual decision hypothesis and the distinction between notional and effective demand, according to which quantity constraints (i.e., realized transactions) affect adjustment in output, with full employment that becomes only a special case (on Clower's disequilibrium theory see Backhouse and Boianovsky 2013; Chapter 4; Béraud 2018, p. 29). However, Modigliani did not develop the implications of his argument in the 1963 article from which, on the contrary, it disappeared.

As in 1944, Modigliani's focal point was the (theoretically) equivalence of expansionary monetary policies and wage reduction as anti-depression measures, arguing that the rising of the real volume of money to lower the interest rate can be accomplished either by increasing the money stock or by decreasing money wage. He pointed out that "as for Keynes, they are equivalent . . . except for the great differences in their relative feasibility and political side effects" (1955, p. 89). He also returned, once more on the possibility of the nonexistence of a solution: if full employment income requires a negative interest rate, neither monetary policy nor wage policy would be capable of restoring full employment. On this ground, he remarked:

But although full employment is not reached . . . some unique and stable solution to the system will always exists, given M, as long as [wage] is constant. By contrast, there is no solution to this system if [wage] is a perfectly flexible price since the negative equilibrium interest rate implies ineradicable excess supplies in some markets. Wage rigidity, which leads to the emergence of unemployment, and hence to a fall in the level of real income serves to reduce the level of supplies faster than the fall in demand. Thus, there will be somewhere be an end, though not a very satisfactory one, to the process of cumulative deflation.

(1955, p. 90)

The last parts of Modigliani's "Preliminary Notes" are devoted to the cases in which some prices are rigid relative to wages, wage are rigid downward, and the Pigou effect under non-unit elasticity of expectations. As in his previous analysis of price expectations he showed that whenever the elasticity is less than unity, this effect works in the same direction as the Pigou effect: a fall in current prices will raise the level of expected future prices relative to the current ones, thereby encouraging consumption and investment. If, instead, the elasticity is larger than unity, the Pigou effect and the expectation effect work in opposite direction: a fall in prices encourages consumption via a rise of wealth but discourages consumption and investment via the expectations of further falls in prices. Thus, he concluded that "if price expectations are sufficiently elastic, wage reductions may not only be less effective but may actually have a perverse effect, reducing rather than raising income; monetary policy would then represent again the only way (except fiscal policy) of raising income and employment, despite the Pigou effect".

(1955, p. 130)

His analysis, Modigliani remarked, provides further reasons to support monetary policy as a more practical tool than wage-level manipulation: 1) there is no way to enforce wage cuts, whereas monetary policy is always within the power of government and monetary authority; 2) monetary policy is a more reliable tool (indeed, when government bonds and non-bank money represent a substantial fraction of aggregate net worth, it may also turn out to act in the wrong direction); 3) wage cuts may exert a significant deterrent effect on investment by redistributing income and wealth against risk taking, as already mentioned in the PhD dissertation.

Real wage rigidity: inflation and oligopoly

With respect the PhD dissertation and the 1944 article, Modigliani also discussed real wage rigidity by referring to the example of the Italian minimum wage legislation, in which neither monetary policy nor fiscal policy succeeded in reducing unemployment (1955, p. 104). An increase of money supply only leads to a rise of money wages without affecting real variables, whereas government spending only drives up interest rates. Therefore, Modigliani pointed out, the only solution is to raise labor productivity.[15]

His discussion of real wage rigidity is strictly related to cost-push and demand-pull inflation analysis. Modigliani defined cost-push inflation a situation in which the upper bound on the level of real output is set by full employment in the labor market, despite the existence of unused plant capacity. Once it has been reached, further expansion of aggregate demand and expanding output bids up wages and, then, prices because of the rise of costs. On the other hand, the upper limit may be set by a shortage of productive capacity with considerable manpower still available. Expansion of money demand after this point would lead first to a sharp rise in commodity prices, a rise that is soon be followed by demand for higher wages to compensate for the increase in the cost of living.[16]

Modigliani finally mentioned the case of oligopolistic markets and markup, which he examined more in depth in the1963 article in which firms' price-setting behavior was analyzed on the basis of the so-called Bain–Sylos–Labini–Modigliani model he developed in the late 1950s (see Modigliani 1958; also see Rancan 2015).

Modigliani's preliminary notes remained unpublished. The most relevant content was then summarized in Modigliani's (1963) article he delivered at a conference Lee Bach organized at Carnegie in 1962 on monetary economics, when Modigliani was leaving for Northwestern University to join, a year later, MIT. The 1963 article was the departure point for the specification of the macroeconometric model, whose building and development absorbed Modigliani (along with Ando and a number of PhD students) from the late 1960s through the 1970s.

Notes

1 Also see Modigliani (2001, pp. 51, 57–59), where he remarked that he and Brumberg were challenging the idea that savings rise with a rise of income and that savings is a luxury good that accumulate in patrimony.
2 Also see Robert Eisner (1956, 1961), who was working on the project.
3 In his reply Modigliani mentioned Christ, Klein, Duesenberry and Brown among people who had already read the paper.
4 Modigliani claimed to have done little to revise the essay, however adding that three of his lectures in Italy had been devoted to that area of work: "Incidentally my lectures on the subject have been very well received – of course not everybody is ready to accept the word but even those that don't are sufficiently stirred up about it to make feel good" (Modigliani to Stroz, May 16 1954, MP).
5 The possibility of carrying out empirical tests was at that time the main problem for the life cycle hypothesis because the lack of data providing joint information on age, assets (net worth) and average expected income; therefore, they were most of the time only indirect. Regarding Reid's tests, Modigliani and Brumberg referred to a communication she provided at a 1952 conference at Minnesota on "Savings, Inflation and Economic Progress", which Modigliani also mentioned in the autobiography. Modigliani recalled that when going back from the conference with Brumberg, they "were rewarded with

a ray of light": the role of savings is to accumulate resources to maintain a stable average consumption over the life span (Modigliani 2001, p. 59).

6 On this, also see Modigliani's letter to Sylos Labini in 1956.

7 Modigliani and Brumberg also referred again, as in the1954 article, to the unrecorded comments of Brady, and the contributions of William Hamburger (1951) and James Tobin (1947) in their unpublished PhD dissertations on consumption and savings at the University of Chicago and at the University of Harvard, respectively. On Tobin's dissertation see Dimand (2014, Chapter 3).

8 Ando and Modigliani had already published in 1957 some tests on the life cycle hypothesis and in 1960 a comparison with Friedman's (1957) theory of permanent income. Important implications of the life cycle hypothesis for macroeconomics referred to the incorporation of finite lifetime models; the consumption and savings life cycle model also played a seminal role for the building of the overlapping generation approach to modeling as in the case of Allais, Samuelson and Dimand (see Barnett and Solow 2000, p. 222).

9 See for example Eisner's (1969) analysis of the weak effect of the 1968 surcharge tax on inflation because it was provisional.

10 As Modigliani wrote to Sylos Labini, they were "a set of notes covering a dozen lessons from my last year classes, which serve as an introduction to a kind of general treatise on the theory of money and interest, written partly before the course and partly based on the course itself, and which constitutes the starting point of what I hope will be a book on the subject" (Modigliani to Sylos Labini: September 14, 1956, MP).

11 In an unpublished reply to Hahn's (1955) critique to the "Liquidity Preference" article, Modigliani remarked that his model was not stated in general equilibrium language "as it become fashionable since the time of its appearance", however, recognizing that he went further in that direction (undated, MP).

12 "I must add that the plan to proceed systematically with the analysis of the effect of market forms on employment according to the lines drawn in Rome still exists but I have to continue to postpone it due to other previous commitments. We will come back to talk about it at the right time" (Modigliani to Sylos Labini: September 14, 1956, MP).

13 Apparently Modigliani's discussion of different kinds of money supply was independent from Gurley and Shaw. Commenting Modigliani's early draft of the 1963 article, Patinkin pointed out the similarity between Modigliani's and Gurley and Shaw's distinction and called Modigliani's attention to their volume, which Modigliani then quoted in the 1963 article (Patinkin to Modigliani: May 2, 1962, MP).

14 Modigliani devoted a section to Hicks's (1939) and Mosak's (1944) dynamic general equilibrium analysis and the indeterminacy of price level under unit elasticity of price expectations. According to him, the problem arises because they fixed the interest rate and, therefore, the system became overdetermined: "regardless of the elasticity of expectations if the interest rate (or any other variable) is fixed arbitrary it is of course impossible to clear all markets" (1955, p. 56).

15 Modigliani had spent the first six months of 1955 in Italy, where he discussed at some length with Sylos Labini about market structures and Keynesian unemployment and the role of rigidities (see their correspondence).

16 As showed by Boianovsky and Trautwein (2006), the "prehistory" literature on the relation between the employment level and inflation was extensive in the 1940s and 1950s, pre-announcing the advent and the standard interpretation of the Phillips curve.

References

Ando, K. A. 1959. *A Contribution to the Theory of Economic Fluctuations and Growth (1959)*, PhD Dissertation, Carnegie Tech.

————. 1974. "Some Aspects of Stabilization Policies, the Monetarist Controversy, and the MPS Model", *International Economic Review*, 15 (3): 541–571.

Ando, A., and F. Modigliani. 1957. "Tests of the Life Cycle Hypothesis of Savings: Comments and Suggestions", *Bulletin of the Oxford University Institute of Statistics*: 99–124.

————. 1959. "Growth, Fluctuations and Stability." *American Economic Review*, 49 (2): 501–524.

————. 1960. "The 'Permanent Income' and the 'Life Cycle Hypothesis' of Saving Behavior: Comparison and Tests", in *Consumption and Saving*, vol. 2, Wharton School of Finance and Commerce, Philadephia: University of Pennsylvania, 74–108.

————. 1963. "The 'Life Cycle' Hypothesis of Savings: Aggregate Implications and Tests", *American Economic Review*, 33 (1), part 1: 55–84.

Arrow, K., and G. Debreu. 1954. "Existence of an Equilibrium for a Competitive Economy", *Econometrica*, 22 (3): 265–290.

Backhouse, R. E., and M. Boianovsky. 2013. *Transforming Modern Macroeconomics. Exploring Disequilibrium Microfoundations, 1956–2003*, Cambridge, New York: Cambridge University Press.

Bain, J. S. 1956. *Barriers to New Competition*, Cambridge, MA: Harvard University Press.

Barnett W. A., and R. Solow. 2000, "An Interview with Franco Modigliani November 5–6 1999", *Macroeconomic Dynamics*, 4: 222–256.

Béraud, A. 2018. "Modigliani et la question de l'existence d'un équilibre dans un modèle à prix flexible", *HAL archives-ouvertes.fr.* 1–38.

Boianovsky, M., and H.-M. Trautwein. 2006. "Price Expectations, Capital Accumulation and Employment: Lindahl's Macroeconomics from the 1920s to the 1950s", *Cambridge Journal of Economics, 30* (6): 881–900.

Brady D., Rose D. Friedman, 1947. "Savings and the Income Distribution", *Studies in Income and Wealth*, National Bureau of Economic Research, New York: 247–265.

Clower, R. 1965. "The Keynesian Counterrevolution: A Theoretical Appraisal", in *Theory of Interest Rates*, ed. by F. H. Hahn and F. P. R. Brechling, London: Macmillan.

Dimand, R. W. 2014. *James Tobin*, U. K. Palgrave Macmillan.

de Scitovszky, T. 1941. "Capital Accumulation, Employment and Price Rigidity", *Review of Economic Studies*, 8 (2): 69–88.

Duarte, P. G., and G. T. Lima, eds. 2012. *Microfoundations Reconsidered: The Relationship of Micro and Macroeconomics in Historical Perspective*, Edward Elgar Cheltenam (UK) and Northampton (US).

Duesenberry, J. S. 1949. *Income, Savings and the Theory of Consumer Behavior*, Cambridge, MA: Harvard University Press.

Eisner, R. 1956. "Determinants of Capital Expenditures: An Interview Study", in *Bureau of Economics and Business Research*, University of Illinois.

————. 1961. "Interview and Other Survey Techniques in the Study of Investment", in *Problems of Capital Formation*, Princeton, NJ: Princeton University Press.

————. 1969. "Fiscal and Monetary Policy Reconsidered", *American Economic Review*, 59 (5): 897–905.

Fisher, S. 1988. "Recent Developments in Macroeconomics", *Economic Journal*, 98 (391): 294–339.

Friedman, M. 1957. *A Theory of the Consumption Function*, Princeton: Princeton University Press.

Gurley, J. G., and E. S. Shaw. 1960. *Money in a Theory of Finance*, Washington: The Brookings Institutions.

Hahn, F., 1955. "The Rate of Interest and General Equilibrium Analysis", *Economic Journal*, 65 (257), 52–66.

Hamburger, W. 1951. *Consumption and Wealth*, unpublished PhD dissertation, University of Chicago.

Hicks, J. 1939. *Value and Capital: An Inquiry into Some Fundamental Principles of Economic Theory*, Oxford: Oxford University Press.

Mehrling, P. 2011. *The New Lombard Street: How the Fed Became the Dealer of Last Resort*, Princeton, NJ: Princeton University Press.

Metzler, L. A. 1951. "Wealth, Savings and the Rate of Interest", *Journal of Political Economy*, 59 (2): 93–116.

Modigliani (Franco) Papers. David M. Rubenstein Rare Book and Manuscript Library, Duke University.

Modigliani, F. 1944a. "Liquidity Preference and the Theory of Interest and Money", *Econometrica*, 12, January: 45–88.

———. 1944b. *The General Theory of Employment, Interest and Money under the Assumptions of Flexible Prices and of Fixed Prices*, Thesis, Doctorate for Social Science New School for Social Research, Franco Modigliani Papers.

———. 1947. "L'Organizzazione e la Direzione della Produzione in un'Economia Socialista," *Giornali degli Economisti e Annali di Economia*, 6: 441–514.

———. 1949. "Fluctuations in the Saving- Income Ratio: A Problem in Economic Forecasting," *Studies in Income and Wealth*, National Bureau of Economic Research, no. 11, New York: 371–441.

———. 1955. "Theory of Money and Interest in the Framework of the General Equilibrium Analysis. Preliminary Notes", Franco Modigliani Papers.

———. 1958. "New Developments on the Oligopoly Front", *Journal of Political Economy*, 66 (3), June: 215–232.

———. 1963. "The Monetary Mechanism and Its Interaction with Real Phenomena", *The Review of Economics and Statistics*, 45 (1), Part 2, Supplement, February: 79–107.

———. 1975. "The Life-Cycle Hypothesis of Savings Twenty Years Later", in *Contemporary Issues in Economics*, ed. by M. Parkin and A. R. Nobay, Manchester: Manchester University Press.

———. 1980. *The Life Cycle Hypothesis of Saving.* Vol. 2. *The Collected 812 Papers of Franco Modigliani*, 6 vols, Cambridge MA: MIT Press.

———. 1986. "Life Cycle, Individual Thrift, and the Wealth of Nations", *American Economic Review*, 76 (3): 297–313.

———. 2001. *Adventure of an Economist*, New York, London: Texere.

Modigliani, F., and R. Brumberg. 1953 (1980). "Utility Analysis and Aggregate Consumption Functions: An Attempt at Integrating", in *The Collected Papers of Franco Modigliani, Vol. 2: The Life Cycle Hypothesis of Saving*, Cambridge, MA: MIT Press.

———. 1953. *Utility Analysis and Aggregate Consumption Functions: An Attempt at Integrating*, Franco Modigliani Papers.

———. 1954. "Utility Analysis and the Consumption Function: An Interpretation of Cross-Sectional Data", in *Post Keynesian Economics*, ed. by K. K. Kurhiara, New Brunswick: Rutgers University Press.

Modigliani, F., and F. E. Hohn. 1952. "Solutions to Certain Problems of Production Planning over Time Illustrating the Effect of Inventory Constraints", Appendix to Cowles Commission Paper, Economics No 2038, April.

———. 1955. "Planning Over Time and the Nature of the Expectations and Planning Horizon", *Econometrica*, 23 (1): 46–66.

Mosak, J. 1944. *General Equilibrium Theory in International Trade*, Bloomington: Principia Press.

Ohlin, B. 1937. "Some Notes on the Stockholm Theory of Savings and Investment", *Economic Journal*, 47 (185): 53–69.

Patinkin, D. 1948. "Price Flexibility and Full Employment", *American Economic Review*, 38 (4): 543–564.

———. 1956 (1965). *Money Interests and Prices: An Integration of Monetary and Value Theory*, 2nd ed., New York: Harper & Row.

Rancan, A. 2014. "Modigliani's Comments on Sylos Labini's Theory of Unemployment (1956–58)", *PSL Quarterly Review*, 67: 269–282.

———. 2015. "The Origin of the Sylos Postulate: Modigliani's and Sylos Labini's Contributions to Oligopoly Theory", *Journal for the History of Economic Thought*, September: 431–448, Cambridge University Press.

———. 2019. "Income Distribution, Consumption, and Economic Growth in Italy: Kaldor's Theory *versus* the Life Cycle Hypothesis (1960s–1970s)", *History of Political Economy*, 51 (5): 867–900.

———. 1950. "Effect of Income Concept upon Expenditure Curves of Farm Families", *Conference on Research in Income and Wealth*, 15: 131, 174.

Sylos Labini, P. 1956. *Oligopolio e Progresso Tecnico*, Milano: Giuffré.

Szenberg, M., and L. Ramrattan. 2008. *Franco Modigliani a Mind That Never Rests*, Palgrave Macmillan.

Tobin, J. 1947. A Theoretical and Statistical Analysis of Consumer Savings, unpublished PhD dissertation, Harvard University.

7 Becoming Keynesian

Introduction

In his autobiography Modigliani recalled that at the end of 1959 he was invited to spend a research period at MIT as visiting professor, but the Carnegie administration was against it, also adding that he had the impression that the administration did not intend to invest resources in the economics sector, "To my dismay, they decided not to replace an excellent economist, Alexander Henderson, who had worked alongside me" (2001, p. 91).

But, above all, behind Modigliani's decision to leave the Carnegie Institute, there was his desire to come back to more traditional researches. In a letter to Luigi Pasinetti, Modigliani explained that he wanted to be part of a "wider department of economics, more traditional in its interests, and to be more free in the courses to offer and the researches to carry out" (January 31, 1960, MP). Jaques Drèze, his student at Carnegie, also recalled that his impression at the time was simply "that Modigliani wanted to pursue his career in a department of economics (hopefully MIT) rather than a business school" (Letter to the author, September 3, 2010).[1]

It is with his arrival at MIT, in 1962, that the image of Modigliani as a Keynesian took fully shape. The 1944 article provided to the young Modigliani wide prominence among leading economists and was influential in subsequent interpretations of Keynes's theory. Nonetheless, Modigliani did not publish anything else on classical and Keynesian economics in the following fifteen years, that is, until the publication of the 1963 article on the monetary interactions with real phenomena. The only exception is the article with Albert Ando on economic growth and fluctuations (Ando and Modigliani 1959), an outgrowth of Ando's PhD dissertation, in which they explained business cycles by looking at rigidities and market imperfections. The article, however, went quite unnoticed. Modigliani lengthy "Preliminary Notes on the Theory of Money", which represented his major effort to develop Keynesian economics along the lines of the 1944 article, remained in fact unpublished, although circulated among a few colleagues (see his correspondence with Luigi Pasinetti, Patinkin and Sylos Labini).

According to Paul Samuelson (1987), Modigliani's 1944 article set the basis for the subsequent microfoundational program of Keynesian economics:

"[Modigliani] wrote a seminal article setting Model-T Keynesianism on its modern evolutionary path and probing its microfoundations in rigid, nonmarket clearing prices" (p. 29). However, at that time Modigliani only assumed wage rigidity as a realistic assumption, eventually explained by historical or institutional reasons without providing any theoretical basis for the labor market behavior. It will be only with the challenge to the price and unemployment long-run trade-off (Friedman's 1968; Phelps's 1967, 1968 critiques of the Phillips curve) that a search for proper microfoundations of this sector eventually began. Modigliani's contributions to the microfoundations of macroeconomics mainly came, in the 1950s and 1960s, within mainstream neoclassical economics, as in the case of the life cycle theory and the so-called Bain–Modigliani–Sylos Labini model of price setting in oligopolistic markets (Modigliani 1958, see Rancan 2015).

Perry Mehrling (2014), discussing postwar monetary economics at MIT, argued that Modigliani, who was the leading figure in the field, was never interested in providing theoretical foundations for the Keynesian or monetary theory. It was Tobin (1956, 1958) at Yale not Modigliani who took the lead for the Keynesian. Despite Modigliani's early interest in money, his research agenda took another direction in the late 1940s and 1950s. Modigliani himself acknowledged in the introduction to his *Collected Papers* (vol. 1 1980) that it was almost twenty years after the publication of the 1944 *Econometrica* article before he returned to work on this topic. His main interests were the life cycle theory and the Modigliani and Miller theorem, with the latter falling outside "traditional" Keynesian theory, for which he was awarded the Nobel Prize in 1985.

Only after Modigliani joined MIT did he turn his attention to monetary issues and Keynesian economics with the 1963 article and, more important, start a collaboration with the Federal Reserve Board to build its first macroeconometric model for the U.S. economy (the Fed–MIT–University of Pennsylvania model), which also involved a large number of scholars and PhD students.[2] The model later became identified with the mainstream Keynesian theory of the 1950s and 1960s. Oliver Blanchard's entry on the "Neoclassical Synthesis" refers to the model as its "apotheosis" because it embodied successfully most of the contributions of Keynesian economists such as Hicks, Solow, Tobin and Modigliani himself in "an empirically based and mathematically coherent model". According to Blanchard, "by the early 1970s the synthesis appeared to have been highly successful and the research program laid down after the war to have been mostly completed" (2008, pp. 635–636; see also Goodfriend and King 1997; Mankiw 1990 among others). Modigliani himself in his recollection looked at the 1960s as the "golden age of Keynesianism", having in mind Samuelson, Solow, Tobin, Haller and "others of their kind" (2001, p. 99).

Certainly, with the 1944 article and his focus on a monetary explanation and solution of involuntary unemployment, Modigliani placed himself among the few postwar Keynesians who ascribed a crucial role to the quantity of money rather than to real (investment) variables to explain economic fluctuations. As discussed (Chapter 2), Modigliani's close attention to monetary phenomena was to a large extent the result of his education at the New School and the influence exerted by Marschak (see Hagemann 2005; Dimand and Hagemann 2019) along with Lange and Lerner, Lowe and Neisser. Moreover, in the 1930s his approach to economics mainly came from his reading about price control and inflation (see Chapter 1). It is not a coincidence that Friedman in a seminar with Modigliani organized by the St. Louis Federal Reserve to discuss Modigliani's 1976 American Economic Association Presidential Address refers to Modigliani as a monetarist ante-litteram:

> I may say that I've always thought that Franco, insofar as you use these terms, has always been a monetarist, in very important ways. His famous 1944 paper certainly qualifies as a major element in the so-called monetarist structure.

(Friedman 1977, p. 12)[3]

Modigliani also labelled himself a monetarist, quoting from Friedman's newspaper heading: "We are all Keynesians, now". He said, "We are all monetarists", if it means to ascribe a crucial role to the quantity of money (Modigliani 1977a, p. 1).

Along with Modigliani, Markowitz (1952), Patinkin (1956) – also Marschak's students (see Dimand and Hagemann 2019; Mehrling 2002, 2010) – and Tobin were among the leading economists who attempted to introduce money in the Walrasian system of equations, thus reconciling neoclassical economics with Keynesian. They largely contributed to establish the postwar mainstream that Mehrling (1998, p. 204) labels "monetary Walrasianism" – Walrasian because the economy was represented by a set of simultaneous equations and monetary because one set of equations referred to the demand for and supply of money.[4]

According to Mehrling (2014), it was precisely because of Modigliani's focus on money that Samuelson wanted him at MIT. For Samuelson Friedman's monetarism was more about engineering than science as it was Friedman's claim about discretionary policy versus rules.[5] This was the approach Modigliani also pursued. Differently from Patinkin and Tobin, he was less interested in providing foundations to Keynesian monetary theory and much more concerned with its policy implications. As Merhling further noticed, "after all, on the scientific fundamentals of the theory of money there was no really difference between Samuelson and Friedman" (2014, p. 183). The same is even truer for Modigliani, who explicitly acknowledged it in the 1977 seminar with Friedman on the Keynesian and monetarist dispute:

> Well, let me first say that the conclusion of my work is very clear: namely, that there are no significant differences of analysis between able, intelligent, open-minded monetarists and non-monetarists. . . . It seems to me that the framework is the same, . . . Then the question is: Where is the main source of difference?

Modigliani answered that they are on value judgments and confidence on policy makers (1977a, pp. 6–7).[6] Samuelson had positioned MIT as the anti-monetarist school and, therefore, he needed someone to defend and support this position, along with the Keynesian policy agenda, someone "serving as the public face of MIT's view on money for the next generation. Modigliani would fill both the inside and the outside roles" (see Mehrling 2014, pp. 184–185).

Modigliani at MIT

Modigliani had visited MIT in 1960, then he joined Northwestern University with the agreement that he would move to MIT the following year, where he would remain for the rest of his career.

In 1962 Modigliani attended a symposium Lee Bach[7] organized at Carnegie on monetary economics, sponsored by the National Bureau Committee. The conference was devoted to reexamine the role of money and monetary policy in economic growth and fluctuations. It was organized into two sessions: one to devoted to theoretical issues, the other to policy issues. The former session hosted Friedman and Anna Schwartz, who anticipated the results of their forthcoming monumental study on U.S. monetary history (Friedman and Schwartz 1963a), James Duesenberry, with a paper on portfolio theory and Modigliani who discussed the paper on monetary interactions with real phenomena. The other session discussed the reports of the Commission on Money and Credit (see Bach 1963, p. 3).

At the center of the theoretical debate, there was Friedman and Schwartz's empirical study devoted to provide factual evidence on the crucial role of money stock in business fluctuations rather than changes of autonomous expenditures.[8] However, they only sketch the channels through which changes of money supply affect the real economy by referring to its direct influence on prices (through the cash balances effect the and real assets substitution) rather than through changes of interest rates, as stated by the Keynesians. Friedman and Schwartz admitted to having "little confidence" in their knowledge of the transmission monetary mechanism, concluding that this was "the challenge our evidence poses: to pin down the transmission mechanism *in specific enough detail*" (1963b, p. 55 emphasis added).

The need for empirical research on monetary channels was acknowledged by all participants at the symposium.[9] Bach also remarked that Friedman and Schwartz's rediscovery of money, along with the agreement that seems to emerge among economists on the portfolio approach to the demand for money, could lead to a rapprochement of the monetarist and Keynesian views (1963, pp. 3–4).

A possible integration of Friedman's quantity theory with the Keynesian analysis was discussed by Modigliani in the paper he presented at the same session. Although Modigliani's (1963) article is especially known as an updated version of his early 1944 Keynesian model, as Modigliani himself introduced it, its second part is devoted to the monetarists' debate and stabilization policies.[10] He analyzed the modus operandi of monetary and fiscal policy through the standard IS-LM apparatus, focusing on the role of money through changes in interest rates. In the last section of the article, Modigliani rejected Friedman and Meiselman's (1963) "dichotomy" between the income-expenditure model and the quantity theory of money (read as a demand for money), arguing that the two might be integrated through the recognition that money affects income through both changes in the demand for money and a reduction of the cost of capital (see also Ando and Modigliani's 1965 reply to Friedman and Meiselman's 1963 paper).[11]

Modigliani's (1963) IS-LM model became the theoretical framework underlying the Federal Reserve Board, MIT and University of Pennsylvania macroeconometric model (FMP), integrated by a modified Solow's neoclassical growth model to examine the system's dynamics towards a steady state.

The origin of the Fed-MIT-Penn model

The Keynesian and monetarist debate peaked with Friedman and Meiselman's (1963) challenge to the Keynesian income expenditure model and Friedman and Schwartz's (1963a) empirical demonstration of the crucial role of money to explain economic fluctuations. Friedman's emphasis on the role of money contributed to revitalize the field of monetary economics and the monetary policy debate over the 1960s. Postwar Keynesian skepticism towards money had confined monetary policy to the subordinate role of accommodating fiscal policy by committing to support the prices of government securities through a low and stable interest rate (the so-called peg era). The 1951 Treasury-Fed accord represented a first step to liberate the monetary authority from the Treasury policy with the Federal Reserve that regained its control over interest rates (Mehrling 2011, pp. 54–55; also see Stein 1969, p. 277; Hetzel 2008; Meltzer 2003).

In 1955 Samuelson, in his testimony before the Joint Economic Committee, supported a fiscal and monetary policy mix: easy money to stimulate investment and budget surpluses to provide the savings to sustain economic growth and full employment (Stein 1969, p. 363). The same year, at the joint meeting of the American Economic Association and the American Financial Association, the New York Fed explicitly endorsed the goals of the 1946 Employment Act, pointing out the importance of the Federal Reserve for achieving them, and asked for academic help: "your study and your published finding" (quoted from Mehrling 2011, p. 56).[12] The economic advisers of the Kennedy administration (Galbraith, Harris, Samuelson and Tobin) believed that the economic problem was to achieve high and rapid economic growth to maintain full employment through fiscal and monetary policy "with the former being the senior partner in the combination". As noticed by Stein (1969, p. 382), once monetary policy had been reincorporated into Keynesians' thinking, the distinction between Keynesians and non-Keynesians ceased to be relevant. As Friedman stated in the mid-1960s, "We are all Keynesians now and nobody is any longer a Keynesians" (*Time*, December, 1965, p. 65, quoted in Stein 1969, pp. 381–382). A consensus on the effects of monetary and fiscal policy on aggregate demand and the level of money income, at least in the short run, seemed to emerge. Thus, in the 1960s money mattered again, and the issue became that of integrating "the new appreciation of money with the largest institutional and intellectual framework of macroeconomics" (Mehrling 2011, p. 60).Once the importance of money for the economic activity was accepted, what remained to understand was the mechanisms through which it influenced real variables. The increasing attention to monetary issues, along with the rising of inflation since 1966, required a rigorous approach to monetary policy that explains the Fed Board's search for closer relationships with academia. To identify the channels and to estimate the impact of monetary policies on aggregate demand was the main objective of the Fed–MIT–Penn macroeconometric model.

In 1964 the Federal Reserve Chairman, William McChesney Martin, asked Bach to arrange a series of informal discussions on monetary economics among a small group of academic monetary economists and the Federal Reserve Board. Thus, in 1964 the Fed Board established the so-called academic consultants meetings, which were expected to replicate the Treasury consultant meetings launched by Seymour Harris in 1960. Bach arranged the meetings, explaining to Modigliani that

> [t]he Board feels that has not active contacts with academic economists. While this plan has some parallel with the Treasury Consultants' meetings . . . the discussion more sharply focused on issues which are of direct responsibility of the Board, to discuss immediate current policy issues and some major issues of analysis and policy.

(Bach to Modigliani: November 1963, MP)

Each of the three annual sessions was devoted to analyze the Economic Report of the President and the outlook for the subsequent year, especially with reference to its implications for monetary policy, with discussions that should be on practical rather than technical issues because, as Bach explained to Modigliani, at the Board "they are rather allergic to what they consider theoretical and up with clouds discussion" (Bach to Modigliani: January 8, 1964, MP).

Over the 1960s and 1970s both Keynesian economists like James Duesenberry, Arthur M. Okun, Samuelson and Modigliani, and monetarists like Friedman and Allan Meltzer, regularly attended the meetings.

Around the same time, at the Fed Division of Research and Statistics, Modigliani and Chairman Martin launched an empirical seminar series for better coordination of empirical research (Robert C. Holland to Modigliani: January 20, 1964, MP). Martin advocated for these empirical seminars to become regular "for a better understanding of our problems and, I hope, for a better formulation of our monetary policy" (Martin to Modigliani: February 4, 1964, MP). Both the empirical seminars and the academic consultants meetings reinforced the relationships between the Fed Board and academic monetary economists and probably represented the foundational gatherings for the design and the building of the Fed–MIT–Penn econometric model (on this see Rancan 2019, pp. 450–456). Modigliani recalled (2001) in 1964 the Fed Board asked him to build an econometric model for the U.S. economy for forecasting and economic policy purposes (also see Bodkin et al. 1991, Chapter 4; Szenberg and Ramrattan 2008 Chapter 6). The model was completed in 1970 with the collaboration of Albert Ando and a number of PhD students and economists both from the academia and from the Fed Board, and was operative until the mid-1990s (Szenberg and Ramrattan 2008, Chapter 6; also see Brayton and Mauskopf 1987).[13]

The Fed Board wanted the model to be conceived and understood as an independent tool of economic policy that did not reflect the Fed Board's view. Therefore, it financed the project through the Social Science Research Council (SSRC), which had to coordinate the work around a common research project, with the implicit assurance that the council entrusted the project to MIT under Modigliani's direction (Modigliani 2001, p. 101).[14]

The model was, thus, the outgrowth of a research team formed by academic economists and professional economists from the Fed Board, under Modigliani's, Ando's and Frank de Leeuw's (from the Fed Board) supervision. Their aim was to provide the Fed Board with an econometric model to guide the monetary discretionary policy through a qualitative and quantitative study of the mechanisms through which monetary and fiscal actions influenced aggregate demand (Modigliani SSRC research project, 1966, MP). The model changed names, along with its sponsors, from FRB–MIT to FMP (Fed–MIT–Penn) with the inclusion of Albert Ando from the University of Pennsylvania and finally MPS (MIT–Penn–SSRC), with the disappearance of the Fed Board's name at the end of its financial support in 1970 with the delivering of the model. As for the academic side of the research, the model was then assigned to Wharton Econometric Forecasting Associates, which became responsible for its maintenance (updating) and distribution to universities and other public institutions and to private organizations (see Ando's reports in MP).

The Fed-MIT-Penn (FMP) econometric model was especially conceived to analyze and quantify the impact of stabilization actions with half of its behavioral equations containing fiscal and monetary policy variables (it was the model with the largest number of policy variables). In particular, as Modigliani stated in the research project he submitted to the SSRC, the focus should have been on the channels linking the monetary and real sectors, with reference "to the ways, the intensity and the effectiveness by which changes in monetary variables affect the effective demand and its components" and the their spread over time (Modigliani 1966; MP). Its departure point should have been the Brookings model (1965–1969), particularly the financial sector. Another important source of inspiration was Stephen Goldfeld's econometric model (1966), an outgrowth of his PhD dissertation at MIT where the crucial role of commercial banks behavior in the monetary transmission mechanism was emphasized.

Due to its large scale the building of the FMP model was organized around research areas, each one assigned to members of the research team, formed by a large number of scholars, especially PhD students (Modigliani's "informal group" as he labeled it in the project). Charles Bischoff was the main responsible for the investment sector, whose model was an outgrowth of his dissertation on the "Study of Distributed Lags and Business Fixed Investments" (1968); Richard Sutch was responsible for the financial sector (PhD 1968, see also Modigliani and Sutch 1966, 1967); George de Menil also earned his PhD in 1968 with a dissertation on wage determination and was responsible for the building of the wage and price sector. Dwight Yaffe discussed a dissertation on "Credit Rationing and the Commercial Loan Market" in 1968 and was responsible for this sector. Robert Shiller contributed to the financial sector, after 1970, with a theory on the determination of real interest rates that incorporated price expectations (see Modigliani and Shiller 1973). It was an outgrowth of his dissertation on "Rational Expectations and the Structure of Interest Rates" (1972).[15] Robert Rasche from the University of Pennsylvania was Ando's closest assistant and the man responsible for computational and organizational aspects. After 1968, Arnold Zellner (from the University of Chicago) collaborated with Ando for the implementation of simulation programs.

From the Fed Board the economists most involved in the research were Edward Gramlich, Robert Enzler and Frank de Leeuw. Ando was especially concerned with the real sector and the impact of fiscal policy, on which he had worked for the Brookings model and the Commission for Money and Credit, whereas Modigliani and de Leeuw were devoted to the design of the financial sector. They were all responsible for the entire structure of the model. Modigliani and Ando supervised each contribution both from academia and from the Fed Board and, as appeared from their correspondence and Ando's several reports and memoranda, he was the main responsible in organizing and coordinating the research teamwork. The model estimations and simulations were carried out contemporaneously at the University of Pennsylvania (under Ando and Rasche's responsibility) and at the Fed Board by de Leeuw and Gramlich.[16]

The macroeconometric model was not only applied by the Fed Board for a qualitative and quantitative understanding of the working of stabilization policies, and to forecast, but also became the tool by which Ando and Modigliani engaged with the struggle against the monetarists contentions, particularly Friedman and Schwartz (1963a, 1963b), Friedman and Meiselman (1963) and the St. Louis econometric models' empirical results (Andersen and Jordan 1968). Modigliani relied on its estimates in his American Economic Association presidential address devoted to the monetarist and the Keynesian controversy and to challenge the emergence of the new classical macroeconomics (Modigliani 1977a; also see Ando 1981).

The model theoretical purposes

In the several reports Ando wrote for the Fed Board and the SSRC committee, he emphasized the close connections between the Keynesian theory, he referred in particular to Modigliani's 1963 IS-LM model and the FMP econometric model.[17] Its building provided to Modigliani the opportunity to test empirically his most innovative theories, all incorporated in the econometric model, such as the life cycle theory, the Modigliani and Miller theorem, and his oligopolistic theory. More in general the model represented the opportunity to prove empirically Modigliani's monetary view, already advanced in 1944 and reaffirmed with the 1963 article.[18] Since the beginning of his Keynesian studies, Modigliani was interested in analyzing the links between the monetary and real side of the economic system, and their policy implications. In his influential 1944 article, he had challenged the Keynesians' orthodoxy, arguing that the unemployment equilibrium originated from a disequilibrium in the money market rather than a fall in the propensity to invest, and therefore, what was required was an increase of money supply (see Chapter 2). Under this perspective the FMP model represented an attempt to fill a lacuna within the traditional Keynesian view and macroeconometric models that in the 1950s and early 1960s still concentrated on real variables and fiscal policy. As Modigliani explained, the FMP model was built "along Keynesian lines – but our sort of Keynes, where money is very important" (2001, p. 100). Modigliani aimed to challenge the idea that for Keynesians money did not matter. Therefore, the model was intended to demonstrate the influence of monetary variables on real ones, highlighting the anti-cyclical role of monetary policy. Most of the large-scale models of that time were inspired by Lawrence Klein, who concentrated on the investment's interest elasticity (see Klein 1947). The Klein–Goldberg model (1955) and the Klein's Postwar Quarterly model (1964) were devoted to analyze the functioning of the real sector and the impact of fiscal policies with the money market that played a minor role. When monetary policy effectiveness was discussed, the Keynesian models mainly concluded in favor of fiscal policy, as in the case of the Brookings model, according to which "monetary policy shifts must be substantial if the course of the economy is to be changed, at least in a recessionary situation" (see Bodkin et al. 1991, pp. 96, 104; Intriligator 1978, p. 452). As Marc Nerlove's (1966) survey showed, in 1966 of the six econometric models estimated from postwar data, only two had more than two endogenous financial variables, and three had no monetary sector at all.

The FMP model also represented a reply to the monetarists challenge to both the income expenditure theory and the Fed Board discretionary policy. Whereas in their first report on the FMP model, de Leeuw and Gramlich explained that the econometric model was needed because "no other model has as its major purpose the quantification of monetary policy" (1968, p. 11), in their subsequent report of May 1969, which followed the publication of the St. Louis monetarist model, they explained that their departure point was the lack of consensus on the role of money in the economic system, with macroeconometric models reaching opposite conclusions (1969, pp. 265–266). To them, the inability of empirical studies to solve the theoretical dispute was due to the lack of reference to the channels by which money influences the rest of the system. The FMP model was aimed to fill this lacuna. Indeed,

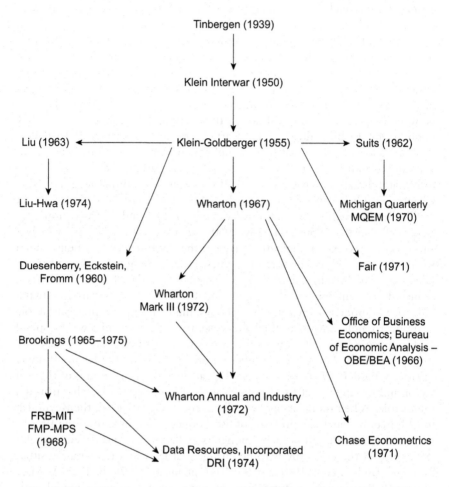

A 'Family Tree' of Macroeconometric Models of the US" in Intriligator 1978, p. 452

de Leeuw and Kalchbrenner (1969) and Gramlich (1971) were involved in the dispute with monetarist economists from the St. Louis bank.

Modigliani's SSRC research project also made explicit reference to Friedman's empirical findings, explaining that one of the purposes of the FMP model was to confront with his direct estimation approach: "One especially interesting issue we hope to pursue is to devise method for testing Friedman view that . . . there is little point in bothering with the analysis of individual channels and one should concentrate on highly aggregate type of analysis" (Modigliani 1966, MP). Growing literature discussing the performance of Keynesian macroeconometric models, the monetarist single equation approach and their ability to track past data and to forecast appeared at the beginning of the 1970s (see Gramlich 1971; Ando 1974; Benjamin Friedman 1975; Gordon 1974; Cooper and Fisher 1972; Modigliani 1971; Modigliani and Ando 1976, among others).[19]

The FMP real sector and its policy implications

In their reports to the Fed Board and to the SSRC, Ando and Modigliani emphasized that differently from other macroeconometric models, the most important equations of the FMP model were derived from explicit behavioral assumptions (also see Ando 1981).

Attempts to bridge micro and macroeconomic analysis were common long before Lucas's new classical economics, as in the case of the disequilibrium research agenda set up by Patinkin in the 1950s (Backhouse and Boianovsky 2013; on postwar microfoundational programs see Duarte and Lima 2012). Modigliani's research on microeconomics was always followed by an examination of its macroeconomic implications. A combination of micro and macroeconomic analysis already appears in his early study on the workings of a socialist economy where the two levels of analysis were entangled, and Modigliani's Meat Plan, whose fiscal policy recommendations were the result of empirical estimates of substitution and income effects. Modigliani's unpublished notes on monetary theory (1955); Modigliani and Brumberg's life cycle hypothesis (1953, 1954); Holt, Modigliani, Muth and Simon's research on firms' behavior under uncertainty (1960); and Ando and Modigliani's (1959) study on economic fluctuations and growth went in this direction. The idea underlying each research line was to have a more rigorous approach to macroeconomics still providing concrete answers to economic problems and advice to policy makers. The policy implications of economic theory had been since the beginning at the basis of Modigliani's interest in the study of this discipline. In a letter to his mentor Marschak of November 1947 (when Modigliani was working on the Meat Plan) about Marschak's paper on money illusion, Modigliani explained:

> [f]or this moment, I would like to add that I have a feeling that the refinements of analysis suggested in this paper is more valuable and more promising from a practical point of view, than some of the methodological refinements recently worked out at the Cowles Commission, which are logically very interesting, but on the practical application of which I still have my doubts. I devoted myself whit enthusiasm to work out the details of the Plan because I saw here, perhaps for the first time, a situation in which my training in economic theory and statistics could be of practical immediate use.

(November 21, 1947)

This same attitude is evident in the 1970s when facing the stagflation problem. In his 1976 presidential address Modigliani pointed out that what was urgent was not the academic dispute but to provide answers to policy makers:

> There are of course, in principle, policies other than aggregate demand management to which we might turn. . . . But so far such policies, at least those of the wage-price control variety, have proved disappointing. The

design of better alternatives is probably the greatest challenge presently confronting those interested in stabilization.

(1977a, p. 15)

And, again, in the 1986 Mattioli lecture "The Debate over Stabilization Policies" pointed out that "[w]hether or not the Phillips curve is vertical . . . an issue which has generate much controversy – does not seem to be crucial" (1986, p. 83). To him the crucial parameter was the relative cost of inflation and unemployment, and the greatest challenge was to develop "alternatives to aggregate demand managements and selling them to politicians" (1986, p. 83).

Modigliani focused in the 1970s on policy issues against the monetarists and new classical macroeconomists' prescriptions, while Ando defended the macroeconometric model against methodological attacks. Ando (1981) explained that they wanted a model as close as possible to the real world; therefore, they evaluated any theoretical hypothesis on the basis of its approximation to reality. On this ground, Ando remarked, they admitted deviations from the optimization principle and the market clearing assumption. According to Ando,

if the purpose of economic investigation is to describe how the economic system works in reality as accurately as possible, the maximizing principle cannot be a teleological principle, but it must be thought as a working hypothesis, an approximation to reality, and it must be specific enough to have strong empirical content.

(1981, p. 344)

As mentioned, the investment block was an outgrowth of Bischoff's dissertation (see Bischoff 1968). Its most important feature was the adherence to the putty-clay assumption because of a closer representation of the real working of the economy with respect to the neoclassical perfect substitution hypothesis.[20] The putty-clay assumption established that once a specific technology satisfying the production function had been chosen, the capital invested in this technology became irrevocably specialized and produced output only by being combined with labor in the initially chosen fixed proportion. In other words, existing equipment could not be modified in response to changes in relative factor prices. Under a theoretical perspective, this assumption acknowledged the working of the economy out of equilibrium with price factors that could deviate from factors' marginal productivity. The putty-clay assumption also had relevant policy implications because it weakened the short-run sensitiveness of investment demand to variations of interest rates, making the impact of fiscal stimulus stronger (because it delayed the crowding-out effects) and monetary policy weaker and effective only after longer delays.[21]

The consumers' expenditure sector responded to Ando, Brumberg and Modigliani's life cycle hypothesis. The presence of wealth in the consumption function implied a direct channel of influence from monetary policy to consumption that moved from the short-term interest rate to the long-term rate, the market value of shares and, hence, to wealth, with important consequence in terms of stabilization actions. Indeed, the resulting impact on aggregate output of monetary policy was estimated of the same order of magnitude as the response of the components of gross investment but relatively faster (Modigliani 1975, pp. 249–250). Moreover, because current consumption depended on expected resources over life, short-run variations in income, caused by shocks, appeared largely absorbed into saving (thus reducing the crowding-out effects). In other words, the life cycle model weakened the magnitude of the multiplier and the impact of transitory fiscal actions because of the distinction between permanent and transitory changes in income, but strengthen that of monetary actions.[22]

Finally, the wage and price sector, the most crucial and debated one, was introduced endogenously only in the last version of the model after a number of alternative specifications and the contributions of different scholars from the Fed Board and academia. Still in a 1968 memorandum to the Board, apparently written by Tella, it was concluded that despite all the econometric attention, on a theoretical level the wage equation was still the weakest one: "We are not still clear as to whose behavior is being represented and what the basis is for some of the variables in the equation" (April 1968, MP). This equations block was finally specified by Enzler (from the Board) and de Menil (1972).

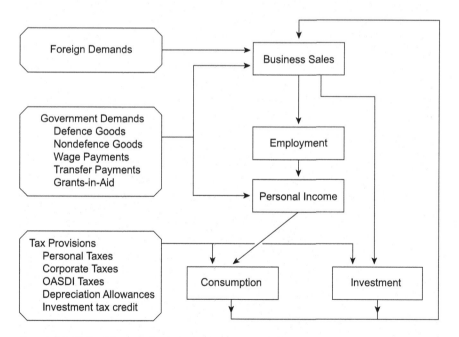

Franco Modigliani Papers, D.M. Rubenstein Rare Book and Manuscript Library, Duke University.

They referred to an augmented Phillips curve to explain the rate of change of wages as a function of the unemployment rate and past changes of prices; while firms set prices in accordance with the Bain, Modigliani and Sylos Labini's oligopolistic model. Relative prices are thus determined through a markup over costs, the most relevant of which are labor costs (de Menil and Enzler 1972; Modigliani 1958; also see Ando 1974 and Modigliani 1975). Once embedded in the FMP model, the wage and price sector remained almost unchanged until the dismissal of the macroeconometric model in the mid-1990s, however acknowledging since the mid-1970s the verticality of the long-run Phillip curve (Pierce and Enzler 1974; see Rancan 2020).[23]

Modigliani went on to work on the Phillips curve with Lucas Papademos and with Ezio Tarantelli through the 1970s, outside the context of the FMP model but within that of the stabilization policies debate, to which I return next.

The FMP financial sector

As Modigliani emphasized in the 1966 SSRC research project for the FMP model, the most relevant effort in its building concerned the design of the financial sector and its links with real ones. Indeed, the sector counted the greater number of behavioral equations becoming "the most elaborate financial sector of any econometric model so far constructed" (Szenberg and Ramrattan 2008, p. 136). As mentioned, its departure point was the Brookings model financial sector that although detailed did not deeply investigate the connections with real variables (Bodkin et al. 1991, pp. 91–96; also see Acosta and Rubin 2019).

The other important source of inspiration was Stephen M. Goldfeld's econometric model of commercial banking behavior (1966). Starting from Tobin's unpublished monetary notes, Goldfeld analyzed banks' portfolio behavior, its link with investment and consumption and the impact of monetary policy under a quantitative perspective. His model anticipated some of the FMP model features, such as the representation of banks as rational profit-maximizing entities whose investment decisions under uncertainty (concerning future yields and maturities) are an important source of money supply. Both in Goldfeld's and the FMP models, short- and long-run interest rates represented major links with the real sector, with two term-structure equations reflecting the consolidated behavior of the financial system. Goldfeld concluded that the portfolio approach did not weaken the impact of monetary policy on national income which, instead is quite significant. Thus, "monetary policy is capable of playing a more important role in stabilization than heretofore generally assumed" (1966 p. 196).[24]

The crucial role of interest rates in the monetary transmission mechanism explained the major attention to the theory of interest rate determination in the building of the FMP model. The most original contributions appeared in a series of articles, in particular Modigliani and Sutch (1966, 1967) and

Modigliani and Shiller (1973) on the determination of long-run interest rates and Modigliani et al. (1970) on the determination of short-run interest rates. From these contributions it appears the increasing attention to the role of expectations and the distinction between real and nominal interest rates as the result of the inflationary process initiated in the late 1960s, along with the recognition of the relevance of financial (stochastic) variables (in particular of assets returns).

Modigliani and Sutch (1966)[25] suggested a model for the determination of the maturity structure of yields, later incorporated in the FMP model, that combined Hicks's Risk Premium Model (Hicks 1939) with Culberston's (1957) Market Segmentation Hypothesis. In Modigliani and Sutch's model the yield structure was controlled by the Hicksian principle of the equality of expected returns modified by the risk premium. Next, following Culberston's model, Modigliani and Sutch agreed that traders do not necessarily have a preference for short-period returns (as, e.g., for the life cycle model of savings). Different traders have different habitats; that is, might have funds that they intend to keep invested for *n* periods (1966, p. 183). It followed that the spread between the long rate and short rate should depend primarily on the expected change in the long rate, but it was also influenced by the supply and demand of long- and short-term securities to an extent reflecting the prevailing risk aversion, transaction costs and facilities for effective arbitrage operations.

In estimating the habitat hypothesis, Modigliani and Sutch's departure point was the idea de Leeuw developed for the Brookings model, according to which expectations on future yields were both regressive (à la Keynes); that is, people expect the interest rate to regress towards a normal level based on past experience, and extrapolative as suggested by Duesenberry (1958). Under this latter hypothesis, an increase of interest rate leads to expectations of a further rise and vice versa. A combination of both hypotheses led to a model of expectations formation in which "the prevailing expectations of long-term rates were the result of the extrapolation of very recent changes and the regression toward a long term normal level" (1966, p. 12). Modigliani and Sutch simply expressed the expected long rate as an approximation of the weighted average of past short rates, and it was estimated by Bischoff, using for the first time the Almon distributed lag technique.

Modigliani and Sutch's model on the determination of the term structure of interest rates was later refined by Modigliani and Shiller (1973). The paper was an outgrowth of Shiller's PhD dissertation (under Modigliani's supervision) on "Rational Expectations and Term Structure of Interest Rates" (1972) in which expectations of future changes in prices enter in the determination of long-run yields. Modigliani and Shiller's shift of attention from nominal to real interest rates is here further explained by the emerging of rational expectations models. One of their aims was, in fact, to demonstrate the consistency of their term structure model with the rational expectations hypothesis. According to Modigliani and Shiller, their evidence showed that the distributed lags of their term structure equation were consistent with rational expectations.

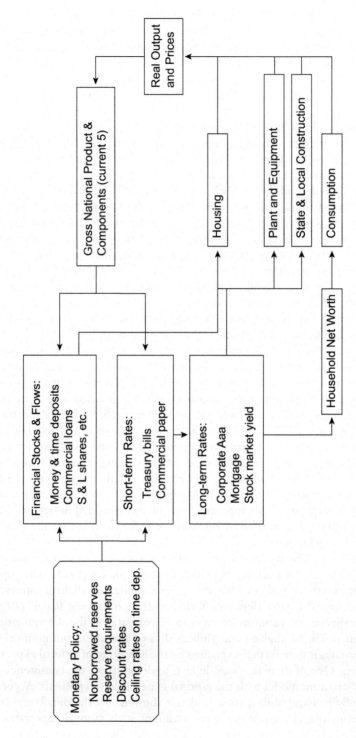

From Franco Modigliani Papers, David M. Rubenstein Rare Book and Manuscript Library, Duke University.

The relation between the long rates and past short rates and prices estimated in the process of fitting the term structure equation was in fact similar to the relation that would hold if the long rates were an average of expected future rates. Moreover, according to them, because their term structure equation fitted the current long term closely, it was also demonstrated that past rates and prices were the two major variables on which markets based their forecasts of the future course of short-term interest rates.

The introduction of changes in price expectations provided an important feedback mechanism from the real to the monetary sector and created the conditions for a greater instability of the economic system with the model that in the case of an expansive demand shock and flexible expectations became explosive (see Ando's notes, undated, MP, Ando 1974; Visco 1991, p. 309).

In summary, the financial sector was characterized by a chain of relationships among interest rates that extended their influence on the real sector through rental rates and the rate of return on equities. In particular, the discount term influenced the short-term money rate and the money supply. In turn, short-term interest rates entered in the determination of the long-term rate that had a direct influence on the rental rate, and thus on investment demand, and an indirect influence on output and employment thorough the market value of equities and, thus, on wealth and household expenditures because of the life cycle hypothesis.

The FMP model and the Yale school

Ando and Modigliani discussed a refined version of the FMP financial sector at the 1972 conference on the Brookings model, emphasizing that it represents an attempt to implement empirically the Yale portfolio model (also see also Bodkin et al. 1991, p. 113; Mehrling 2010, p. 211).[26] However, in his comments Smith and Tobin (1975) were critical. They remarked that Ando and Modigliani's financial model did not obey any of the three "Yale precepts" underlining its general equilibrium approach such as 1) an explicit balance equation of supply and demand specified for every asset with interest rates or asset prices that adjust to clear the market; 2) every behavioral sector adjusting those items in the balance sheet that it controls; 3) all the asset demand and supply equations of a behavioral sector being explicitly specified and all containing the same list of variables (Smith and Tobin 1975, p. 565). Instead, in Ando and Modigliani, "the form of each equation, the list of variables in it, the lags, all have been adjusted to get the best explanation case by case. Variables have been omitted when they were statistically insignificant or conceptually remote" (1975, p. 566). On this basis, Smith and Tobin especially rejected the term structure approach for the determination of yields, in which the asset supplies played only a minor role.

Ando and Modigliani remarked the different purposes of their model, that is, to investigate the connections between the financial and real sector and, most important, estimation problems as the reasons explaining their different framework, in particular the use of the term structure approach and the excess demand approach. It followed from the need to reconcile data availability with considering securities of various maturities, and the impossibility to have data about all assets' supply and demand.[27] In other words, to construct a theoretical model on the one side, and an econometric model on the other responds to different tasks and implied different problems. The design and specifications of the macroeconometric model were the result of compromises among rigor (economic theory), data availability, computational problems and estimates along with attention to the model performance in fitting data and to forecast (on this see Backhouse and Cherrier 2019).[28]

The main connections between economic theory, namely, the Keynesian theory, and the macroeconometric model should be the object of a monograph Ando and Modigliani were writing since 1969 but they never finished. The difficult combination of the theoretical and policy purposes of the model is also apparent from the different agenda the academic team led by Ando and Modigliani and the Fed Board team followed, with the latter that wanted a model operative already since 1968 while the academic side concentrated on improvement of each equations and in putting the separate blocks of the model together (see Ando to Brill: January 10, 1969). Since each single sector was specified and estimated by different research groups that worked mainly separately also within academia, one of the main difficulties faced was to conceive the entire model as a unified, consistent model (see Backhouse and Cherrier 2019, pp. 431–437).[29] Thus, what should be considered among Modigliani's most important contributions to Keynesian macroeconomics (as argued by Blanchard 2008) is hardly recognizable under a theoretical perspective while it is more in terms of policy prescriptions.

Modigliani and the Phillips curve tradeoff

Modigliani's contributions to economics of the late 1960s and 1970s is closely connected with the development of the FMP model. How much his research agenda was shaped by his work on the macroeconometric model (and partly contemporary on the building of the first Bank of Italy's econometric model) clearly appears from the reports to the dean of MIT Economics Department. Since 1966 all his study and publications revolved around the model.[30] It also appears that his engagement with economic policy and his attempt to influence policy decisions increased rapidly over the 1970s especially regarding the inflation and unemployment tradeoff.

With the exception of his work on finance, most of Modigliani's research time and publications since the mid-1960s were devoted to development of single blocks of the macroeconometric model. Modigliani spent a semester of the 1967–1968 academic year in Italy working on the first Bank of Italy macroeconometric model and simultaneously working on the FMP model. The 1968–1971 reports to the dean were also about Modigliani's progress in completing the FMP model, along with the monograph about the model and its uses in the analysis of stabilization forces. In 1969 he reported that he expected "to devote the summer and the coming fall semester to the completion of a monograph. . . . I have been especially concern in revision of the wage and price sector" (1969–1970, MP) and again in 1971: "Substantial progress has been made on a monograph reporting on the construction of the model" (1970–1971, MP).

The collaboration with the Federal Reserve Board formally ended in 1970 with the delivering of the model, and the other copy of the model transferred to the Wharton Associates of the University of Pennsylvania for its maintenance. However, Modigliani and Ando's research team still continued to improve some aspects of the model (as in the case of the financial sector, short-run interest rate determination and the investment block), and a number of simulations continued to appear to establish the effectiveness of stabilization policies and compare discretionary actions versus fixed rules.

With the building of the model, Modigliani also became increasingly involved in policy issues. In the early 1970s, his counseling activities particularly to the Fed Board and the Treasury occupied little time but then, with the peak of the economic recession and stagflation, Modigliani reported to the dean that a

> large part of the professional activities has been devoted to areas quite unusual such as endeavor to persuade our government to pursue more sensible economic policies, especially in the area of stabilization . . . several meetings of the Federal Reserve Board, papers in the AER

(Modigliani 1974–75)

> And again, in the 1975–76 academic year he explained to have "devoted a major proportion of my activities to an effort to influence economic policy away from its current emphasis on larger unemployment to reduce inflation; real vs monetary causes of inflation".

(Modigliani 1975–76, MP)[31]

The breakdown of the unemployment and inflation trade-off was at the center of the theoretical and political debate of the 1970s. Friedman's 1968 presidential address and Phelps's 1967 and 1968 papers had challenged the Phillips curve long-run tradeoff through the accelerationist mechanism. According to them, the effects of expansionary policies on real income and employment level appeared only temporary. As soon as people revise their expectations on future prices, wages and prices start to rise and employment to fall towards its natural rate.

In the mid-1970s Modigliani put forward the so-called noninflationary rate of unemployment (NIRU) in a paper with his PhD student Lucas Papademos (Modigliani and Papademos 1975) as an alternative to Friedman's natural rate hypothesis and to support expansionary policies against the monetarists' campaign.

Modigliani and Papademos' aim was to show that expansionary policies were not inflationary for high levels of unemployment and that, therefore, stabilization actions still played a role. Modigliani had already discussed the topic at the February 1974 academic consultant meeting at the Fed Board to support real versus monetary targets and discretionary versus fixed-rule policies, arguing that expansionary policies did not accelerate inflation.[32] At the meeting, as in the paper with Papademos soon after, Modigliani explained that the NIRU, defined as the rate at which prices change was stable, was consistent with both "the vertical and non-vertical Phillips curve schools", being the rate emerging from the intersection of a negative sloping or vertical Phillips curve with a negligible rate of inflation (Modigliani and Papademos 1975, p. 142). Modigliani and Papademos stressed that the NIRU avoided the "conceptual question of the shape of the Phillips curve at extreme values" (1975, p. 145), addressing instead the more relevant question of what unemployment path was consistent with slowing inflation. To them the verticality of the Phillips curve was only of academic interest; the issue was not theoretical but practical relative to the estimate of the value and the stability of the noninflationary rate that would justify a "fiscal stimuli and an accommodating monetary policy".[33]

At the 1974 Fed Board meeting, Modigliani also rejected the key role monetarists ascribed to money supply and particularly to expectations in the inflation process independently from initial conditions. To him the monetarists' expectations view "makes no sense" unless one presume that entrepreneurs follow closely all monetary statistics and immediately change their prices (Modigliani 1974, MP).[34] On theoretical grounds, what appeared unacceptable to Modigliani, as clearly stated in subsequent articles, was the explanation of unemployment in terms of expectations errors instead of lack of jobs and attempts to read the phenomenon in an equilibrium context (see Modigliani 1977a, 1986).

In spite of their different meanings, Modigliani and Papademos's NIRU was quickly associated in the literature with Friedman's natural rate hypothesis, considering the NIRU a first step Keynesian economists used to move towards the acceptance of Friedman's analysis (see Hall and Sargent 2018, p. 126). Unlike Friedman's natural rate hypothesis, the NIRU was a political benchmark to be reached through an active role of stabilization policies. By contrast, Friedman's natural rate hypothesis was understood as a theoretical concept derived from Wicksell's natural rate of interest, defined as the equilibrium level that prevails in the long run as the result of frictional and structural market forces, with deviations from it explained by errors in expectations.

Modigliani's 1974 memorandum and Modigliani and Papademos's 1975 Brookings paper were devoted to convincing policy makers that inflation accelerates only when unemployment falls below the NIRU, whereas in the case of a slack economy unemployment would approach it from the above, through a mix of fiscal (expansive) and monetary (accommodating) policy (1975, p. 160).[35]

Modigliani and Papademos's Phillips curve combined a traditional reading of the wage equation in terms of a disequilibrium in the labor market with Charles Holt's search theory (in Phelps 1970). The appearance of search models in the 1970s is associated with legitimation of the concept of voluntary unemployment within a choice theoretic framework and equilibrium model (Phelps 1970).[36] By contrast, Modigliani and Papademos applied Holt's theory to dismiss under specific circumstances, such as the existence of a large amount of structural unemployment, the inflationary consequences of expansive policy and to rationalize wage stickiness (also see Modigliani 1977a, 1986).[37]

Modigliani had already applied Holt's search theory in a paper with Ezio Tarantelli (1973) on the Phillips curve for a developing economy (they referred to Italy). They worked on a modified Phillips curve that took care of vacancies, explaining the rate of change of wages in terms of the stock of vacancies (average duration of vacancies) and the reciprocal of unemployment (the same average length of unemployment).

Their starting point was the segmentation of the labor force into trained and untrained unemployed to demonstrate that an expansion of aggregate demand induces inflation but also creates the conditions for its subsequent dampening. By increasing the pool of trained labor force relative to the unskilled, the competitiveness in the labor market rises, and therefore, for any given increase of the aggregate demand there will be a reduced pressure on wages (for a similar approach see Rees 1970, p. 232).[38] Modigliani and Tarantelli pointed out that there is not a unique relation between the rate of growth of wages and the unemployment level because it depends on the composition of unemployment between trained and untrained laborers. This is not associated with an unstable Phillips curve but with a family of possible curves. To them, a reduction of unemployment below some initial natural rate does not necessarily accelerate inflation, rather it could be consistent with any stable value of price and wage change (1973, p. 221).[39]

Over the 1970s and still in the 1980s, Modigliani defended the Phillips curve relationship with a shift of attention from Friedman to the rational expectation movement in macroeconomics. Starting from the assertion that the long-run vertical Phillips curve is consistent with a variety of models such as the Keynesians' inflationary gap (i.e., Keynes's notion of a unique upper bound to sustainable employment) and the classical neutrality of money, Modigliani strongly rejected the reading of fluctuations of unemployment within an equilibrium context based on wage and price flexibility, perfect competition and voluntary unemployment (Modigliani 1977a, 1986).

The dispute over theoretical, methodological and policy issues continued through the 1970s and 1980s. Looking at Modigliani's writings he was engaged to defend Keynesian economics, especially those policy contentions connected with it both in United States but also in Italy. In particular in Italy we was active in informing public opinion as a columnist of the most important newspapers (see Asso 2007; Camurri 2019). He was also active in training a new generation of Italian economists with an increasing number of young Italian economists who went to study at MIT. As Samuelson recalled, "a revolving circle of Italian graduate students spiced our common rooms (2005, p. 6).

Modigliani's struggle to defend Keynesian economics under a theoretical and policy perspective since the 1970s was a battle also to defend an idea of economics as devoted to practical issues, and a view about the relationships among policy interventions, the market system and individuals he had progressively matured over his academic career. A long way separates the rhetorical articles he wrote in the 1930s in support of the corporative economy from the building of the macroeconometric model for a rigorous analysis of the workings of a market economy and the effect of policy actions. Nonetheless he still recognized in the 1970s the role of value judgments in economics:

> I do have something to say about value judgements. Just a few words. I think there is no question but that value judgements play a major role in the differences between economists. And I think it is unfortunate, but true, that value judgements end up by playing a role in your assessment of parameters, and of the evidence we consider. . . . And there is no question that Milton [Friedman] and I, looking at the same evidence, may reach different conclusions as to what it means.

(1977b, p. 10)

Although postwar economic discipline is characterized by an increasing formalization, and Modigliani became one of the main advocates of this methodological turn since his arrival in United States, economics remained for him a normative and applied science whose aim was to provide concrete answers to concrete problems, with the aim of improving social welfare. Modigliani acknowledged the role of value judgments and expressed his own in terms of choice between unemployment and inflation, and recognized the shortcomings of the market system and the active role of policy actions. Thus, in the opening of his 1976 presidential address to the American Economic Association he argues that the economy *needs to* be stabilized, *can be* stabilized, and therefore *should* be stabilized by appropriate monetary and fiscal policies (1977a, p. 1), a fundamental practical message he ascribed to the *General Theory*; a message on which Modigliani was already reasoning before his encounter with Keynes. The idea of an equilibrium in the economy which is not mechanically achieved but is constructed as the result of agents' will was the departure point of his criticisms to classical economics in the 1930s (see Chapter 1). Modigliani's confidence in the individual decision-making process that emerges from his microeconomic research on savings and firms' behavior under uncertainty, along with his belief in discretionary policy represents in some way a re-affirmation of that early view. The market equilibrium is not a mechanical achievment but the result of interactions among individuals and the institutional set up.

Notes

1 The chapter is partly based on Rancan (2019).
  Modigliani left Carnegie in 1961, moving to Northwestern University with the agreement of joining MIT a year later. At Northwestern University Modigliani taught macroeconomics to Axel Leijonhfvud, who was following him from MIT.

Leijonhfvud's influential book on Keynesian economics was partly written as critique to Modigliani's equilibrium approach to Keynes's theory (Backhouse and Boianvosky 2013, Chapter 4).

2 However, according to Mehrling (2014, p. 12), it came too late: the Fed-MIT-Penn model became for a time the new orthodoxy, but the criticism of Tobin and William Brainard (1968) proved decisive, and the alternative framework of Tobin (1969) became the starting point for the next generation of macroeconometric modeling.

3 See "The Monetarist Controversy: Discussion by Milton Friedman and Franco Modigliani", *Federal Reserve Bank of San Francisco Economic Review*, Supplement, Spring 1977: 5–27.

4 Mehrling did not consider the disequilibrium line of thought, which put in dispute the Walrasian market clearing approach and that focused on providing a microfoundation for money market behavior. This line of thought had in Patinkin an important departure point (see Backhouse and Boianovsky 2013).

5 On the analogy of Keynesian economics with engineering, see Mankiw (2006).

6 On the role of ideology in economic analysis and discourse, particularly regarding the debate on inflation and unemployment over the 1970s, see Romani (2018).

7 It was Bach (dean of the newly created GSIA) who asked Modigliani to join him at Carnegie in 1952 to reinforce the study of monetary, mathematical and quantitative economics. They were colleagues until Modigliani moved in 1961 to Northwestern University and then MIT. Bach moved to Stanford University in 1963. Since WWII he was a Federal Reserve Board consultant.

8 Similar conclusions were published by Friedman and Meiselman in their report to the Commission on Money and Credit (1963), which initiated the so-called radio station debate with Ando and Modigliani (FM AM debate).

9 See especially Bach (1963) and Minsky (1963). Minsky also complained about neglecting the monetary and financial sectors in postwar macroeconometric models, arguing that it was "a defect that should be corrected" (1963 p. 65–66).

10 In 1963 Modigliani was also working on empirical tests of monetary policy, and of rules versus discretion" aimed at assessing the role of monetary policy in the postwar period, and the feasibility and desirability of replacing discretion with a rule", see Modigliani 1964, 72 (June) issue of the *Journal of Political Economy*.

11 According to Minsky, the belief that money was important was not inconsistent with the acceptance of the modern income expenditure approach to business cycles (1963). Similarly, according to Bach, Friedman and Schwartz's rediscovery of money and the emerging agreement on portfolio analysis, although through different adjustment mechanisms, could lead to a rapprochement of the monetarists and the Keynesians views (1963, pp. 3–4).

12 Robert Hetzel (2008) in his narrative about the Federal Reserve postwar monetary policy distinguished between the *stop-go monetary policy* (1965–1979), which had the objective of a low stable unemployment, and the *lean against the wind policy* (1955–1965; and after 1979), which had the main task of price stability. The *stop-go* era, on which my narrative focused, is described as the result of the Keynesians' belief that inflation was a real phenomenon and that "fiscal policy and direct intervention by government in price setting should substitute for monetary authority to control inflation and business cycles" (2008, p. 58).

13 Ando, Modigliani and Rasche published the complete list of equations (about 200 equations) only two years after the completion of the model, in 1972 in the *American Economic Review* (without comments and with reference to the 1969 version). It was followed by two other reports years later, published by the Fed Board in 1985 and 1987 by Brayton and Mauskopf and in 1996 by Brayton and Tinsley. For a brief historical reconstruction of macroeconometric models at the Fed Board, see Brayton et al. (1997).

14 The Fed Board had refused to finance the project for building a large-scale model of the U.S. economy sponsored by the SSRC and submitted to the Board by Lawrence Klein and

Duesenberry that resulted in the Brookings model (see Acosta and Pinzón-Fuchs 2018, pp. 11–12). In 1966 Modigliani submitted a research project on the modus operandi of monetary policy to the SSRC. In his memoranda to the Fed Board and the SSRC, Ando partly provided a different reconstruction of the beginning of the collaboration with the Fed Board (see Rancan 2019).

15 None of Modigliani's students involved in the building of the model remained at MIT after 1968: Bischoff moved to the Cowles Commission at Yale (1968–1975), Sutch became an assistant professor at the University of California, de Menil went to Princeton, and from 1970 to 1975 he was the director of the quarterly modeling project of the Ministry of Finance in France. Yaffe also moved to Princeton soon after his PhD.

16 Until the end of 1969 there were two separate econometric models, one at MIT and Penn the other at the Fed Board, and they were merged only at the end of 1970. The reasons were organizational. The two research teams worked mainly separately also due to academia and the Fed Board's different purposes. As Ando explained to Brill, economists from the "academic side" wanted to postpone the work involved in putting together the model and concentrated on improvements of each equation, whereas de Leeuw and Gramlich from the Fed Board "must have a functioning system as soon as possible." Thus, the Fed Board's version had been functioning since November 1967, whereas the MIT–Penn version became operational for practical purposes a year later (Ando Report 1969, MP; also see Backhouse and Cherrier 2019).

17 Ando also emphasized the possible use of the econometric model for teaching purposes: "its theoretical structure was somewhat more transparent and easily understood by other economists" so that the model "may provide a better research vehicle for academic economists and a more convenient teaching device in graduate schools" (undated MP).

18 See Modigliani (1944, pp. 75–76); see also Chapter 2. Regarding empirical validation of his monetary view, Modigliani recalled in his autobiography that he was "very happy" to know that Gerard Tinter would have tested empirically his 1944 model.

19 On the FMP model and the debate with monetarists, see Rancan (2019).

20 It was derived from a constant elasticity of substitution (CES) neoclassical production function (see Rasche and Saphiro 1968).

21 According to Hall (1977, p. 90, endnote 25), the putty-clay assumption was proposed for the first time by L. Johansen, "Substitution versus Fixed Production Coefficients in the Theory of Economic Growth: A Synthesis", *Econometrica*, 27, April 1959. A bibliography of others' contributions are in C. Bliss, "On Putty-Clay", *Review of Economic Studies*, 35 (68): 105–132. Regarding the FMP model investment function also see Ando, Modigliani, Rasche and Turnovsky (1974).

22 See for example Eisner's (1969) analysis of the weak effect of the 1968 surcharge tax on inflation because it was provisional.

23 On the history of the Phillips curve myth, see Forder (2014).

24 In a 1968 letter for a seminar at Yale, Ando referred to Goldfeld as "my consultant on everything" (February 22, 1968).

25 Modigliani and Sutch's model was developed to test empirically the results of the Kennedy *Operation Twist* (1961), aimed at reducing the spread between long-term and short-term maturities through the Fed open market and the Treasury debt management operations, to encourage capital inflow.

26 Ando and Modigliani's revised financial sector should have been part of the monograph on the FMP model Ando and Modigliani were preparing.

27 Theoretical differences referred to Ando and Modigliani's dismissal of Brainard and Tobin's (1963) "adding up constraint" because, to them, big corporations followed a satisfying behavior that led them to have residual assets or liabilities in their balance sheets to simplify their decision process. They also replaced Tobin's q, the ratio of the market value of capital assets to their replacement cost, to determine investment. It was substituted with the expected profitability of production activities using new capital. According to Ando and Modigliani, the introduction of the putty-clay assumption made

meaningless the concept of reproduction cost if technology and price factors changes. In other words, in the FMP model investment decisions depended on the comparison of the expected rate of return on capital and investment costs (i.e., long-run interest rate). On these differences, also see Ando 1974. On "Tobin's q" theory of investment, see Dimand (2014, Chapter 5).

28 On the FMP model financial sector, see Acosta and Rubin (2019).

29 Since February 1968 Ando began a collaboration with Arnold Zellner with the aim of formalizing "the statistical inference procedure for large scale models including the question of interpreting simulation results" (February 22, 1968 MP). The problem, Ando explained to Modigliani, was "to develop a more systematic procedure for choosing among alternative specifications of the model" (September 9, 1968 MP). Ando also remarked that the next task was to have a unified model and "to perform extensive diagnostic simulations to understand the characteristics of the model" (September 9, 1968). In April 1968 Daniel Brill wrote to Ando how impressed he was by the "stable full of young horses Zellner has at his command there at Chicago" (April 29, 1968, MP).

30 The theoretical and practical efforts behind the building of the FMP model (and macroeconometric models in general) also contributed to shape for at least a decade the way of doing macroeconomics by involving a large number of scholars and PhD students. On the practice of macroeconomics in connection with macroeconometric model building, see Acosta and Pinzon Fuchs 2019.

31 The battle Modigliani tackled, especially at the Fed Board, and the progressive isolation in which he found himself is evident from the reports of the Fed Board academic consultant meetings of the late 1970s. In the conclusion of the February 1981 meeting, Bach, like "some other consultants, expressed concern that Modigliani wanted to revert to fine tuning" ("Summary of Discussion", Academic Consultant Meeting, February 27, 1981, MP). Modigliani was critical about the anti-inflationary policy of the Board and claimed that Fed's independence should be strictly confined to the choice of the most effective monetary policy to accomplish the goals set by the administration of Congress.

32 Modigliani had already criticized the CEA report for 1974 (Modigliani 1974), a copy of which he sent to Fed Chairman Burns and to Robert Holland writing about his concern with the "extremely tight policy" of the last weeks.

33 Still in the 1976 presidential address Modigliani considered empirical evidence inadequate to discriminate between a vertical and nonvertical Phillips curve, particularly because of the asymmetry between upward and downward wage rigidity (Modigliani 1977a; see also Modigliani 1986, p. 79).

34 As for empirical evidence Modigliani argued that in most years from 1957 to 1970, the acceleration of money stock and the acceleration of inflation went against each other and that until 1974 the correlation between changes in inflation and changes in money supply, current and lagged, was about zero, concluding once again, that the only influence of money on prices was indirect through aggregate demand and employment.

35 Most of the audience's attention at the Brookings session (especially of Keynesians like Klein and Tobin) did not concentrate on the introduction of a concept similar or even interchangeable with that of Friedman but on the estimate of NIRU and the feasibility of the policy mix it would support. Modigliani himself, recognized the difficult task he was pursuing in trying to convince the Board: "you feel that I am out of my mind and that a South America style rate of growth of money of 12 or 15% is totally unacceptable" (Modigliani 1974, MP).

36 Although Holt's theory became especially known through Phelps's 1970 book on microfoundations, Holt began to work on this model already in the 1950s, when he was Modigliani's colleague at Carnegie (see *Organization*, edited by J. M. March and H. Simon, 1958). Holt's model followed a satisfactory approach to laborers' and firms' decisions making according to which the employee compared the "utility of an alternative

state to that of his present state: If the alternative is enough 'better' to outweigh the costs of the transition, the change was made, otherwise not" (Holt 1970, p. 60). Holt's key concept was represented by the adaptive "wage aspiration level", in the sense that it changes as conditions change. This is the "behavioral hypothesis" or "rational research strategy" on which basis the unemployed makes a choice. The initial wage aspiration level is set on the basis of the worker's previous experience (the most recent wage), knowledge of what other workers have achieved, and perceptions of what job opportunities are currently available in the market; and it is inversely related to the unemployed time. In other words, in Holt's search model the rate of change of money wages depends upon the behavior of unemployed and employed workers "in searching the market for their best opportunities" and on "employers' efforts to maintain work forces at their desired levels in the face of quits and recruiting problems" (1970, p. 69).

37 Holt's theory was the only one in Phelps's volume that did not introduce the natural rate hypothesis.

38 Interesting enough, by applying the standard Phillips curve to Italian data (1952–1968), the coefficient of inflation was already larger than unity. Modigliani and Tarantelli said that this result was already reported by Sylos Labini, in 1967, with no reference to the Phillips curve, who explained it by the increasing of trade union pressure on wages (Modigliani and Tarantelli 1973, p. 210).

39 Modigliani also emphasized the heterogeneity of the labor force in his 1976 presidential address to rationalize price and wage stickiness. According to him in oligopolistic markets, firms respond to changes in demand by endeavoring to adjust output and the employment level without significant changes in prices relative to wages, with effects on vacancies and search time. The rationale behind firms' behavior is that if wages decrease, the first to quit are likely to be the best workers; therefore, a reduction of demand could be accomplished more economically not by reducing wages but by firing or by layoffs (Modigliani 1977a, p. 7).

References

Acosta, J., and G. Rubin. 2019. "Bank Behavior in Large-Scale Macroeconometric Models of the 1960s", *History of Political Economy*, 51 (3): 471–492.

Acosta, J., E. Pinzon-Fuchs 2019. "Peddling Macroeconometric Modeling and Quantitative Policy Analysis: The Early Years of the SSRC's Committee on Economic Stability, 1959–1963", *OEconomia*, 9 (3): 537–558.

Andersen, L. C., and J. L. Jordan. 1968. "Monetary and Fiscal Actions: A Test of Their Relative Importance in Economic Stabilization", *Federal Reserve Bank of St. Louis Review*, 50 (November): 11–24.

Ando, A. K. 1974. "Some Aspects of Stabilization Policies, the Monetarist Controversy", *International Economic Review*, 15 (3): 541–571.

———. 1981. "On a Theoretical and Empirical Basis of Macroeconometric Models", in *Large-Scale Macro-Econometric Models*, ed. by Kmenta and Ramsey, North-Holland Amsterdam.

Ando, A. K., and F. Modigliani. 1959. "Growth, Fluctuations and Stability", *American Economic Review*, 49 (2): 501–524.

Ando, A. K., and F. Modigliani. 1965. "The Relative Stability of Monetary Velocity and the Investment Multiplier", *American Economic Review*, 55 (4): 693–728.

———. 1969. "Econometric Analysis of Stabilization Policies", *American Economic Review*, 59 (2): 296–314.

———. 1975. "Some Reflections on Describing Structures of Financial Sectors", in *The Brookings Model: Perspective and Recent Developments*, ed. by G. Fromm and L. R. Klein, Amsterdam: North Holland, 524–563.

Ando, A. K., F. Modigliani, R. Rasche, and S. J. Turnovsky. 1974. "On the Role of Expectations of Price and Technological Change in an Investment Function", *International Economic Review*, 15 (2): 384–414.

Asso P. F., ed. 2007. *Franco Modigliani. L'impegno civile di un'economista*, Siena: Fondazione Monte dei Paschi di Siena.

Bach, G. L. 1963. "Introduction", *Review of Economics and Statistics*, 45 (1), Part 2, Supplement: 3–5.

Backhouse, R. E., and M. Boianovsky. 2013. *Transforming Modern Macroeconomics: Exploring Disequilibrium Microfoundationss, 1956–2003*, Cambridge and New York: Cambridge University Press.

Backhouse, R., and B. Cherrier. 2019. "The Ordinary Business of Macroeconometric Modelling: Working on the MIT-Fed-Penn Model (1964–1974)", *History of Political Economy*, 51 (3): 425–448.

Bishoff, C. 1968. "Lags in Fiscal and Monetary Impacts on Investment in Producers Durable Equipment", *Cowles Foundation Discussion Papers* no 250, Cowles Foundation for Research in Economics, Yale University.

Blanchard, O. J. 2008. "Neoclassical Synthesis", in *The New Palgrave: Dictionary of Economics*, ed. by S. N. Durlauf and L. E. Blume, vol. 5, 2nd ed., London: Macmillan Press Ltd, 634–637.

Bodkin, R. G., L. Klein, and K. Marwah. 1991. *A History of Macroeconometric Model-Building*, Edwar Elgar.

Brainard, W. and J. Tobin, 1963. Financial Intermediaries and the Effectiveness of Monetary Controls", *American Economic Review*, 53 (2): 383–400.

———. 1968. "Pitfalls in Financial Model Building", *American Economic Review*, 58 (2): 99–122.

Brayton, F., A. Levin, R. Lyon, and J. C. Williams. 1997. "The Evolution of Macro Models at the Federal Reserve Board", *Carnegie-Rochester Conference Series on Public Policy*, 47: 43–81.

Brayton, F., and E. Mauskopf. 1985. "The Federal Reserve Board MPS Quarterly Econometric Model of the US Economy", *Economic Modelling*, 2 (3): 170–292.

———. 1987. "Structures and Uses of the MPS Quarterly Econometric Model of the United States", *Federal Reserve Bulletin*, 93: 93–109.

Brayton, F., and P. Tinsley, eds. 1996. "A Guide to FRB/US A Macroeconometric Model of the United States." Version 1.0, October, 1–47.

Camurri, R. ed. 2019. *I modesti consigli di un premio Nobel. Franco Modigliani. Rischio Italia. L'Italia vista dall'America (1970–2003)*, Donzelli Editore.

Cooper, J. P. and S. Fisher. 1972. "Stochastic Simulation of Monetary Rules in Two Macroeconomic Models", *Journal of the American Statistical Association*, Vol. 67 (340): 750–760.

Culberston, J. M. 1957. "The Term Structure of Interest Rates", *The Quarterly Journal of Economics*, 71 (4): 485–517.

de Leeuw, F., and E. M. Gramlich. 1968. "The Federal Reserve: MIT Econometric Model", *Federal Reserve Bulletin*, January: 11–40.

———. 1969. "The Channels of Monetary Policy: A Further Report on the Federal Reserve: MIT Model", *The Journal of Finance*, 24 (2): 265–290.

de Menil, G., and J. J. Enzler. 1972. "Prices and Wages in the FRB_MIT-Penn Econometric Model", O. Eckstein, ed. *The Econometric of Price Determination Conference* October 30–31, Board of Governors of the Federal Reserve System, Washington, D.C.: 277–308, Sponsored by the Governors of the FED and SSRC.

Dimand, R. W. 2014. *James Tobin*, Palgrave Macmillan.

Dimand, R., and H. Hagemann, 2019. "Jacob Marschak and the Cowles Approaches to the Theory of Money and Assets". Cowles Foundation Discussion Paper no 2196. https://www.researchgate.net/publication/335677051. Last access November 29, 2019.

Duarte, P. G and G. Tadeu Lima ed. *Microfoundations Reconsidered: The Relationship of Micro and Macroeconomics in Historical Perspective*. Cheltenham, UK, Northampton MA, US. Edward Elgar Publishing.

Duesenberry, J. C. 1958. *Business Cycles and Economic Growth*, New York: McGraw-Hill Book Co. Ltd.

Eisner, R. 1969. "Fiscal and Monetary Policy Reconsidered", *American Economic Review*, 59 (5): 897–905.

Friedman, B. 1975. "Rational Expectations Are Really Adaptive After All," unpub. paper, Harvard Univ.

Friedman, M. 1968. "The Role of Monetary Policy", *American Economic Review*, 58 (1): 1–17.

———. 1970. "A Theoretical Framework for Monetary Analysis", in *Milton Friedman's Monetary Framework: A Debate with His Critics*, Chicago and London: University of Chicago Press, 1–62.

———. 1977. "The Monetarist Controversy: Discussion by Milton Friedman and Franco Modigliani", *Federal Reserve Bank of San Francisco Economic Review*, Supplement, Spring: 5–27.

Friedman, M., and A. J. Schwartz. 1963a. *Monetary History of the United States, 1867–1960"*, Princeton, NJ: Princeton University Press.

———. 1963b. "Money and Business Cycles", *The Review of Economics and Statistics*, 45 (1), part 2: 32–64.

Friedman, M., and D. Meiselman. 1963. "The Relative Stability of Monetary Velocity and the Investment Multiplier in the United States, 1987–1958", in *Stabilization Policies: Commission on Money and Credit*, Englewood Cliffs, NJ: Prentice-Hall, 165–268.

Forder, J. 2014. *Macroeconomics and the Phillips Curve Myth*, Oxford: Oxford University Press.

Fromm, G., and L. R. Klein eds., 1975. *The Brookings model: Perspective and Recent developments*, Amsterdam: North Holland.

Goldfeld, S. M. 1966. Commercial bank behavior and economic activity: a structural study of monetary policy in postwar United States, Amsterdam, North Holland publishing company.

Goodfriend, M., and R. King. 1997. "The New Neoclassical Synthesis and the Role of Monetary Policy", *NBER Macroeconomics Annual 1997*, vol. 12, Cambridge: MIT Press, 231–296.

Gordon, J. R., ed. 1974. Milton Friedman's Monetary Framework. A debate with his critics, University Chicago Press.

Gramlich, M. Edward. 1971. "The Usefulness of Monetary and Fiscal Policy as Discretionary Stabilization Tools." *Journal of Money, Credit and Banking*, 3 (2 part 2): 506–32.

Hagemann, H. 2005. "The Influence of Jacob Marschak, Adolph Lowe, and Hans Neisser on the Formation of Franco Modigliani's work", in *Franco Modigliani and the Keynesian Legacy*, Schwartz Center Conference at the New School University, New York, April 1–25.

Hall, R. 1977. "Investment, Interest Rates, and the Effects of Stabilization Policies", *Brookings Papers on Economic Activity*, 1: 61–103.

Hall, R. E. and T. J. Sargent. 2018. "Short and Long Run Effects of Milton Friedman's Presidential Address". *Journal of Economic Perspectives*, vol. 32 (1): 121–134.

Hetzel, R. L. 2008. *The Monetary Policy of the Federal Reserve: A History*, Cambridge: Cambridge University Press.

Hicks, J. 1939. *Value and Capital. An Inquiry into Some Fundamental Principles of Economic Theory*. Oxford: Clarendon Press.

Holt, C. 1970. "Job Search, Phillips' Wage Relation, and Unemployment Influence: Theory and Evidence", in *Microeconomic Foundations of Employment & Inflation Theory*, ed. by E. Phelps, Macmillan, 53–123.

Holt, C. C., F. Modigliani, J. F. Muth, and H. Simon. 1960. *Planning Production, Inventories and Work Forces*, Prentice-Hall.

Intriligator, M. D. 1978. *Econometric Models, Techniques, and Applications*, Oxford: North Holland.

Klein, L. R. 1947. Klein, L., 1947 (1966). *The Keynesian revolution*, New York: Mcmillan.

Klein, L. R. 1964. "A Postwar Quarterly Model: Description", *Models of Economic Determination*, NBER Studies Income and Wealth no. 28, Princeton: Princeton University Press.

Klein, L. R., and A. S. Goldberger. 1955. *An Econometric Model for the United States, 1929–1952*. Amsterdam: North Holland.

Mankiw, N. G. 1990. "A Quick Refresher Course in Macroeconomics", *Journal of Economic Literature*, XXVIII: 1645–1660.

———. 2006. "The Macroeconomist as Scientist and Engineer", *The Journal of Economic Perspective*, 20 (4), Fall: 29–46.

Markowitz, H. 1952. "Portfolio Selection", *Journal of Finance*, 7 (1): 77–91.

Mehrling, P. 1998. *"The Money Muddle: The Transformation of American Monetary Thought", 1920–1970*, History of Political Economy, 30 (Supplement): 293–306.

———. 2002. "Don Patinkin and the Origin of Postwar Monetary Orthodoxy", *European Journal of Economic Thought*, 9 (2): 161–185.

———. 2010. "A Tale of Two Cities", *History of Political Economy*, 42 (2): 201–219.

———. 2011. *The New Lombard Street: How the Fed Became the Dealer of Last Resort*, Princeton: Princeton University Press.

———. 2014. "MIT and Money", in *MIT and the Transformation of American Economics*, ed. by E. R. *Weintraub History of Political Economy* 46 (Supplement): 177–197.

Meltzer, A. 2003. *A History of the Federal Reserve, Volume 1: 1913–1951*, Chicago: Chicago University Press.

Minsky, H. P. 1963. "Comments on Friedman's and Schwartz' Money and the Business Cycles", *The Review of Economic Statistics* 45 (1), part 2: 64–78.

Modigliani (Franco) Papers. David M. Rubenstein Rare Book and Manuscript Library, Duke University.

Modigliani, F. 1944. "Liquidity Preference and the Theory of Interest and Money", *Econometrica*, 12, January: 45–88.

———. 1955. "Theory of Money and Interest in the Framework of the General Equilibrium Analysis. Preliminary Notes", Franco Modigliani Papers.

———. 1958. "New Developments on the Oligopoly Front", *Journal of Political Economy*, 66 (3): 215–232.

———. 1963. "The Monetary Mechanism and Its Interaction with Real Phenomena", *Review of Economics and Statistics*, 45 (1), part 2 Supplement, 79–107.

———. 1964. "Some Empirical Tests of Monetary Management and of Rules Versus Discretion", *Journal of Political Economy*, 72 (3): 211.

———. 1966. "Outline of Proposal Research Project on the Links between Monetary Policy and Aggregate Demand", To the Members of the Subcommittee on the Monetary Mechanism of the Social Science Research Council Committee on Economic Stabilization (Bank of Italy Historical Archive.): 1–7.

Modigliani, F. 1971. "Monetary Policy and Consumption: Linkages via Interest Rate and Wealth Effects in the MPS model." *Federal Reserve Bank of Boston Conference Series no 5* (June): 9–84. pdfs.semanticscholar.org/eb34/e1fd0e32274568f20f70d-6296c3b0001369a.pdf.

————. 1975. "The Channels of Monetary Policy in the Federal Reserve-MIT-University of Pennsylvania Econometric Model of the United States" in *Modelling the Economy Based on Papers Presented at the Social Science Research Council's Conference on Economic Modelling, July 1972*, ed. by G. A. Renton, London: Heinemann Educational Book, 240–267.

————. 1977a. "The Monetarists Controversy or, Should We Forsake Stabilization Policies?", *American Economic Review*, 67 (2): 1–19.

————. 1977b. "The Monetarist Controversy: A Seminar Discussion: Paper by Franco Modigliani", *Federal Reserve Bank of San Francisco Economic Review*, Supplement, Spring.

————. 1980–1989. *The Collected Papers of Franco Modigliani* (5 voll.), ed. by A. Abel, Cambridge, MA: MIT Press.

————. 1986. *The Debate over Stabilization Policy*, Cambridge: Cambridge University Press.

————. 1987. *Macroeconomics and Finance: Essays in Honors of Franco Modigliani*, ed. by R. Dornbusch, S. Fisher, and J. Bossons, Cambridge, MA: MIT Press.

————. 2001. *Adventure of an Economist*, New York and London: Texere.

Modigliani, F., and A. K. Ando. 1976. "Impacts of Fiscal Actions on Aggregate Income and the Monetarist Controversy: Theory and Practice" (with the assistance of J. Giangrande). In *Studies in Monetary Economics*, vol. 1, ed. by Jerome L. Stein, New York: American Elsevier, 17–42.

Modigliani, F., and R. Brumberg. 1953 (1980). "Utility Analysis and Aggregate Consumption Functions: An Attempt at Integrating", in *The Collected Papers of Franco Modigliani, Vol. 2: The Life Cycle Hypothesis of Saving*, Cambridge, MA: MIT Press.

————. 1954. "Utility Analysis and the Consumption Function: An Interpretation of Cross-Sectional Data", in *Post Keynesian Economics*, ed. by K. K. Kurhiara, New Brunswick: Rutgers University Press.

Modigliani, F., and L. Papademos. 1975. "Targets for Monetary Policy in the Coming Year", *Brooking Papers on Economic Activity*, 1: 141–165.

Modigliani, F., R. Rasche, and P. J. Cooper. 1970. "Central Bank Policy, the Money Supply and the Short Term Rate of Interest", *Journal of Money, Credit and Banking*, 2 (2): 166–218.

Modigliani, F., and R. Sutch. 1966. "Innovations in Interest Rate Policy", *American Economic Review*, 56 (1/2): 178–197.

————. 1967. "Debt Management and the Term Structure of Interest Rates: An Empirical Analysis", *Journal of Political Economy*, 75: 569–589.

Modigliani F., Shiller R. J., 1973. "Inflation, Rational Expectations and the Term Structure on Interest Rate", *Economica. New Series* 40 (157): 12–43.

Modigliani, F., and E. Tarantelli. 1973. "The Consumption in a Developing Economy and the Italian Experience", *American Economic Review*, 65 (5): 825–842.

Nerlove, M. 1966. "Tabular Survey of Macro-Econometric Models", *International Economic Review*, 7 (2): 127–175.

Patinkin, D. 1956 (1965). *Money Interests and Prices: An Integration of Monetary and Value Theory*, 2nd edn, New York: Harper & Row.

Phelps, eds. E. 1970. *Microeconomic Foundations of Employment and Inflation Theory*, New York: W. W. Norton & Company, Inc.

Pierce, J. L. and J. J. Enzler. 1974. "The effects of external inflationary shocks. *Brookings Papers on Economic Activity*, 1: 13–61.

Rancan, A. 2015. "The Origin of the Sylos Postulate: Modigliani's and Sylos Labini's Contributions to Oligopoly Theory", *Journal for the History of Economic Thought*, (September), Cambridge University Press: 431–448.

————. 2019. "Empirical Macroeconomics in a Policy Context: The Fed-MIT-Penn versus the St. Louis Model (1965–1975)", *History of Political Economy*, 51 (3): 449–470.

————. 2020. "The 'place of the Phillips curve' in Macroeconometric Models: The Case of the Fed's Macroeconometric Model (1966–1980s)". https://papers.ssrn.com/sol3/papers.cfm?abstract_id=3414864.

Rasche, R. H, and H. T. Saphiro. 1968. "The F.R.B.-M.I.T. Econometric Model: Its Special Features". *The American Economic Review*, 58 (2): 123–149.

Rees, A. 1970. "The Phillips Curve as a Menu for Policy Choice", *Economica*, 37 (147): 227–238.

Romani, R. 2018. "On Science and Reform: The Parable of the New Economics, 1960s–1970s", *The European Journal of the History of Economic Thought*: 1–33.

Samuelson, P. A. 1987. The 1985 Nobel Prize in Economics, in *Macroeconomics and Finance: Essays in Honor of Franco Modigliani*, ed. by R. Dornbusch, S. Fisher, and J. Bossons, Cambridge, MA: MIT Press, 29–35.

————. 2005. *Franco: A Mind Never at Rest, Franco Modigliani between Economic Theory and Social Commitment*, Proceeding of the International Conference Organized by the Accademia Nazionale dei Lincei, Roma, February 17–18, Banca Nazionale del Lavoro, Quarterly Review, 58: 5–10.

Smith, G., and J. Tobin. 1975. "Discussion (on Some Reflections on Describing Structures of Financial Sectors)", in *The Brookings Model: Perspective and Recent Developments*, ed. by G. Fromm and L. R. Klein, Amsterdam: North Holland, 564–572.

Stein, H. 1969. *The Fiscal Revolution*, Chicago: University of Chicago Press.

Szenberg, M., and L. Ramrattan. 2008. *Franco Modigliani: A Mind That Never Rests*, Basingstoke, England, and New York: Palgrave Macmillan.

Tobin, J. 1956. "The Interest Elasticity of the Transactions Demand for Cash", *Review of Economics and Statistics*, 38 (3): 241–247.

Tobin, J. 1958. "Liquidity Preference as Behavior Towards Risk," *Review of Economic Studies*, 25 (1): 65–86.

Tobin, J. and W. Brainard. 1968. "Pitfalls in Financial Model Building," *American Economic Review*, 58 (2): 99–122.

Tobin, J. 1969. "A General Equilibrium Approach to Monetary Theory," *Journal of Money, Credit, and Banking*, 1 (1): 15–29.

Visco, I. 1991. "A new round of US model comparisons: a limited appraisal" in L. R. Klein ed. *Comparative Performancec of U.S. Econometric models*, Oxford University Press, New York, pp. 289–315.

Index

Note: Page numbers in *italics* indicate figures on the corresponding page.

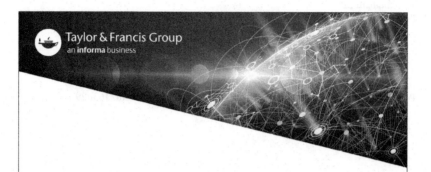

Printed in the United States
By Bookmasters